Eugen Hussak, Erastus Gilbert Smith

**The Determination of rock-forming Minerals**

Eugen Hussak, Erastus Gilbert Smith

**The Determination of rock-forming Minerals**

ISBN/EAN: 9783743325739

Manufactured in Europe, USA, Canada, Australia, Japa

Cover: Foto ©ninafisch / pixelio.de

Manufactured and distributed by brebook publishing software (www.brebook.com)

Eugen Hussak, Erastus Gilbert Smith

**The Determination of rock-forming Minerals**

# THE
# DETERMINATION
## OF
# ROCK-FORMING MINERALS.

BY

DR. EUGEN HUSSAK,

PRIVAT-DOCENT IN THE UNIVERSITY OF GRAZ.

WITH ONE HUNDRED AND THREE WOODCUTS.

AUTHORIZED TRANSLATION FROM THE FIRST GERMAN EDITION

BY

ERASTUS G. SMITH, PH.D.,

PROFESSOR OF CHEMISTRY AND MINERALOGY, BELOIT COLLEGE,
BELOIT, WISCONSIN.

SECOND EDITION.

NEW YORK:
JOHN WILEY & SONS.
1891.

Copyright, 1885, by
JOHN WILEY & SONS.

# PREFACE TO THE FIRST ENGLISH TRANSLATION.

THE following authorized translation of Dr. Hussak's work was undertaken with the view of supplying a want felt in our colleges and universities. Though great progress has been made in the sciences of mineralogy and lithology in later years, through the study of the optical and the other physical properties of minerals, few attempts have been made to condense the exhaustive and original articles scattered through the scientific periodicals and State and national publications, and to put them in suitable shape for use in the laboratory and the class-room. It has been the aim, therefore, to place before the American student a practical work which shall describe the methods and exhibit the results of such investigations.

The translation of a technical work of this character is beset with difficulties appreciable only by those who have undertaken a similar task. Few liberties have been taken with the text, and the attempt has been made to reproduce the original literally so far as possible; at points, however, in order to convey clearly the author's meaning, some recasting of sentences was unavoidable.

The translator will consider it a great favor if any errors noticed either in statement or in translation are communicated to him, in order that they may be eliminated in future editions.

I would express my thanks to Dr. George Williams of Baltimore for several such corrections to the original text already received and incorporated in the translation.

ERASTUS G. SMITH.

BELOIT COLLEGE, BELOIT, WISCONSIN, October, 1885.

# PREFACE.

As the following Manual is designed especially for the use of students, the cost of the work demanded as much abridgment as possible. For this reason much of the knowledge of minerals which belongs to mineralogy proper is passed over, and in the bibliography of Part II. only those works are cited which contain detailed communications concerning the microscopical properties of the rock-forming minerals.

I must, at this time, express my gratitude to Professor Dr. F. Zirkel for his many friendly suggestions; nor am I under less obligations to Professor F. Fouqué, who has most courteously allowed the reproduction of a large number of figures from his well-known work, "Minéralogie Micrographique."

EUGEN HUSSAK.

GRAZ, November, 1884.

# TABLE OF CONTENTS.

## PART I.

### METHODS OF INVESTIGATION.

|  | PAGE |
|---|---|
| Preparation of Microscopical Sections.................................. | 3 |
| The Microscope provided with Polarization Apparatus suitable for Mineralogical and Petrographical Investigation........................... | 7 |
| A. Optical Methods of Investigation..................................... | 16 |
|    1. Examination of Mineral Cross-sections in Parallel Polarized Light................................................................ | 16 |
|       I. Single refracting Minerals................................... | 17 |
|       II. Double-refracting Minerals.................................. | 17 |
|    2. Examination of Minerals in Convergent Polarized Light......... | 29 |
|    3. Behavior of Twinned Crystals in Polarized Light................ | 37 |
|       Twins of the Regular System.................................. | 37 |
|       Twins of the Tetragonal and Hexagonal Systems............. | 38 |
|       Twins of the Rhombic System ................................ | 39 |
|       Twins of the Monoclinic System ............................. | 40 |
|       Twins of the Triclinic System................................ | 43 |
|    4. Determination of the Index of Refraction...................... | 44 |
|    5. Pleochroism of Double-refracting Minerals..................... | 45 |
|       Determination of the Axial Colors............................ | 45 |
| B. Chemical Methods of Investigation.................................. | 50 |
|    Microchemical Methods............................................ | 51 |
|       *a.* Bořicky's Microchemical Method........................... | 55 |
|       *b.* Behrens's Microchemical Method.......................... | 59 |
| C. Mechanical Separation of the Rock-forming Minerals................ | 66 |
|    I. Separation with the Solution of the Iodides of Potassium and Mercury...................................................... | 67 |
|    II. Klein's Solution................................................ | 73 |
|    III. Rohrbach's Solution of the Iodides of Barium and Mercury.... | 75 |
|    IV. Methods of Separation based on the Different Action of Acids on Minerals.................................................. | 76 |
|    V. Separation of the Rock-constituents by means of the Electromagnet..................................................... | 79 |

|  | PAGE |
|---|---|
| D. Explanations of the Tables relating to the Morphological Properties of the Rock forming Minerals. | 81 |
|     I. Mode of Occurrence of the Rock-constituents. | 81 |
|     II. Structure of the Rock-forming Minerals. | 87 |
|         Shell formed Structure of Crystals. | 90 |
|         Interpenetration of the Rock-constituents. | 93 |
|     III. Inclosures of the Rock-forming Minerals. | 93 |
|         Gas pores. | 94 |
|         Fluid Inclosures. | 95 |
|         Inclosures of Vitreous Particles. | 97 |
|         Inclosures of Foreign Minerals. | 99 |
|     IV. Decomposition of the Rock constituents. | 101 |

## PART II.

### TABLES FOR DETERMINING MINERALS.

| | |
|---|---|
| Table for Determining the System of Crystallization of the Rock-forming Minerals. | 106 |
| A. Even in the thinnest Sections of Opaque Minerals. | 108 |
| B. Minerals Transparent in Thin Sections. | 112 |
|     I. Single refracting Minerals. | 112 |
|         *a*. Amorphous Minerals. | 112 |
|         *b*. Minerals Crystallizing in the Regular System. | 114 |
|     II. Double-refracting Minerals. | 122 |
|         *a*. Optically Uniaxial Minerals. | 122 |
|             1. Minerals Crystallizing in the Tetragonal System. | 122 |
|                 α. Double-refraction Positive. | 122 |
|                 β. Double-refraction Negative. | 124 |
|             2. Minerals Crystallizing in the Hexagonal System. | 128 |
|                 α. Double-refraction Positive | 128 |
|                 β. Double-refraction Negative. | 132 |
|         *b*. Optically Biaxial Minerals. | 140 |
|             1. Minerals Crystallizing in the Rhombic System. | 140 |
|             2. Minerals Crystalling in the Monoclinic System. | 156 |
|             3. Minerals Crystallizing in the Triclinic System. | 178 |
| C. Aggregates. | 189 |
| Bibliography | 197 |
| Explanation of Cuts accompanying Part II. | 215 |
| Cuts accompanying Part II. | 219 |
| Index. | 229 |

# ON THE DETERMINATION OF ROCK-FORMING MINERALS.

## PART I.

### METHODS OF INVESTIGATION.

F. Zirkel. Die mikroskopische Beschaffenheit der Mineralien und Gesteine. Leipzig, 1873.
H. Rosenbusch. Mikroskopische Physiographie der petrographisch wichtigsten Mineralien. Stuttgart, 1873.
Fouqué et Michel Lévy. Minéralogie micrographique. Paris, 1878.
E. Cohen. Zusammenstellung petrographischer Untersuchungsmethoden. Strassburg, 1884.

There are two methods of examining rocks, the macroscopical and the microscopical.

In the macroscopical investigation of rocks those parts of the mineral mixture discernible with the naked eye can be studied with reference to crystalline form, cleavage, color, lustre, streak, hardness, solubility in acids, etc. For the more exact optical investigation, however, cleavage sections exactly oriented must be obtained, the cleavage angle, when possible, measured in order to determine the plane of cleavage, and the section, if not already transparent, ground thin. Such an investigation of the rock-forming minerals leads in most cases to the goal, provided the particles have a certain magnitude, at least 1–2 mm. Isolated particles of minerals can be examined before the blow-pipe; yet, because of their minuteness, such a purely macroscopical examination is insufficient in most cases. This is especially true in porphyritic or very fine-grained rocks, and therefore for these rocks the microscopical examination is employed. It is necessary in such a case that the pieces of rock under examination shall be ground into thin transparent leaves. In such sections the single constituents are cut in most varied directions. By these minute cross-sections the crystals and the rock-forming minerals can be determined by optical methods with the polarization-microscope, and by combination of the optical with the crystallographical properties, i.e., with the form of the cross-section, i.e., crystalline form, and cleavage.

This determination is more difficult if the minerals occur only as grains. Of course here also the human eye has its limitations: if the separate particles are so minute that they cannot be observed in section, i.e., afford no cross-sections; or, when examined under the highest possible magnifying power, they give no figures suitable—i.e., large enough—for optical study, their determination by the polarization-microscope is impossible.

In the following pages is given a description of the method of producing preparations from rocks suitable for microscopical study; of the application of the polarization-microscope adapted to the complete exposition of the optical and chemical methods of determination; then follows the discussion of the mechanical separation of the rock-constituents according to their specific gravity and by the electro-magnet; and, finally, a short chapter on the structure of the rock-forming minerals and a systematic survey of them.

## The Preparation of Microscopical Sections.

In order to prepare a thin section from a rock, either a suitable tablet is cut with a section-cutter from the rock, or a convenient fragment, about 2 ccm. large, is broken off with a hammer, and as even a face as possible is ground, using either an emery-disk of a section-grinder or grinding by hand on an iron plate with coarse emery-powder and water. The size of the emery used depends entirely upon the hardness of the rock. Evenness of the emery-powder, and an iron plate as smooth as possible and free from furrows, are chief factors in obtaining an even surface on the ground fragment.

If the face is sufficiently even, it is polished on a glass plate with fine floated emery, or emery-flour, and water. The fragment is then cemented by this face with boiled Canada balsam to an ordinary glass plate (preferably one that is quadratic) somewhat larger than the fragment, and rather thick, so that it can be better grasped.

Certain precautionary measures must be observed. The fragment must be first well cleaned and dried, the Canada balsam sufficiently heated, boiled neither too much nor too little, so that the emery-powder may not become distributed through it or the balsam crack off from the glass. The balsam may be boiled over an alcohol-lamp, either in an iron spoon or directly on the object-glass. Care must be taken that the balsam does not inflame. It is impossible to state the exact instant when the balsam is sufficiently boiled, as this depends on its state of dilution and must be determined by several experiments. The balsam is sufficiently boiled if, after it has already begun to fume rather strongly, large bubbles rise from the bottom, or the balsam begins to evaporate from the edges of the glass plate. The boiling of the balsam is conducted most safely in an oven with thermometer attachment, such as are sold by Fuess of Berlin. If the balsam has been boiled in an iron spoon, a small portion is placed on an object-glass, and this gently warmed until the balsam becomes a thin liquid.

The evenly-ground rock-section is firmly pressed into the boiled, still fluid, balsam, with the plane surface downward. In the operation care must be taken that no bubbles of air remain between the rock and glass, as often happens when the surface ground on the rock is not perfectly even. The plate thus prepared is allowed to thoroughly cool. If the balsam on the plate about the rock-tablet receives no impression, or appears free from fissures, it is sufficiently boiled.

The natural surface of the rock-fragment is next ground with coarse emery-powder. This is continued until the larger mineral particles or even the plate itself begins to be translucent, i.e., until the thickness is about $\frac{1}{2}$–1 mm. Here, again, care must be exercised that the surface is as even as possible, and that the Canada balsam surrounding and protecting the plate is not completely cut away. The grinding, as before, is continued on glass plates with fine emery, and finally with emery flour, until the tablet of rock becomes perfectly transparent. It is then cleaned from the emery, the surrounding Canada balsam is carefully scratched away, and is then dried. For the final preparation a better object-glass is selected, one well polished and freed from dust-particles or clinging threads, dried, and a larger drop of Canada balsam placed upon it. The balsam may be boiled directly on the object-glass or in a spoon, and then transferred as in the previous case.

The thin rock-tablet, to which another small drop of balsam has been added, is made movable by carefully and gently heating the object-glass, and with a pointed bit of wood is pushed over on to this second glass, which in turn is gently warmed so that the balsam again becomes mobile and surrounds the rock-section on every side; the covering-glass, of course previously cleaned and warmed, is laid upon and carefully pressed down upon the rock-section so that the excess of balsam and the air-bubbles escape. The preparation is allowed to cool slowly until the balsam has solidified, and is then cleaned by carefully scratching away the excess of balsam with a knife and washing with alcohol.

As by scratching away the balsam the covering glass is often liable to break away, owing to the overheating of the balsam, it is advisable to shave away the balsam with a warmed knife, and then wash the preparation with alcohol.

Many rocks, especially those of a coarse granular structure, exceedingly porous or decomposed, cannot thus be transferred, and are shattered in the preparation. Sections from such rocks therefore must be placed on a better object-glass at once, and, after they are ground thin, must be finished on this same glass by pouring boiling balsam on the dried and cleaned section, and the rapid laying on and gentle pressing down of the covering-glass. Here care must be taken neither to warm the object-glass a second time, nor to press down the covering-glass too firmly, as in either case the section is often broken; it is therefore necessary to finish the preparation as rapidly as possible in order that the balsam upon the glass may not cool and thus necessitate a second warming.

Such rocks as pumice-stone which are exceedingly porous or full of cavities, or of a drossy character, or friable and fragile, as tufa, must be boiled in Canada balsam first, to make possible the grinding of a plane surface, as the balsam forcing its way into the cavities, and becoming solid on cooling, imparts to the whole a greater degree of consistency. Such thin sections must of course be finished according to the method last described, upon the same object-glass on which it was ground.

Sections easily shattered may be prepared most safely by Canada balsam dissolved in ether or chloroform. The preparation must not be heated, and must be allowed to dry very slowly. It is advisable to use rather more balsam than is ordinarily taken, as in the process of drying, i.e., the evaporation of the ether, air-bubbles may enter the balsam beneath the covering-glass. It is also advisable to avoid spotting the covering-glass with balsam, as cleaning the preparation cannot be undertaken for several weeks, until after the balsam is completely dried.

Thoulet has described a method of cutting isolated mineral particles, sand, etc.

The powder to be examined is mixed with about ten times its volume of zinc oxide, and the mixture is rubbed up to a thick mud with potassium silicate (soluble glass). This is then pressed into a mould conveniently made from a short piece of thick glass tubing, placed on an object-glass, and allowed to stand several days and harden. When thoroughly dried, the mass is easily slipped from the glass, is solid, and can be worked into a thin section exactly as any rock fragment.

In order to grind friable rocks, or those become rotten through advanced decomposition, according to A. Wichmann (Tschermak's Min. u. petr. Mitth. V, 1882, 33) the best course is the following: The fragment broken away is first shaved on one side as even as possible with a knife, and this is polished on a dry glass plate; the fragment is then cemented to the plate with Canada balsam, previously cooled so that the rock may not be further changed by its high temperature, and again shaved on the opposite side until as thin a section as possible remains, which is finally prepared with Canada balsam dissolved in ether.

### The Material for the Preparations.

The emery should be as pure as possible, i.e., unadulterated and rich in corundum, the size of the coarser granules about 0.3–0.5 mm.; the fine emery should be like flour. The coarser variety is known as "No. 70," the fine variety as "emery flour."

The Canada balsam should be clear and rather liquid.
The object-glasses are not generally more than 18 mm. square.
Labels for microscopical preparations are to be had in book-form.
Thin rock-sections are prepared by Fuess, Berlin, S. W., Alte Jakobstrasse, 108, and by Voigt & Hochgesang, Göttingen; large collections, also, of thin sections, systematically arranged, can be obtained from the same firms. Both houses supply excellent microscopes especially adapted to mineralogico-petrographical investigations.

## The Microscope provided with Polarization Apparatus suitable for Mineralogical and Petrographical Investigation. (Also often called the "polarization-microscope.")

TH. LIEBISCH. Bericht über die wissenschaftlichen Instrumente auf der Berliner Gewerbeausstellung. Berlin, 1879. p. 342.
H. ROSENBUSCH. N. Jahrb. f. Miner. u. Geol. 1876. p 504.
  Ueber die Anwendung der Condensorlinse bei Untersuchungen im convergentpolarisirten Lichte:
V. LASAULX. N. Jahrb. f. Miner. u. Geol. 1878, p. 377.
E. BERTRAND. Société minéralogique de France. 1878, 9 Mai p. 22 and 14 Nov. p. 96.
C. KLEIN. Nachr. d. k. Ges. d. Wissensch. z. Göttingen. 1878, p. 461
  Ueber stauroskopische Methoden:
H. LASPEYRES. Groth's Zeitschr. f. Krystallographie, VI. Bd. p. 429.
L. CALDERON. Groth's Zeitschr. f. Krystallographie, II. Bd. p. 68.

The completely equipped polarization-microscope (Figs. 1 and 2) differs from the ordinary microscope by (1) the presence of a graduated object-stage revolving horizontally (Fig. 1, $c$), with vernier attachment suitable for the determination of the directions of extinction, measurement of angles, etc.; (2) two Nicol's prisms (Fig. 2, $ss$ and $rr$) for investigations in parallel polarized light; (3) a condenser (Fig. 2, $TT$) for investigations in converging polarized light; (4) a plate of quartz (Fig. 2, $ZZ$) for determining feebly double-refracting minerals, which is cut perpendicular to the chief axis, has parallel planes, and can be introduced over the objective by a slit (Fig. 2, *tt*); (5) a calcite plate for stauroscopic investigations cut perpendicular to the chief axis, with parallel planes —that is, a Calderon's double-plate (Fig. 2, *c*) or a Brezina's calcite plate set in an ocular; (6) a fourth undulation mica plate and a Dove's quartz compensation-plate, i.e., a thin wedge of quartz for the determination of the character of the double-refraction, which either enters or is just below the analyzer; and finally (7) an apparatus for centring the object-stage (Fig. 1, *m* and *n*; Fig. 2, *N*, *nn*, *mm*), and various minor pieces of apparatus, as the cross-threads in the ocular, an ocular- and stage-micrometer, blende (Fig. 2, *dd*) for investigations in converging polarized light, the graduation of the head of the micrometer-screw and of the plate on the stage.

For mineralogico-optical investigations one Nicol's prism, *the polarizer* (Fig. 2, *rr*), is fixedly adjusted beneath the stage and above the reflector; and the second, *the analyzer* (Fig. 2, *ss*), is graduated and is above the ocular. For investigations in parallel polarized light it is very convenient if the polarizer is fixed in such a position that the *directions of vibration* of both nicols are at right angles to each other, i.e., the nicols are crossed when the zero-point of the analyzer coincides with a mark on the tube, and at the same time the ocular with its cross-threads so adjusted in the tube that the arms of the cross-threads are exactly parallel with the directions of vibration of both nicols.

If this is not the case, the nicols must always first be crossed by turning the analyzer until complete darkness occurs and this position of the analyzer is noted. Moreover, the arms of the cross-threads must be parallel to the nicol chief sections. This may be done in the following manner: We place on the stage of the microscope, and between the crossed nicols, an object-slide to which is firmly cemented either a small quartz-crystal or a rock-section containing a longitudinal section of an apatite crystal, and turn the stage until the quartz or the

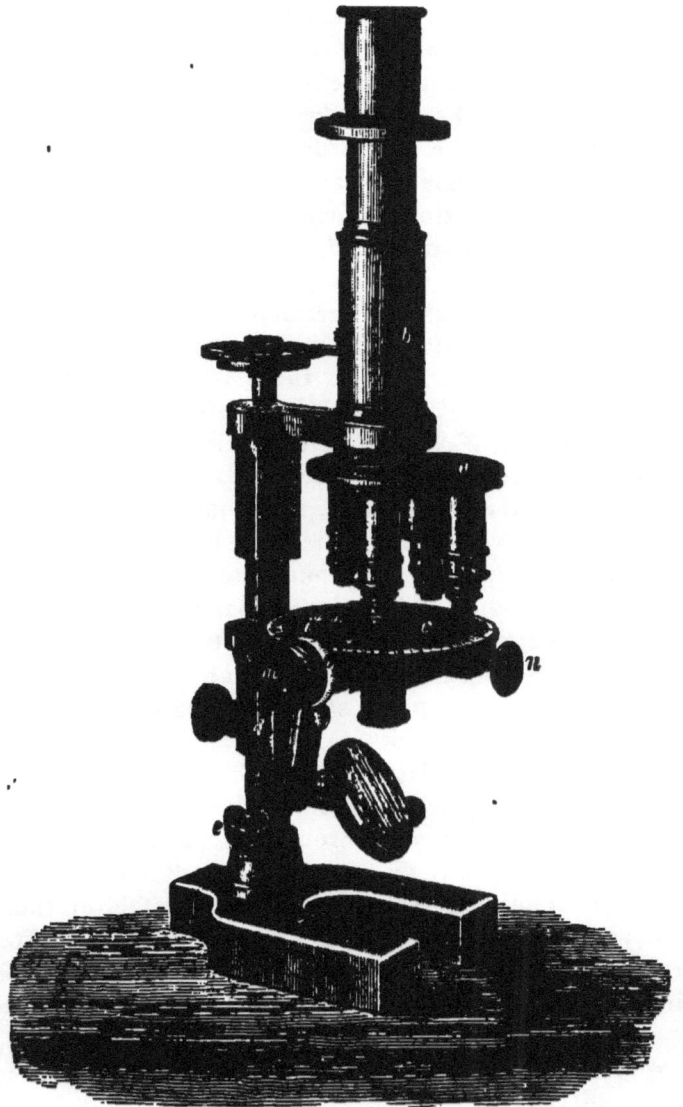

Fig. 1.—Polarization-microscope, by R. Fuess. (New model.)

apatite crystal is completely darkened. The analyzer is now removed from the ocular, and the ocular is revolved until one arm of the cross-threads within the ocular is exactly parallel to the prismatic edge of the quartz crystal or the longitudinal edge of the apatite needle. In order to determine the directions of extinction in minerals, care must be taken that the ocular carrying the cross threads, when correctly placed in the manner described, is not displaced, as can easily occur in removing the analyzer.

The **Condenser** (the Lasaulx-Bertrand lens) for producing converging polarized light in the microscope is formed from two plano-convex lenses. One of these is screwed directly above the polarizer, and the second, in a suitable setting, laid upon the first (Fig. 2, $TT$). In investigations in convergent light, the ocular is removed and the nicols crossed. Objective 7 and ocular 3, Hartnack, is the best combination, though a more acute objective system can often be advantageously employed. In examining very diminutive crystalline cross-sections, a blende (Fig. 2, $dd$) is placed above the analyzer for the purpose of isolating the cross-section to be examined. The Bertrand lens can be inserted within the tube in place of the ocular (removed for the purpose), should an enlargement of the interference-figures be required.

The **Biot-Klein's Quartz Plate** (Fig. 2, $ZZ$), about 2 mm. thick, with parallel planes cut perpendicular to the optic axis, and brass-mounted, is introduced through a suitable opening directly above the objective (Fig. 2, $tt$). In order to use this quartz plate in examining feebly-refracting minerals or those of marked zonal structure, the upper nicol is revolved, after the quartz plate is introduced and the polarizer, objective, and ocular are in suitable positions, until the extremely sensitive red (the so-called "*teinte-sensible*") of the circular polarizing quartz appears. The mineral to be examined is then placed beneath the objective.

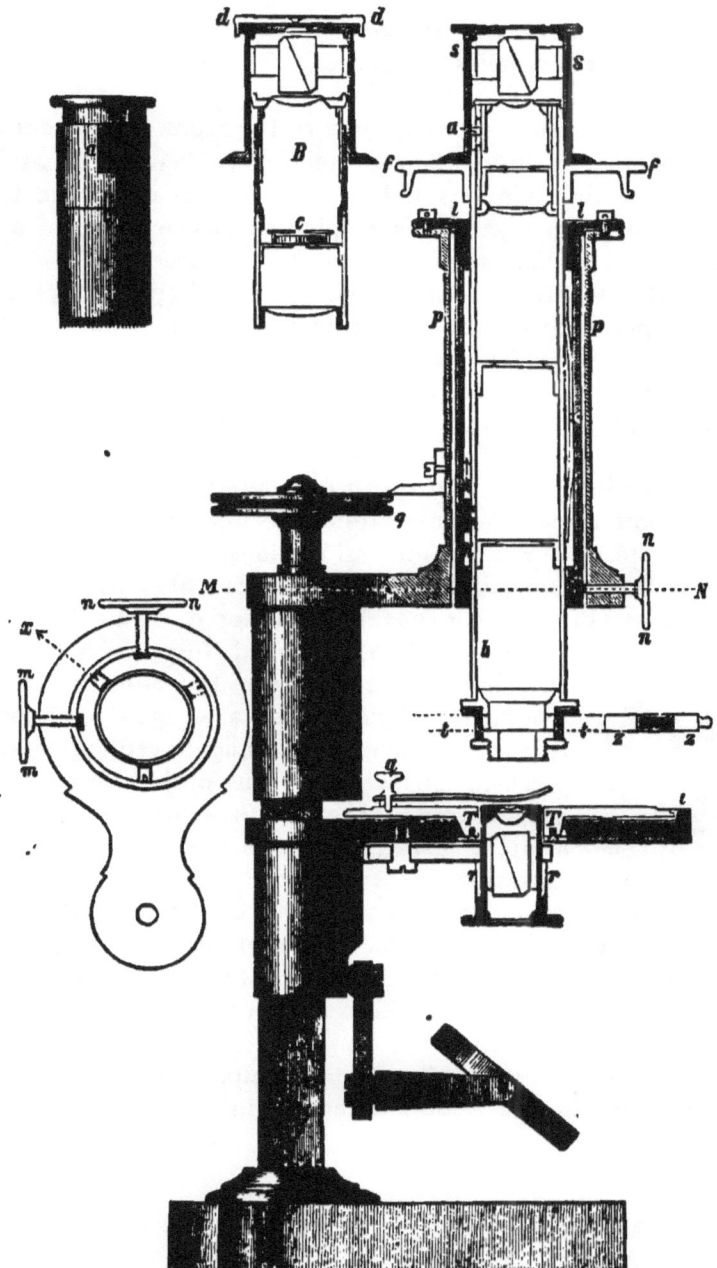

FIG. 2.—POLARIZATION-MICROSCOPE, BY R. FUESS. (Older model. Cross-section.)

Minerals with feeble double-refraction, as leucite, or those showing optic anomalies, as garnet, will induce a change of color.

The quartz plate is also applied to the more exact determination of the position of the directions of vibration, as all double-refracting minerals undergo a change of color, and this remains unchanged only in isotropic sections or when an axis of elasticity coincides with a nicol chief section.

The **Calcite Plate,** about 2 mm. thick, with parallel planes, and cut perpendicular to the optic axis, is set in a cork ring, and when in use is laid between the ocular and the analyzer. The nicols are crossed, and the interference-figures of the calcite plate then appear on the section under examination. The arms of the cross-threads must again coincide with the arms of the interference-cross of the calcite plate. More exact stauroscopic investigations cannot be undertaken with this plate except on the larger mineral sections.

For the microstauroscopical measurements the **Calderon Double-plate** (Fig. 2, *c*) is peculiarly adapted. This is made from a twin of calcite artificially formed (Fig. 3, *abcdef*) by

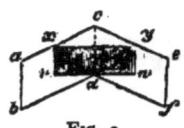

FIG. 3.
CALDERON DOUBLE-PLATE.

cutting a rhombohedron through the short diagonals, grinding away a wedge-shaped portion from either half, and again cementing the polished surfaces. If the projecting and re-entrant angle of the twin thus formed be ground away, a plane plate *xyvw* is obtained, divided by the plane separating the two pieces of calcite *c, d*. This plane appears from above as an extremely fine straight line. This double-plate is so mounted in one of the oculars that the boundary-line of the plate is parallel to the chief section of a nicol; .i.e., that both halves between crossed nicols show the same degree of extinction.

A **Fourth Undulation Mica Plate** is employed to determine the character of the double-refraction in uniaxial minerals;

in biaxial minerals, either a plate of quartz about 2 mm. thick and cut perpendicular to the optic axis, or a wedge of quartz with one plane parallel to the optic axis and the other inclined at an angle of about 5°, is used.

In making use of the interference-figures obtained with the condenser, to determine the character of the double-refraction in optically-uniaxial minerals, the mica plate is laid on the tube so that the plane of the optic axis of the mica, generally indicated by a mark on the setting, makes an angle of 45° with the planes of vibration of the nicols.

In investigating optically-biaxial minerals the quartz wedge is inserted by an opening in the analyzer so that the chief axis of the quartz forms an angle of 45° with the plane of vibration of the analyzer. The interference-figures of the mineral under examination are brought, by revolving the stage, into such a position that the plane of the optic axis is at first parallel and then perpendicular to the chief axis of the quartz wedge.

If but a single quartz plate cut perpendicular to the optic axis is at hand, the analyzer must be raised with one hand from the tube of the microscope, from which the ocular is removed, so that the quartz plate can be used beneath it, care being taken that both nicols remain exactly crossed. Then with the other hand the quartz plate is turned a little about a horizontal axis so that the rays of light must pass through a thicker layer of quartz, and so that the axis of revolution is at first parallel to the plane of the optic axis of the mineral and afterwards perpendicular to it.

In order to **Centre** exactly any particular point of an object under examination, and revolve about its own centre, so often necessary in the measurement of angles especially, either the revolving-stage can be moved in two directions at right angles to each other (Fig. 1, *m*, *n*), or the tube acting within a socket can be moved by two screws (Fig. 2, *mm*, *nn*). There must be a new centring of the stage or tube for each combination of ocular and objective.

If the stage can be centred, one of the centring-screws (Fig. 1, *m*) can serve at the same time as **Micrometer.** Each revolution of this screw, the total number being read off from a circle (*p*) placed beside it, corresponds of course to a definite magnitude of displacement of the stage, that is, of the object lying upon it; e.g., in the new microscope made by Fuess, one interval of the micrometer-screw corresponds to a horizontal movement of the stage of 0.002 mm. An ocular-micrometer often accompanies the microscopes instead of this stage-micrometer. Such a micrometer is made of glass, circular and fitted to the ocular, with a fine millimetre-scale engraved on it.

The method of Duc de Chaulnes is best adapted to determine the thickness of thin sections, i.e., the **Index of Refraction,** in sections of minerals with parallel plane surfaces. The micrometer-screw (Fig. 2, *g*) moving the tube in a vertical direction has a graduated circle attached, from which the revolutions of the screw, and therefore the extent of vertical movement of the tube, can be read. In Fuess's instrument, already mentioned, the tube micrometer-screw is divided into 500 degrees, each of which corresponds to a vertical movement of 0.001 mm.

The index of refraction is determined according to the formula $n = \dfrac{d}{d-r}$, where *d* represents the thickness of the mineral leaflet, and *r* the movement of the tube which is necessary to see a point as clearly through the plate after it is introduced as before its introduction.

In order to easily find a second time such places on the preparation as may be desired, two scales are placed at right angles to each other on the stage (Fig. 1, *c*), which run from the centre of the circular stage towards the 0° and 90° points of the outer graduation of the same and are graduated into whole or half millimetres. Then it is only necessary to place the object-slide upon the stage so that it lies directly over the two scales with two of its sides parallel to the marks of graduation. By noting the numbers of these marks of graduation, the position of the preparation as to right and left is fixed. Should the object-glass be laid a second time on the stage in the same position, the desired point will fall within the field.

Finally, those microscopes manufactured by Fuess or by Voigt & Hochgesang are supplied with a **Heating-stage**, with thermometer attached, to be placed upon the circular revolving-stage. This can be heated by an alcohol-flame placed within a mica chimney, and often does good service, e.g., in determining the fluid inclosures in minerals.

Different blendes are also added, suitable for placing either upon the ocular, i.e., the analyzer, or of introduction in place of the polarizer.

A heating-apparatus far more to the purpose than the one just mentioned, and first suggested by Max Schultze, is described by Vogelsang (Poggend, Ann. CXXXVII, p. 58). In it the object is warmed by a platinum wire heated by means of a galvanic current. With such an instrument a temperature of 200° C. can easily be attained, the rapidity of changes of temperature regulated, and any degree of heat once reached continued quite constant.

The number of different ocular- and objective-lenses by whose combination the object can undergo a varying enlargement is a matter of choice. In mineralogico-petrographical investigations, oculars 1, 2, 3, 4 and objectives 3, 5, 7, 9 of Hartnack's system generally suffice. These are usually considered as the best, and are supplied with the Fuess instrument as described.

## A. Optical Methods of Investigations.

### 1. Examination of Mineral Cross-sections in Parallel Polarized Light.

ROSENBUSCH. Mikr. Physiographie, etc., p. 55–107.
GROTH. Physikalische Krystallographie. Leipzig, 1876.
E. KALKOWSKY. Gr. Zeitschrift f. Kryst., IX, 486

For observations in parallel polarized light both nicols are exactly crossed; the short diagonals corresponding to the direction of vibration in the nicols are thus perpendicular to each other, total darkness of the field following; the ocular and objective for the desired magnifying power are inserted in the tube, and the cross-section to be examined is so placed that on revolving the stage it remains within the field, and its behavior in polarized light throughout a total revolution of the stage noted. The gathering-lens, or condenser, above the polarizer inducing converging polarized light can be left *in situ*, as it does not impede the investigations because a withdrawal of the ocular is unnecessary.

As is well known, a discrimination is made between single- and double-refracting minerals; the amorphous minerals and those crystallizing in the regular system belonging to the first class. The double-refracting minerals are further distinguished according to the number of the optic axes and of the axes of elasticity as *optically-uniaxial* and *optically biaxial* minerals. Those minerals crystallizing in the tetragonal and hexagonal systems belong to the optically-uniaxial, and those in the rhombic, monoclinic, and triclinic systems to the optically-biaxial minerals.

In the following pages the behavior of the minerals as regards the different systems of crystallization to which they belong will be discussed.

## I. *Single-Refracting Minerals.*

**Amorphous and Regular.**—If such a mineral is placed under the microscope with crossed nicols, all of its cross-sections remain perfectly dark throughout a complete revolution of the stage; i.e., they are isotrope.

The darkness of the field induced by crossing the nicols is not changed by introducing a section of an amorphous or regularly crystallizing mineral, because isotrope bodies cause no change in the direction of vibration of the penetrating light, and the elasticity of the ether in such bodies is equal in every direction. The index of refraction $n$ is constant for all directions.

In the stauroscope, with the calcite plate, no change of the interference-figures occurs during a complete horizontal revolution, nor any change in the shading of either half of the Calderon double-plate; as they remain equally dark, the separating-line is invisible.

A series of amorphous and regular minerals, including opal, garnet, analcime, perowskite, which occasionally appear as rock-constituents, show often optical anomalies, in that thin sections of them in parallel polarized light often brighten on revolving the stage. The reason for these phenomena lies probably in the internal tension produced during the growth of the crystal; a detailed zonal structure is generally noticeable in such optical anomalies.

## II. *Double-Refracting Minerals.*

A mineral is double-refracting when a part of its cross-section exhibits color-phenomena during a complete revolution in parallel polarized light, i.e., shows *polarization-colors*. Such cross-sections become four times colored and dark, the latter always occurring in turning from 90° to 90°; i.e., it extinguishes the ray so soon as one axis of elasticity coincides with a chief section of a nicol. The double-refraction depends upon the difference of the elasticity of the ether according to definite directions within these minerals. The color-phenomena are a consequence of the interference of the light-rays caused by the double-refraction, and depend upon the magnitude of the index of refraction, the direction of the section, and the thickness of the mineral leaflet.

By **uniaxial** minerals, embracing the tetragonal and hexagonal systems, are understood those in which the elasticity of the ether differs in two directions, parallel or perpendicular to the chief axis. Here $\mathfrak{a}$ = the axis of greatest elasticity, and $\mathfrak{c}$ the least; and there is but one direction where no double-refraction occurs, viz., in the direction of the **optic axis**, which coincides with the chief axis. The index of refraction of the ordinary ray ($= \omega$) vibrating perpendicularly to the optical chief section (i.e., that plane which is parallel to the optic axis and perpendicular to the entering face of the light) differs from that ($= \varepsilon$) of the extraordinary ray vibrating in the optical chief section. If the chief axis, i.e. the optic axis, coincides with the axis of greatest elasticity, $c = \mathfrak{a}$, and $\omega > \varepsilon$, and the mineral is *negative;* if $c = \mathfrak{c}$ and $\omega < \varepsilon$, the mineral is *positive.* The greater the difference between the indices of refraction, the more powerful is the double-refraction of the mineral.

A section of a tetragonal or hexagonal mineral, cut perpendicular to the chief axis and parallel to $oP$, appears isotrope in parallel polarized light throughout a complete horizontal revolution, and as one of the single-refracting minerals; i.e., it remains perfectly darkened. Sections parallel to the chief axis and one of the prismatic faces are generally rectangular, and between the crossed nicols are always dark when one of the sides of the rectangle, i.e., one of the planes of cleavage parallel to the chief axis, is parallel to one of the chief sections of a nicol or an arm of the cross-wires. This occurs four times during one complete revolution. The longitudinal section is then said to EXTINGUISH PARALLEL to the crystallographic axes.

Fig. 4 gives a clear idea of *this parallel extinction* in an optically-uniaxial mineral cross-section *abcd*. *c* is the chief axis, and *vw* and *xy* are the cross-sections of both crossed nicols, whose optical chief sections coincide with the short diagonals of the rhombic transverse section.

So soon as the chief axis, i.e., one of the sides, forms any angle with the nicol chief section and the cross-wires, the longitudinal section shows the polarization-colors.

Sections inclined to the chief axis, e.g., parallel to a pyramidal plane, of course always extinguish parallel to the chief axis, but not always parallel to the sides. Thus a triangular or pentagonal cross-section extinguishes parallel to one of the sides, as the chief axis in such sections is perpendicular to the direction of one of these sides, while a rhombic cross-section will extinguish parallel to the diagonals of the figure.

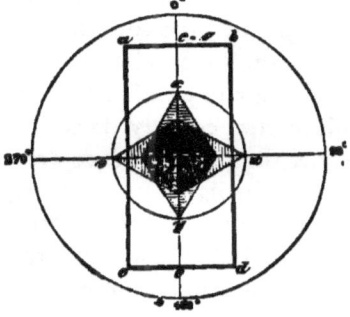

FIG. 4.—PARALLEL EXTINCTION.

The behavior of various cross-sections of a uniaxial crystal in parallel polarized light can be easily demonstrated on a glass crystal model in which the chief axis is marked, if one will always bear in mind that the extinction occurs parallel to the chief axis.

In the stauro-microscope (with calcite plate) transverse sections of optically-uniaxial minerals always show the calcite interference-figures. In longitudinal sections they are undisturbed only when the chief axis or one of the contour-lines of the crystal parallel to it coincides with one of the arms of the cross-wires already in conjunction with the nicol chief sections in the microscope.

Transverse sections behave like isotrope cross-sections when examined with the Calderon double-plate. Longitudinal sections always induce a different shading of both halves of the plate when the chief axis is not parallel to the principal direction of vibration of the nicol, the arms of the cross-wires, or the line of junction in the Calderon plate, three objects which are exactly parallel to each other in the microscope. If the chief axis is parallel to the line of junction, both halves of the plate are equally dark with crossed nicols; if this is not the case, then both halves are unequally shaded, the one dark and the other light, or both are equally clear.

It is possible to determine whether a mineral under examination belongs to the tetragonal or hexagonal system only from the character of the contour of the section cut at right angles to the chief axis. If it is square or octagonal it belongs to the *tetragonal;* if hexagonal or dihexagonal, it belongs to the *hexagonal* system.

In the **optically-biaxial** minerals there are two directions wherein no double-refraction takes place, i.e., there are two optic axes; and further, we assume three axes of elasticity at right angles to each other, i.e., three directions in which the elasticity of the light-ether differs. The direction of the greatest elasticity is designated by $\mathfrak{a}$, that of middle value by $\mathfrak{b}$, and that of the least by $\mathfrak{c}$.

The optic axes do not coincide with the crystallographic axes, and form an angle with each other. The line dividing equally the acute angle is called the *first middle line,* or *acute bisectrix;* the line bisecting the more obtuse angle, the *second middle line,* or *obtuse bisectrix.* The optic axes and both middle lines lie in a single plane, THE PLANE OF THE OPTIC AXES (A.P.); the *optic normal* lies perpendicular to the plane of the optic axes. The axis of elasticity of middle value ($\mathfrak{b}$) always coincides with the optic normal, while the axes of greatest and least elasticity coincide with either the first or the second middle line. If $\mathfrak{a} = 1.$ M., then $\mathfrak{c} = 2.$ M., and the mineral is negative; if $\mathfrak{c} = 1.$ M., and $\mathfrak{a} = 2.$ M., the mineral is positive.

There are three different indices of refraction, $\alpha$, $\beta$, $\gamma$, corresponding to these three axes of elasticity.

Minerals crystallizing in the rhombic, monoclinic, and triclinic systems belong to the optically-biaxial minerals.

**Rhombic Minerals.**—In these minerals the three axes of elasticity $\mathfrak{a} > \mathfrak{b} > \mathfrak{c}$ coincide with the three crystallographic axes $\breve{a}, \bar{b}, c'$; $\mathfrak{a}$ does not always equal $\breve{a}$, etc., yet each of the crystallographic axes can coincide with each of the axes of elasticity. $\mathfrak{a}$ and $\mathfrak{c}$ are always middle lines, and the plane of the optic axes $(AP)$ is always parallel to one of the three pinacoids. The following cases may therefore occur:

If $AP \parallel oP$, then $\left.\begin{array}{l}\breve{a} = \mathfrak{a}, \bar{b} = \mathfrak{c} \\ \breve{a} = \mathfrak{c}, \bar{b} = \mathfrak{a}\end{array}\right\} c' = \mathfrak{b}$;

If $AP \parallel \infty \breve{P} \infty$, then $\left.\begin{array}{l}c' = \mathfrak{a}, \breve{a} = \mathfrak{c} \\ c' = \mathfrak{c}, \breve{a} = \mathfrak{a}\end{array}\right\} \bar{b} = \mathfrak{b}$;

If $AP \parallel \infty \bar{P} \infty$, then $\left.\begin{array}{l}c' = \mathfrak{a}, \bar{b} = \mathfrak{c} \\ c' = \mathfrak{c}, \bar{b} = \mathfrak{a}\end{array}\right\} \breve{a} = \mathfrak{b}$.

Figs. 5 to 8 serve as examples of these cases. These are schematic representations of the optic orientation of rhombic augite and hornblende in sections parallel to the plane of the optic axes. $A$ and $B$ represent the two optic axes; the middle lines or axes of elasticity are designated by German, the crystallographic axes by italic letters.

Cross-sections parallel to the three planes of the pinacoids, in general of rectangular figure, have a parallel extinction, i.e., are dark between crossed nicols only when one of the sides of the rectangle or one of the pinacoidal cleavage-fissures is parallel to a chief section of a nicol. Darkness follows so soon as one of the crystallographic axes coincides with a nicol chief section. This occurs four times in a complete revolution, just as with the longitudinal sections of the uniaxial crystals. The rhombic minerals can, however, be distinguished from them in parallel polarized light, in that the sections *parallel to oP are not isotrope* as in the uniaxial minerals.

Only those sections of rhombic minerals which are cut

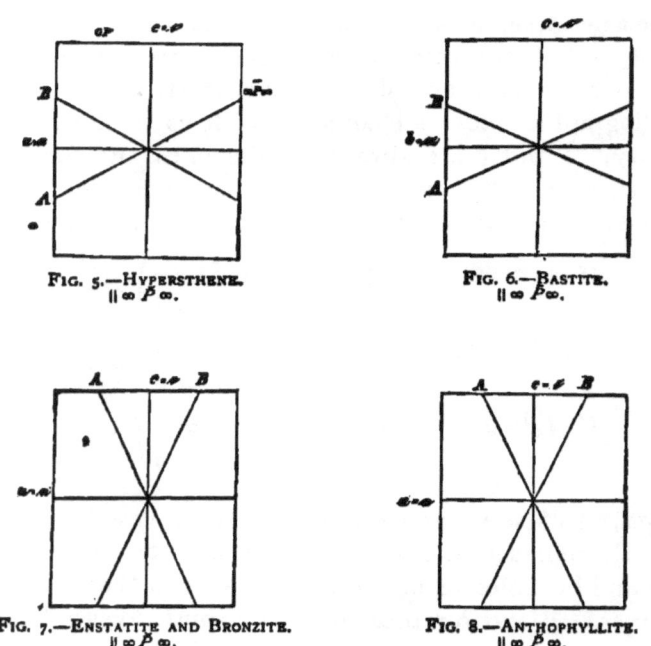

Fig. 5.—Hypersthene.
$\|\infty \bar{P} \infty$.

Fig. 6.—Bastite.
$\|\infty \bar{P} \infty$.

Fig. 7.—Enstatite and Bronzite.
$\|\infty \bar{P} \infty$.

Fig. 8.—Anthophyllite.
$\|\infty \bar{P} \infty$.

exactly at right angles to one of the two optic axes remain perfectly dark throughout a complete revolution, i.e., are isotrope.

Such sections are parallel to $\bar{P}\infty$, $\check{P}\infty$, or a prismatic face, according to the position of the optic axes. It is self-evident that such isotrope sections are more rare in rhombic than in optically-uniaxial crystals, and have, moreover, no such regular forms.

Just as in the pinacoidal sections, i.e., from the zones $oP : \infty P\infty$ and $oP : \infty \breve{P}\infty$, so all longitudinal sections parallel to the vertical axis ($c'$) from the zone $\infty P\infty : \infty \breve{P}\infty$ extinguish parallel to the sides or one of the cleavage-fissures parallel to the vertical axis. Symmetrical sections inclined to the vertical axis, not belonging to any of the above zones, do not extinguish for the most part according to their axial figures.

When examined with the stauroscope, the calcite interference-figures, i.e., the darkening of the Calderon double-plate, appear undisturbed only when one of the crystallographic axes coincides with a nicol chief section; isotrope sections, of course, exert no action on either plate during a complete revolution.

**Monoclinic Minerals.**—In the monoclinic system only the orthodiagonal axis $\overset{\shortmid}{b}$ coincides with one of the axes of elasticity; both of the remaining axes of elasticity form an angle with the crystallographic axes $\overset{\shortmid}{a}$ and $c'$. The plane of the optic axes is either parallel or at right angles to the plane of symmetry $\infty \breve{P}\infty$. In the monoclinic minerals there are the following possibilities for optical orientation:

If $AP \parallel \infty \breve{P}\infty$, then 1. M. $= \mathfrak{c}$  
or 1. M. $= \mathfrak{a}$  $\Big\} \overset{\shortmid}{b} = \mathfrak{b};$

and $\mathfrak{c}$ and $\mathfrak{a}$ are inclined to $c'$ and $\overset{\shortmid}{a}$.

If, on the contrary, $AP \perp \infty \breve{P}\infty$, then 1. M. $= \overset{\shortmid}{b} = \mathfrak{a}$,  
1. M. $= \overset{\shortmid}{b} = \mathfrak{c}$;  
or 2. M. $= \overset{\shortmid}{b} = \mathfrak{a}$,  
2. M. $= \overset{\shortmid}{b} = \mathfrak{c}$.

In this case $\mathfrak{b}$ and $\mathfrak{c}$, or $\mathfrak{b}$ and $\mathfrak{a}$, are inclined to $c'$ and $\overset{\shortmid}{a}$.

In Figs. 9 to 14 are given schematic representations of several rock-forming monoclinic minerals. The cross-sections are parallel to the plane of the optic axes. $A$ and $B$ are the

24 *DETERMINATION OF ROCK-FORMING MINERALS.*

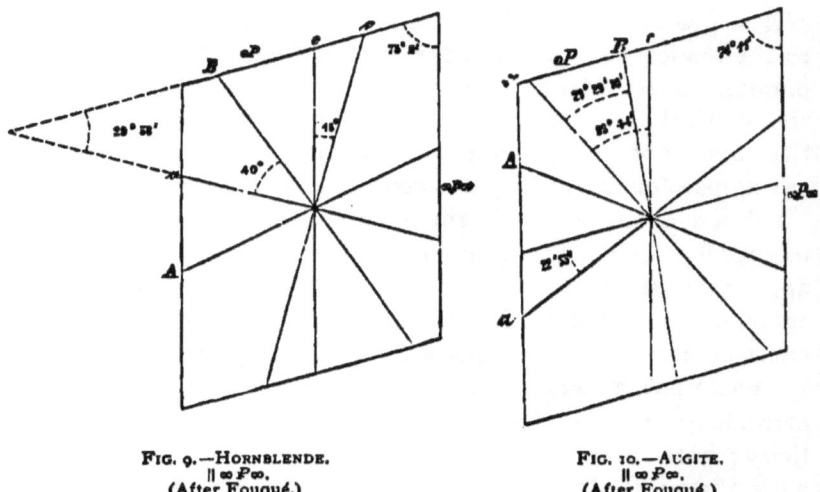

Fig. 9.—Hornblende.
|| ∞P∞.
(After Fouqué.)

Fig. 10.—Augite.
|| ∞P∞.
(After Fouqué.)

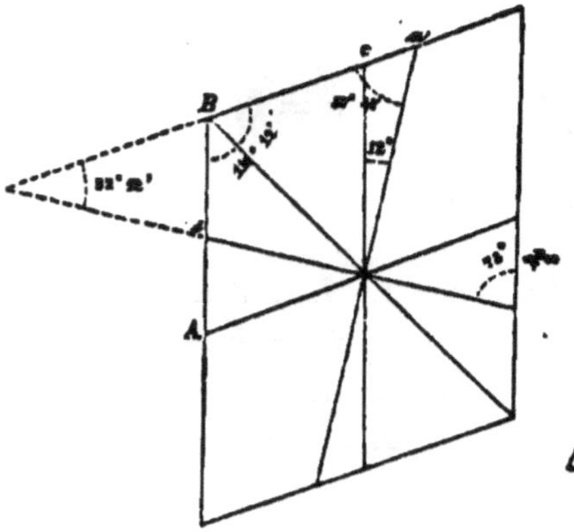

Fig. 11.—Wollastonite.
|| ∞P∞.
(After Fouqué.)

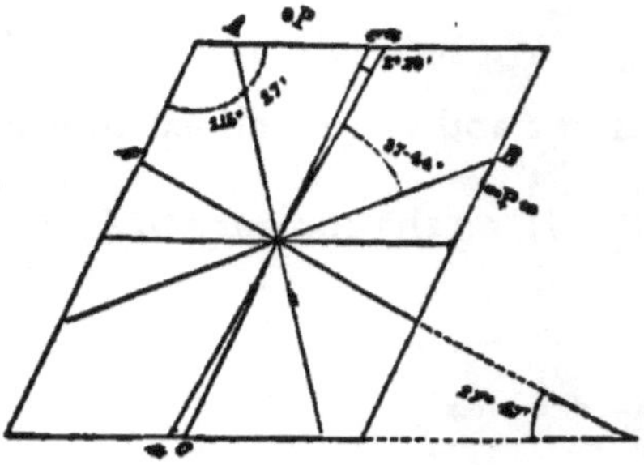

Fig. 12.—Epidote.
|| ∞P∞.
(After Fouqué.)

optic axes, $\mathfrak{a}$ and $\mathfrak{c}$ middle lines, and $c$ the vertical axis. In titanite, Fig. 13, there is shown, in addition, the dispersion of the optic axes $v < \rho$; in orthoclase, Fig. 14, attention is called to the case where the plane of the optic axes is $\perp \infty P \infty$. $A_1 B_1$ are the optic axes where $AP \parallel \infty P \infty$, $A_2 B_2$

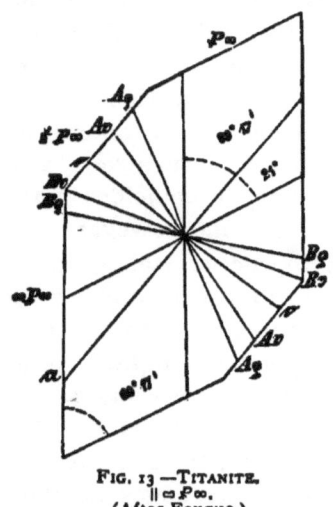

FIG. 13.—TITANITE.
$\parallel \infty P \infty$.
(After Fouque.)

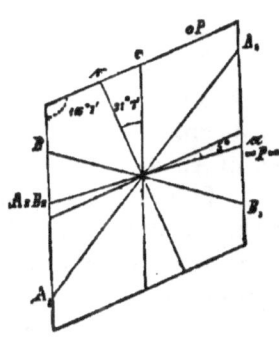

FIG. 14.—ORTHOCLASE.
$\parallel \infty P \infty$.
(After Fouque.)

where $AP$ is $\perp \infty P \infty$; in both cases $\mathfrak{a}$ is at an angle of 5° to the edge $oP : \infty P \infty$.

As a consequence of this inclination of the axes of elasticity to the crystallographic axes, longitudinal sections are not darkened during a complete revolution whenever the crystallographic axes or the cleavage-fissures parallel to these coincide with a nicol chief section, as is the case with rhombic minerals; but in many cases *extinction* (i.e., the section becomes dark under crossed nicols) first takes place when the crystallographic axes are inclined to the nicol chief section; i.e., it *extinguishes obliquely*.

Fig. 15 represents the *oblique extinction* of an optically-biaxial crystal cross-section, *abcd*, wherein *C* represents the vertical axis, and *vw* and *xy* are again the nicol cross-sections. The crystal cross-section is in the position where it completely extinguishes the ray; the inclination of the axis of elasticity lying in the direction *xy* to the vertical axis is 50° in this case.

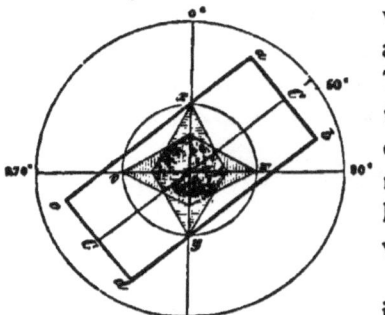

FIG. 15.—OBLIQUE EXTINCTION.

Extinction always follows, as is well known, whenever one axis of elasticity coincides with a nicol chief section; in the monoclinic system, however, two axes of elasticity are always inclined to the crystallographic axes. This angle of inclination is exceedingly characteristic for the various monoclinic crystals (comp. Figs. 9 to 14), and can be readily determined in parallel polarized light. As a consequence of the optical orientation this *oblique extinction* can be accurately determined only in those sections parallel to the plane of symmetry, $\infty P \infty$ (comp. Fig. 15). A cleavage-fissure parallel to the chief axis, or one of the edges parallel to it, is placed in position parallel to an arm of the cross-wires (i.e., a nicol chief section), and the degrees read on the circle of the stage. In this position, between crossed nicols, the cross-section is colored. The stage is then revolved until the cross-section is perfectly darkened. The number of degrees through which the stage must be revolved to cause total darkness gives the angle of inclination of one axis of elasticity to the vertical axis, the "angle of extinction;" e.g., on augite the inclination $c : c = 38°$, therefore $a : c = 52°$. This angle which one of the axes of elasticity forms with the vertical axis of course equals that which the other axis of elasticity makes with the normal to $\infty P \infty$. The angle of extinction can also be measured in relation to another known edge in the section || $\infty P\infty$; e.g., to the edge $oP : \infty P\infty$, i.e., as $oP$ has the same inclination as $\lambda$, the angle of inclination of the other axis of elasticity to the clinodiagonal.

The application of the stauroscope is therefore clear from what has just been stated. This is used, as it is very difficult to determine with the eye alone the exact point of maximum darkness; with the aid of an exceedingly sensitive Calderon double plate, however, this is possible with accuracy to within some few minutes; it is therefore peculiarly adapted to the more exact determination of the position of the plane of the axes of elasticity. Equality of shading in the double-plate of course follows when an axis of elasticity is parallel to the line of junction in the plate.

All sections of monoclinic crystals from the zone $oP : \infty P \infty$ extinguish parallel, as in these the orthodiagonal always coincides with one of the axes of elasticity; extinction follows, therefore, always when one of the edges parallel to the vertical axis or one of the cleavage-fissures parallel to this coincides with a chief section of a nicol. The shading of the Calderon double-plate will therefore be undisturbed only when the orthodiagonal coincides with a nicol chief section, i.e., the line of junction.

Sections from the zones $oP : \infty P\infty$ and $\infty P\infty : \infty P\infty$ always *extinguish* at an angle. The angle of extinction finally reaches 0° when the section is parallel to $oP$ or $\infty P\infty$.

Thus, according to Michel Lévy, the value of the oblique extinction varies in augite and hornblende with the direction of the section in the following manner:

## DETERMINATION OF ROCK-FORMING MINERALS.

| Direction of the section in the zone. | Augite. For $2v = 58° 59'$. | Hornblende. For $2v = 79° 24'$. |
|---|---|---|
| $oP : \infty P \infty$ | $\mathfrak{c} = c = 38° 44'$ <br> $\mathfrak{a} = a = 22° 55'$ } Maximum. <br> In sections parallel to $\infty P \infty$, $\mathfrak{a} : a = 22° 55'$; with more acute inclination of the section the value increases and reaches its maximum on the plane which makes an angle of $67° 14' 6''$ with $\infty P \infty$; it then lessens and becomes 0° in sections parallel to $oP$. | Maximum of $29° 58'$ to $14° 58'$ parallel to $\infty P \infty$, according to the species of hornblende, then decreases and becomes 0° parallel to $oP$. |
| $\infty P \infty : \infty P \infty$ | Maximum of extinction obliquity on $\infty P \infty$, $\mathfrak{c} : c = 38° 44'$. According to the inclination towards $\infty P \infty$ the angle decreases and becomes 0° parallel $\infty P \infty$. | Minimum parallel $\infty P \infty$, between $15°$ (for hornblende) and 0° (actinolite); increases and reaches the maximum (actinolite $= 15° 15' 20''$) in the plane which forms an angle of $38° 18' 25''$ with $\infty P \infty$; then decreases and equals 0° parallel $\infty P \infty$. |
| $oP : \infty \check{P} \infty$ | All sections possess parallel extinction. | |

**Triclinic Minerals.**—In the triclinic minerals no one of the three axes of elasticity coincides with the crystallographic axes.

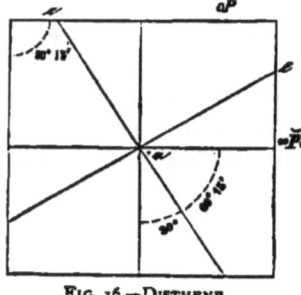

FIG. 16.—DISTHENE. ∥ ∞P∞. (After Fouqué.)

Fig. 16 is an example of the optical orientation of a triclinic rock-forming mineral. $\mathfrak{a}$, $\mathfrak{b}$, and $\mathfrak{c}$ are the three axes of elasticity; the angle of inclination of $\mathfrak{c}$ to the vertical axis in disthene is 30° measured in sections parallel to $\infty P \infty$; $\mathfrak{a}$ is exactly perpendicular to $\infty P \infty$.

All sections, therefore, parallel to the three pinacoidal faces have the oblique extinction. The obliquity of extinction to the faces $oP$ and $\infty \check{P} \infty$

is known in most of the rock-forming minerals, and gives, therefore, an excellent means of determining the minerals of this system. In the thin sections one can in most cases determine from the shape of the cross-section whether it is parallel to one of these pinacoids. If now an oblique extinction is proved on *both* of these pinacoids, it is sufficient for assignment of the mineral to the triclinic system, as in the monoclinic system the oblique extinction obtains only parallel to the plane $\infty P \infty$. Exact measurement of the extinction-obliquity must, however, be made on cleavage-lamellæ parallel $\infty P \infty$ and $oP$.

In the stauroscope the calcite interference-figures, i.e., the shading of the Calderon double-plate, will be disturbed whenever one of the crystallographic axes or a cleavage line or edge *parallel to them is parallel to a nicol chief section.*

## 2. Examination of Minerals in Convergent Polarized Light.

In order to produce convergent polarized light the condenser is placed above the polarizer, and, after the cross-section has been adjusted and centred in the microscope, the ocular is removed and the nicols crossed. If the cross-section is very small, and high magnifying powers must be used, thereby decreasing the interference-figures, the Bertrand lens, for the necessary enlargement, is inserted within the tube in place of the ocular, and the nicols of course are again crossed.

The interference-figures observed with the condenser in different sections of the double-refracting minerals are exactly the same as those obtained on such sections with the Nörremberg instrument. The interference-figures, however, are not so clear and large in the microscope, as the mineral cross-sections are very small, and in the slides are exceedingly thin.  The great advantage gained through the application of the condenser to microscopical petrography, as first recommended by Lasaulx and Bertrand, is evident; e.g., we can determine whether a mineral is a single-refracting, optically uniaxial or biaxial, if but a single isotrope cross-section of the mineral is at hand.  The following observations will demonstrate this.  Of course the examination in parallel polarized light must always precede that in convergent light.

Clear interference-figures can be obtained on using objective 9, Hartnack, and the Bertrand magnifying-lens in convergent light, if the mineral cross-section is not less than 0.05 mm.; if the cross-sections are less, their determination in convergent light is impossible in most cases.  In such cases the examination in parallel polarized light is all the more important.  The behavior of mineral cross-sections in convergent light for the different systems of crystallization is the following:

**Regular and Amorphous Minerals.**—The amorphous minerals and those crystallizing in the regular system remain dark throughout a complete revolution in all cross-sections, and show no interference-phenomena.

**Optically-Uniaxial Minerals** (Fig. 17, I and II).—The isotrope transverse sections of tetragonal and hexagonal minerals show, in case the section is exactly at right angles to the chief axis (Fig. 17, I), a fixed dark interference-cross with several colored concentric rings.  The presence and number of the rings in the cross-section depend on its thickness and the power of double-refraction of the mineral.  If the section is not exactly at right angles to the chief axis, as is evident in ordinary light from the irregular transverse section (e.g., distorted rectangles or hexagons), or the confirmation of an imperfect depolarization in parallel polarized light, the interference-cross in convergent polarized light remains undisturbed throughout a complete horizontal revolution; i.e., it does not open, but moves according to the lesser or greater inclination of the section to the chief axis either within the field or without on the circumference, and in the same direction as the stage is revolved.

If the section is so inclined that the axial point of the interference-figure falls without the field of the microscope (Fig. 17, II), it will not appear in parallel light as isotrope (show polarization-colors and become darkened four times during a revolution); in this case, by revolving the stage from 90° to 90° only one part of the interference-cross will appear as a straight black cloud in the field. The cloud moves, during a revolution of the stage through 90°, from one side of the microscope-stage, i.e., the field of the microscope, to the other in the same plane. As will be shown later, similar pictures will be obtained in sections of optically-biaxial minerals which are cut at right angles to one of the optic axes, yet the black cloud in these moves about an axial point situate within.

**For the Determination of the Character of the Double Refraction** (in sections at right angles to the chief axis) a fourth undulation mica plate is most advantageously employed. As already stated, this is laid on the tube from which the ocular has been removed, and the analyzer placed upon it, with the nicols crossed, and with the plane of the optic axes of the mica inclined at an angle of 45° to a nicol chief section. The black interference cross of a uniaxial crystal diminishes until only two dark points remain and the colored rings are disturbed.

If the two dark points are so situated that the line joining them is perpendicular to the plane of the optic axes of the mica (generally indicated by a mark on the plate), then the mineral under examination is optically *positive;* if the joining line of both the dark points concides with the direction of the axial plane of the mica, the mineral is optically *negative*.

**Optically-Biaxial Minerals** (Fig. 17, III, IV, and V).—If an optically-biaxial mineral be cut at right angles to one of the middle lines bisecting the angle which the two optic axes make

## 32  DETERMINATION OF ROCK-FORMING MINERALS.

### OPTICALLY-UNIAXIAL CRYSTALS.

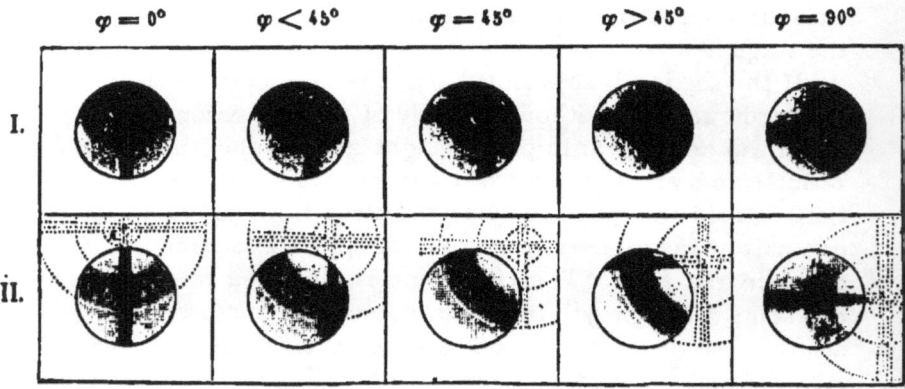

### OPTICALLY-BIAXIAL CRYSTALS.

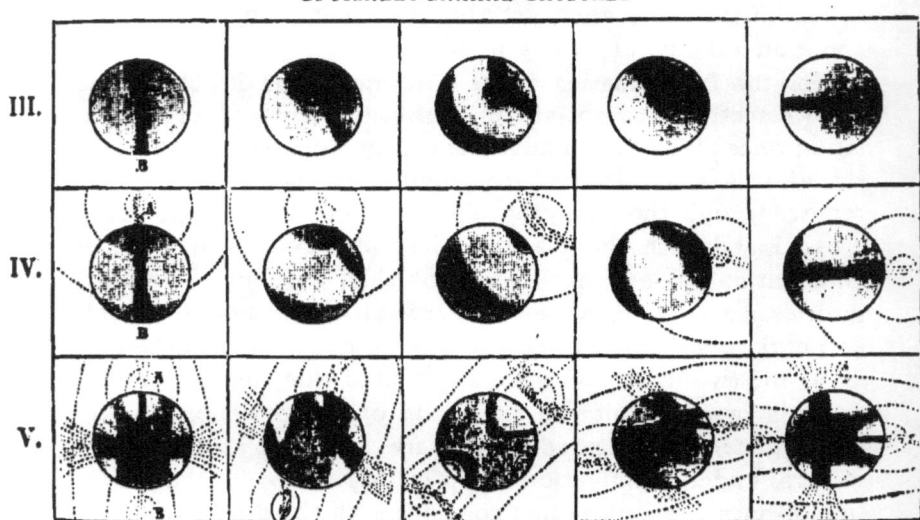

FIG. 27.—INTERFERENCE-FIGURES OF DOUBLE-REFRACTING MINERALS ON USING THE CONDENSER IN THE POLARIZATION-MICROSCOPE. (After Fouqué.)

$\phi$ is the angle which a vertical plane passing through an optic axis $A$ forms with the optic chief section of the polarizer.

with each other (Fig. 17, V), and be examined in convergent polarized light, an interference-figure is seen, in case the plane of the optic axes coincides with a nicol chief section, which is formed from two closed systems of curvature corresponding to the two axial points; these in turn are surrounded by a larger system of curvatures, the lemniscates, and are traversed by a black cross of which one arm, the narrower, passes through the two axial points and thus shows the position of the plane of the optic axes, and whose second arm, much broader, is at right angles to it.

The number of the colored curves depends, again, on the thickness of the mineral leaflet; if this is very thin, as may be expected in rock-sections, only the black cross is visible, thus resembling the interference-figure of optically-uniaxial crystals. The difference is immediately seen on revolving the mineral section on the stage (Fig. 17, V, $\varphi > 45°$); in the optically-biaxial minerals the cross does not remain fixed, but opens and divides into two hyperbolas which move about either axial point and by revolving 90° again close into the cross.

The distance between the two points, or the hyperbolas passing through them, gives both the position of the plane of the optic axes and the magnitude of the axial angle; if this angle is large, then each of the hyperbolas lies without the field, so soon as the plane of the axes forms an angle of 45° with a nicol chief section (Fig. 17, V, $\varphi = 45°$). It can generally be determined from the proximate estimation of the magnitude of the axial angle whether the section is made perpendicular to the first or second middle line. There are cases, as in the rhombic pyroxenes, where the acute axial angle differs but little from the obtuse; in such cases it is impossible to determine by the microscope which axes of elasticity coincide with the first and second middle lines.

If it is known whether the section is at right angles to the first or second middle line, then it can be determined which of the axes of elasticity 𝔞 or 𝔠 coincides with the same, i.e., the optical orientation. If the axial angle is very small, the interference-figure will be similar to the optically-uniaxial mineral and the cross apparently remains closed.

**The Determination of the Character of Double-refraction** in the optically-biaxial crystals is effected in the following manner: The axial figure is placed in such a position that the plane of the optic axis is at an angle of 45° with a nicol chief section, i.e., the cross seems merged into the hyperbolas; the quartz plate described on page 10, or the quartz wedge, is so used beneath the analyzer that the axis of revolution of the quartz plate or quartz wedge is at first parallel and then perpendicular to the plane of the optic axes. In any case, a change of the interference-figure is visible on revolving the quartz plate or on pushing in the quartz wedge; the inner rings move from the circumference of the field towards the centre, the outer lemniscates, on the other hand, in the opposite direction. If this enlargement and movement of the rings occur when the axis of revolution of the quartz plate or the quartz wedge is perpendicular to the plane of the optic axis, the mineral is *positive* double-refracting; under reversed conditions, *negative*.

If the mineral was proved positive double-refracting on sections at right angles to the first middle line, then the axis of the least elasticity coincides with it and the plan is the following:

First middle line = 𝔠 (positive);
Second middle line = 𝔞;
Optic normals always = 𝔟.

**The reverse** is true in case the second middle line is positive:

First middle line = 𝔞 (negative);
Second middle line = 𝔠;
Optic normals = 𝔟.

Sections at right angles to one of the two optic axes appear as isotrope in parallel polarized light, and show in convergent polarized light a spherical or elliptical colored ring-system traversed by a dark cloud (Fig. 17, III). If the section is exactly at right angles to the optic axis, on revolving the preparation the cloud moves in a contrary direction about the axial point lying in the centre of the ring-system; on sections more or less inclined to the optic axes (Fig. 17, IV) a movement of the whole axis-figure is observed concordant with the revolving of the object-stage.

If the section is so oblique to the optic axis (Fig. 17, IV) that the axial point falls without the field, only a part of the cloud ever lies in the centre of the field on revolving from 90° to 90°, just as with the optically-uniaxial minerals cut inclined to the axis; the difference consists, however, in the movement of the cloud itself about the axis-point in the direction opposite to that of the revolving-stage. Sections parallel to the plane of the optic axes, at right angles to b, show no interference-figures in convergent polarized light, become colored as in parallel polarized light, and appear dark whenever an axis of elasticity coincides with a nicol chief section.

**Rhombic Minerals.**—Sections at right angles to the crystallographic axes, consequently parallel to the pinacoidal planes, show perfectly the optical orientation. According to the position of the plane of the optic axes (see page 22), either the vertical axis, the brachy- or macro-diagonal will be the first middle line. One of the pinacoidal sections will show perpendicular to it the first middle line with the smaller angle of the optic axes, a second the appearance of the second middle line with the larger axial angle, and the third parallel to the plane of the axes will show no interference-figures. The transverse sections are the most favorable (at right angles to $c'$); as on the one hand but few of the rock-forming minerals, e.g., olivine, have the axial planes parallel $oP$, consequently in these, at any rate, an interference-figure is seen; and on the other hand, as the predominating cleavage is prismatic or pinacoidal, it can be controlled as to whether the section is made exactly at right angles to the vertical axis.

As a consequence of the dispersion of the optic axes the interference-figure develops in white light a varying color-distribution according as the axial angle for red is greater or smaller than for blue ($\rho \gtrless v$); in the rhombic system the distribution is symmetrical to the middle lines. Where $\rho > v$, in the position: axial plane parallel to the nicol chief section, the inner closed curves are blue on the inner limb, and red on the outer; in the position: axial plane inclined 45° to the nicol chief section, the hyperbolas become red on the inner, the convex surface, and blue on the outer, the concave surface. Where $\rho < v$ the reverse holds true. The phenomena of dispersion, when not too weak, can be studied in convergent light very well in the rock-constituents, e.g., zoisite, etc. Often the simple observation of an hyperbola in relation to the colored edges suffices for the determination of the form of axial dispersion; it is not absolutely necessary, therefore, that the sections should be at right angles to the middle lines.

**Monoclinic Minerals.**—If the plane of the optic axes in monoclinic minerals is parallel $\infty P \infty$, the sections at right angles to the vertical axis and parallel $\infty P \infty$ will not show a perpendicular development of a middle line, as is the case with the corresponding pinacoidal sections of rhombic crystals, but a displaced axial picture ($AP$ parallel to the edge $oP : \infty P \infty$ or $\infty P \infty : \infty P \infty$); or simply an appearance of one of the optic axes according to the degree of inclination of the middle line to the crystallographic axes. Sections at right angles to the middle lines obtain only accidentally and are extremely rare (compare with the rhombic minerals); such, of course, spring from the zone $oP : \infty P \infty$. In prismatic sections the displaced axial picture or appearance of one axis is not visible in the middle of the mineral leaflet, but at one side. If the inclination of the axes of elasticity to the crystallographic axes is very small, as, e.g., from $\mathfrak{a} : c$ in mica, the mineral is apparently

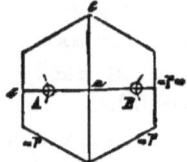
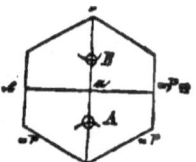

FIG. 18.—MUSCOVITE. $\mid oP$.
Mica I. Class.
(After Fouqué.)

FIG. 19.—BIOTITE. $\mid oP$.
Mica II. Class.
(After Fouqué.)

rhombic (Figs. 18 and 19). In the mica minerals the first middle line $\mathfrak{a}$ differs but little from the normals to $oP$; $A$ and $B$ are the two optic axes; $\mathfrak{a}, \mathfrak{b}$, and $\mathfrak{c}$, the axes of elasticity.

If the plane of the optic axes be at right angles to $\infty \check{P} \infty$, an appearance of one middle line perpendicular to $\infty \check{P} \infty$ may always be observed; yet such an appearance is not shown on sections parallel $oP$ or $\infty \check{P} \infty$; on these a distorted axial picture is again visible, $AP$ parallel to the edge $oP : \infty \check{P} \infty$.

In the **Triclinic Minerals** a perpendicular appearance of a middle line obtains in none of the pinacoidal sections, the plane of the optic axes is neither parallel nor at right angles to a pinacoid, and only portions of the interference-figure can be described in the pinacoidal sections.

The phenomena of dispersion in monoclinic and triclinic minerals cannot be established with great precision by the microscope or prove of value in determining the minerals; in general it can only be determined whether $\rho \gtrless v$.

## 3. Behavior of Twinned Crystals in Polarized Light.

Twins of the **Regular System** cannot be recognized as such either in parallel or convergent polarized light, as both individuals remain equally dark between crossed nicols; therefore the form of the cross-section and the cleavage must be solely regarded in the determination of the law of twinning.

**Twins of the Tetragonal and Hexagonal Systems.**—*a*. With *parallel axial systems.* These also, for the same reason as the regular minerals, cannot be recognized in polarized light.

*b.* On the other hand, twins with inclined axial systems can be recognized easily in parallel polarized light. In these minerals the chief axes and axes of elasticity form an angle with each other, and the twinned crystal will not, therefore, act as a unit in extinguishing the light; e.g., rutile $C:C_1 = 114° 26'$ (Fig. 20). $C,C_1$ are the chief axes of both individuals, and $N$ is the twinning-seam.

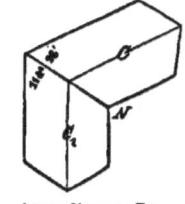

According to 3P∞.   According to P∞.
Fig. 20.—Rutile Twins.

When one individual appears dark between crossed nicols, the second becomes colored. The angle between the two chief axes can therefore be determined, if an edge of one individual parallel to the chief axis be first placed on the centred stage parallel to the nicol chief section so that it is darkened, the stage revolved until the second is darkened, and the number of degrees read through which it was necessary to revolve the stage.

If several individuals are twinned (polysynthetic twins), these are wont to occur in laminations, as, e.g., in calcite, twinning-plane — $\tfrac{1}{2}R$ (Fig. 21): in these, in sections inclined to the twinning-plane, the axes of elasticity of the lamellæ 1, 3, 5, etc., have a similar position, i.e., they extinguish at the same instant. In sections parallel to the twinning-plane no twinning striations can be observed, as in this case but a single individual is met with.

Fig. 21.—Calcite Twin.
According to — $\tfrac{1}{2}R$.
$R$·face.

## METHODS OF INVESTIGATION. 39

If the twinning-plane in calcite is the $R$-face, although never occurring in the rock-forming individuals, the chief axes form nearly a right angle with each other, $C : C_1 = 89° \, 8'$; both individuals therefore extinguish the ray at nearly the same instant.

**Twins of the Rhombic System.**—The most common examples of this system are:

1. Twinning-plane a face of a brachydome.
2.      "      "      pyramid.
3.      "      "      prism.

In the first two cases the crystallographic axes form an angle with each other; in longitudinal sections of such twins, therefore, no unit-extinction between crossed nicols can occur. In staurolite, for example, the vertical axes $c : c_1$, which in this case coincide with the axis of elasticity $\mathfrak{c}$, form with each other an angle of 60° according to the law $\frac{3}{2} P \frac{3}{2}$; but

FIG. 22.—STAUROLITE TWINS ACCORDING TO $\frac{3}{2} P \frac{3}{2}$; $\frac{3}{2} P \infty$.

an angle of 90° according to the law $\frac{3}{2} P \infty$; i.e., in the latter case both individuals extinguish together (Fig. 22).

A further point of recognition for the twinning development in colored minerals lies in the pleochroitic behavior, as both individuals, by virtue of their different position with reference to the chief direction of vibration of the polarizer, will be differently colored.

If one of the prismatic faces is the twinning-plane, a law exemplified, e.g., often on aragonite, rarely on cordierite, etc. (Fig. 23), the longitudinal sections parallel to the vertical axis, when in parallel polarized light, show no difference in the direction of extinction, as the axes of elasticity of both individuals coinciding with the $c'$-axis are again parallel. The two individuals in such sections, however, can be accurately distinguished in convergent polarized light, as the same interference-figure does not appear on both members; but the appearance of a middle line on one side and only one of the

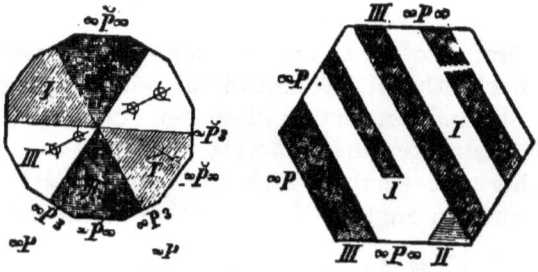

FIG. 23.—CORDIERITE TWINS.
(According to v. Lasaulx.)

optic axes on the other, etc., will be observed, the phenomena depending on the direction of the section.

Penetration twins or trillings after this law often imitate the form of an hexagonal prism. Cross-sections of such twins, however, divide into six sectors in parallel polarized light, two of which in opposite positions will extinguish at the same instant. The axes of elasticity of these three individuals are inclined 60° to each other; an equal inclination of the plane of the optic axes in the individuals can therefore be observed on such twins by convergent polarized light, provided they are not of a mineral with the plane of the optic axes parallel to $oP$.

**Twins of the Monoclinic System.**—The most commonly-occurring twinnings are according to the law: twinning-plane $\infty P \infty$. Twinnings according to a prismatic face seldom occur.

Augite, amphibole, epidote, and gypsum may be brought forward as examples of the rock-forming minerals with repeated twinning according to $\infty P\infty$. Sections perpendicular to the twinning-plane and parallel to $\infty P\infty$ will show, in parallel polarized light, in both individuals, an oblique extinction equally inclined to the vertical axis, i.e., the twinning-seam or line of development, but in opposite directions; e.g., on augite $c : \mathfrak{c} = c_1 : \mathfrak{c}_1 = 38°$ (Fig. 24). Such sections in convergent light show no difference; nor can interference-figures be recognized, as in these minerals the plane of symmetry is at the

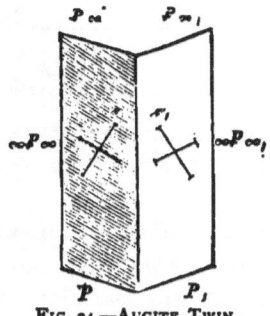
Fig. 24.—Augite Twin according to $\infty P\infty$. ‖ $\infty P\infty$.

Fig. 25.—Polysynthetic Augite Twin according to $\infty P\infty$. Section $\perp c'$-axis.

same time the plane of the optic axes. Such twins, with parallel vertical axes, can be easily recognized in parallel polarized light as belonging to a monoclinic mineral, as both individuals, if rhombic, would extinguish at the same instant. As already stated, several twinning lamellæ are often interpolated according to this law (Fig. 25); therefore in parallel polarized light, especially in sections at right angles to the vertical axis, there is often observed an interchange of brilliantly-colored lines, all parallel to a boundary-line of the apparently simple crystal. Twins occur but rarely after the plane of a dome or pyramid, as in augite according to $-P2$, and more rarely still penetration-twins according to $-P\infty$. In the latter case we are vigorously reminded of the staurolite twinning; but the extinction in these augite twins, so commonly occurring in certain basaltic rocks, does not occur parallel to the vertical axes of both individuals on epidote (Fig. 26). One or more narrow interpolated twinning-lamellæ are often

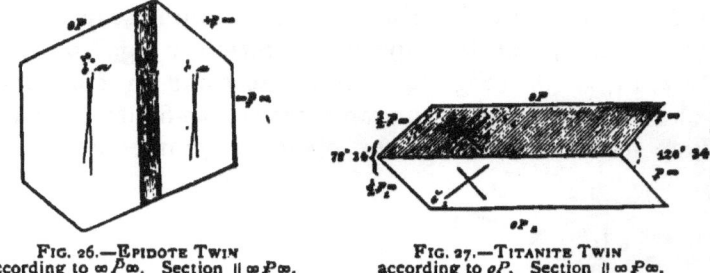

Fig. 26.—Epidote Twin according to $\infty P\infty$. Section ∥ $\infty P\infty$.

Fig. 27.—Titanite Twin according to $oP$. Section ∥ $\infty P\infty$.

noticed in the hexagonal sections parallel to the plane of symmetry, which is the same as the plane of the optic axes parallel to $\infty P\infty$.

In titanite (Fig. 27), contact-twins often occur after the law: twinning-plane $oP$. In this case sections at right angles to the twinning-plane, where they are not parallel to $\infty P\infty$, also develop on either side an angle of extinction equally in-

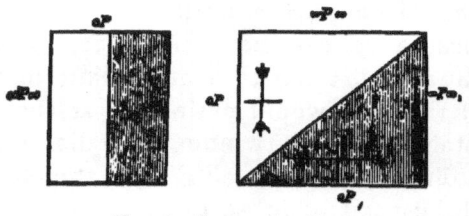

Fig. 28.—Orthoclase Twin according to the Carlsbad and Baveno laws.

clined to the vertical axis. Extinction follows here nearly parallel to the face $\frac{1}{2}P\infty$, as the first middle line is nearly perpendicular to it. Sections parallel $\infty P\infty$ develop in convergent polarized light one optic axis in each individual, but in opposite directions.

## METHODS OF INVESTIGATION. 43

The most varied twinning development occurs on orthoclase (Fig. 28). These will be described more exactly in Part II.

**Twins of the Triclinic System.**—The triclinic rock-forming minerals, especially plagioclase and disthene, are quite commonly polysynthetically twinned; i.e., several parallel twin-lamellæ are interpolated in the crystal. Such twins can be recognized easily also in parallel polarized light, in that the separate twinning-lamellæ appear with varying polarization-colors, and the directions of extinction do not have the same position in two adjoining lamellæ.

In plagioclase the "Albite law" is the most common: twinning-plane $\infty \check{P} \infty$ (Fig. 29). Sections at right angles to this plane from the zone $oP : \infty \check{P} \infty$ will always develop in parallel polarized light the polysynthetic twinning-striations. Such

 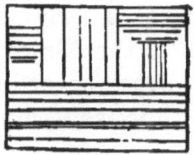

FIG. 29.—POLYSYNTHETIC PLAGIOCLASE TWIN. $\parallel \infty \check{P} \infty$.

FIG. 30.—PLAGIOCLASE TWINNED according to the Albite and Pericline laws.

twins were not possible in the monoclinic system, as the plane in the monoclinic system $\infty P \infty$ corresponding to the plane $\infty \check{P} \infty$ is at the same time a plane of symmetry, and such a symmetrical development gives no twins. Such polysynthetic twins are wanting in orthoclase. It is easy, therefore, to distinguish orthoclase from plagioclase, although it is not impossible for the latter also to occur as a simple twin.

A second less common twinning-law of plagioclase, appearing also combined with the Albite law, is the "Pericline law:" twinning-plane at right angles to the zone $oP : \infty \check{P} \infty$, developed after a plane which, with the prismatic faces, gives a rhombic section.

The twinned developments of plagioclase also will be discussed again at the proper point in Part II. If the Albite and Pericline laws are combined (Fig. 30), one will observe in sections cut approximately parallel to $\infty P \infty$ a double system of twinning-striations cutting each other at nearly right angles.

Disthene occurs, though in rocks more rarely, as twins, according to the following laws:

I. Twinning-plane $\infty P \infty$.
II. " at right angles to the $c'$-axis.
III. " " " " $b$-axis.
IV. " parallel $oP$. This form of twinning is often repeated also, and is commonly observed in the disthene occurring in rocks.

And, finally, it may be mentioned that two twins after one definite law can combine according to another law; e.g., as often occurs in plagioclase, where two plagioclase species twinned after the Albite law (twinning-plane $\infty P \infty$) are united with each other according to the so-called Carlsbad law, common on orthoclase (twinning-plane $\infty P \infty$).

### 4. Determination of the Index of Refraction.

H. Clifton Sorby. On a new method for determining the index of double-refraction in thin sections of mineral substances. Miner. Mag. 1877, No. 6.

H. Clifton Sorby. Determination of minerals in thin sections by means of their refractive indices. Miner. Mag. 1878, No. 8.

J. Thoulet. Contributions à l'étude des propriétés phys. et chim. des minér. microsc. Bull. Soc. minér. 1880, III, 62 et 1883, VI, 184.

Michel Lévy. Bull Soc. minér. 1883, VI, 143 et 1884, VII, 43.

One method of determining the index of refraction in microscopic mineral particles has been mentioned before, under the description of the polarization-microscope (page 14). The following method, applicable in many cases, was proposed first by Thoulet:

Certain minerals, as olivine, different augites, titanite, etc.,

## METHODS OF INVESTIGATION. 45

show on their sections a rough shagreenous surface, considered as almost characteristic for olivine; this is much plainer if the rock-section is not covered with Canada balsam and a covering-glass. This phenomenon is a result of imperfect polishing of the slide, i.e., of the particular mineral, and disappears on a more perfect finishing. By immersion of the mineral showing such a rough upper surface in different liquids whose index of refraction is known, it is possible to determine the index of refraction of the mineral, as the rough upper surface will disappear as soon as a liquid is used whose index of refraction equals or is very near that of the mineral. The liquid filling the depressions in the mineral on immersion thus removes all difference between depression and elevation in the mineral leaflets. Examples of such liquids where $n =$ index of refraction are:

| | |
|---|---|
| Water, | $n = 1.34$ |
| Alcohol, | $n = 1.36$ |
| Glycerine, | $n = 1.41.$ |
| Olive-oil, | $n = 1.47$ |
| Beech-oil, | $n = 1.50.$ |
| Clove-oil, | $n = 1.54$ |
| Cinnamon-oil, | $n = 1.58.$ |
| Bitter-almond-oil, | $n = 1.60.$ |
| Carbon disulphide, | $n = 1.63.$ |

### 5. PLEOCHROISM OF DOUBLE-REFRACTING MINERALS.

*Determination of the Axial Colors.*

GROTH and ROSENBUSCH, l. c.
TSCHERMAK, Sitzungsber. d. k. Akad. d. Wissensch., math.-naturw. Cl., Wien. 1869, 59. Bd., Mai-Heft.
LASPEYRES. Groth's Zeitschr. f. Krystallographie. 1880, IV, p. 454.

We understand by pleochroism that property of double-refracting minerals whereby the light penetrating in different directions shows different colors. Of course only such double-refracting minerals as are colored could show the phenomenon, as it depends upon the varying refraction and partial absorption of the light penetrating in the different directions. Pleochroism, or absorption, stands in closest relationship to double-refraction. Optically-uniaxial colored minerals show differences of absorption in two directions; the optically-biaxial in three directions at right angles to each other and corresponding to the different axes of elasticity.

**Optically-Uniaxial Minerals.**—On looking through such a mineral in a direction at first parallel and then perpendicular to the chief axis, a difference in color will be noted. The color observed on looking through parallel to the chief axis is called the "basal color" (*Basis-farbe*), the color at right angles to it the "axial color" (*Axen-farbe*). If a transverse section of such a mineral be examined in a polarization-microscope, with only the polarizer in position,—the single nicol thus performing the duty of a dichroscope,—and the section be turned through one complete revolution, no difference in color is noticed, as only rays vibrating at right angles to the optic axis are in the field, and there is no double-refraction in the direction parallel to the chief axis. If, on the other hand, a longitudinal section be placed in the microscope, a change of color is noticed on revolving the stage. The greatest difference in absorption is noticed first when the chief axis is parallel to the nicol chief section, and secondly when it is at right angles to it. Thus, e.g., tourmaline (Fig. 31; $xy$ denoting the optical chief section of the polarizer, $c$ the chief axis, $a$ and $c$ the two axes of elasticity), which, as is well known, absorbs the ordinary ray much more powerfully than the extraordinary, appears nearly black when its $c$-axis is at right angles to the shorter diagonal of the polarizer, but shows a light gray or blue color when the $c$-axis is parallel to the nicol chief section. Consequently the ordinary ray ($o$) vibrating at right angles to the chief axis is transmitted with darker colors; the extraordinary ray ($\varepsilon$) vibrating parallel to the chief axis with a lighter gray or bluer color. As the double-refraction of tourmaline is negative, therefore $\mathfrak{a} = c$ and $\mathfrak{c} \perp c$. We can thus express the axial colors: $\mathfrak{a}$ = light gray ($\varepsilon$), $\mathfrak{c}$ = black ($o$). And in general, in minerals with *negative* double-refraction the *ordinary* ray is more strongly absorbed; in those with *positive* double-refraction,

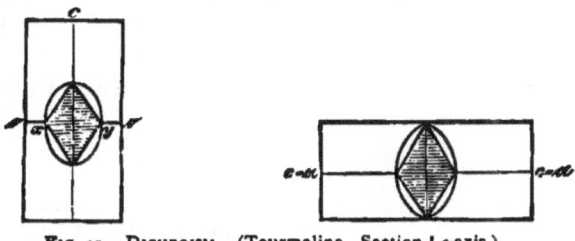

FIG. 31.—DICHROISM. (Tourmaline. Section ∥ $c$-axis.)
(After Fouqué.)

the extraordinary ray. The color with which $o$ is transmitted corresponds with the basal color, while the axial color is compounded from both of the colors for $o$ and $\varepsilon$. In order to observe the colors of the faces, the under nicol, the polarizer, is of course also removed, and the investigation carried on by ordinary light.

**Optically-Biaxial Minerals.**—The differences of absorption are developed in optically-biaxial minerals in three directions at right angles to each other and coinciding with the three axes of elasticity for the most part. We discriminate here, therefore, between three face-colors and three axial colors. The three axial colors corresponding to the axes of elasticity are designated by $\mathfrak{a}$, $\mathfrak{b}$, and $\mathfrak{c}$; each face-color is composed of two axial colors. If one looks through a cordierite crystal, e.g., through the plane $oP$, i.e., in the direction of the vertical axis, here coinciding with the axis of elasticity $\mathfrak{a}$, it appears blue; that is to say, the face-color $A$ which is composed of the axial colors $\mathfrak{b}$ and $\mathfrak{c}$ is blue; parallel $\infty \breve{P} \infty$ ($\mathfrak{c}$) the face-color $C$ is yellowish white from the composition of $\mathfrak{a}$ and $\mathfrak{b}$; and parallel to $\infty \bar{P} \infty$ ($\mathfrak{b}$) the face-color $B$ is a bluish white from composition of the axial colors $\mathfrak{a}$ and $\mathfrak{c}$. On the other hand, the axial colors for cordierite are: $\mathfrak{a}$, yellowish white; $\mathfrak{b}$, light Prussian blue; $\mathfrak{c}$, dark Prussian blue. The determination is effected in the following manner: If a cross-section of a crystal whose optical orientation is known be selected, e.g., a section of hypersthene (Fig. 32) at right angles to the $c'$-axis (parallel $oP$), the axial colors $\mathfrak{b}$ and $\mathfrak{c}$ can be determined in it with the polarizer; on turning the stage, first the brachy-axis ($\breve{a} = \mathfrak{a}$) and then the macro-axis

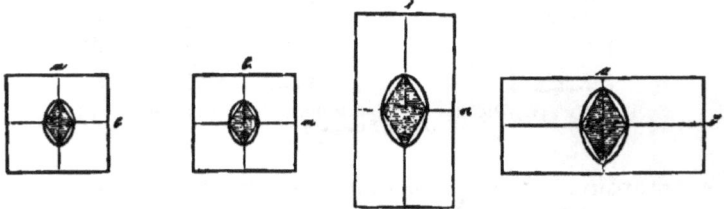

FIG. 32.—TRICHROISM. (Hypersthene. Sections $\perp c'$-axis and $|\infty \breve{P}\infty$.)

($\bar{b} = \mathfrak{b}$) is parallel to the nicol chief section, and above the polarizer. Another cross-section of mineral is needed in order to determine the axial color for $\mathfrak{c}$. This section in the case cited can be either parallel $\infty \bar{P} \infty$ or $\infty \breve{P} \infty$. Parallel to $\infty \bar{P} \infty$ two axial colors, $\mathfrak{a}$ and $\mathfrak{c}$, can again be determined; the axial color $\mathfrak{c}$ is observed so soon as the vertical axis ($c' = \mathfrak{c}$) coincides with a nicol chief section, that for $\mathfrak{a}$ so soon as the brachy-axis coincides. The axial color $\mathfrak{a}$, therefore, was determined twice, and must correspond in both cases if the sections were of equal thickness.

If pleochroitic minerals are examined in extremely thin sections, as is always the case in rock thin sections, the differences of absorption are often imperceptible. This is true of cordierite and andalusite, while tourmaline, e.g., shows the most marked dichroism even in the thinnest needles. For this reason it is advisable to prepare a somewhat thicker section from the rock under examination for the investigation of the optical properties of the larger mineral constituents.

The power of absorption in different directions in any mineral is represented by an $>$ or $<$ annexed to the axes of elasticity; in tourmaline, e.g., $o > \varepsilon$ or $\mathfrak{c} > \mathfrak{a}$, i.e., the ordinary ray is more powerfully absorbed than the extraordinary. In cordierite $\mathfrak{c} > \mathfrak{b} > \mathfrak{a}$, or, as the axes of elasticity in the rhombic minerals coincide with the crystallographic axes, in these according to the optical orientation corresponding $\bar{b} > \breve{a} > \grave{c}$; i.e., the absorption in cordierite is greatest in the direction of the macro-axis.

In tetragonal and hexagonal minerals the directions in which the greatest color-difference can be recognized—Laspeyres calls them "axes of absorption"—coincide with the two axes of elasticity, i.e., are parallel and at right angles to the chief axis; in the rhombic, with the three axes of elasticity, i.e., the crystallographic axes; in the monoclinic and triclinic minerals, however, according to the latest investigations of Laspeyres, the three axes of absorption do not coincide with axes of elasticity, but yet are at right angles to each other.

In the monoclinic minerals there appears to be but one coincidence of an absorption-axis, and that with the orthodiagonal; while each of the others, lying in the plane of symmetry, forms an angle with the axes of elasticity. Colorless double-refracting minerals, e.g., apatite, often show pleochroism as a consequence of the regular inclosures of colored particles or other mineral fragments.

And, finally, it may be mentioned that the axial colors of pleochroitic minerals do not remain constant, in that often on cross-sections of one and the same mineral now $\mathfrak{c} > \mathfrak{a} > \mathfrak{b}$ and now $\mathfrak{c} > \mathfrak{b} > \mathfrak{a}$, and so on, are observed; or one and the same mineral can be now feebly and now powerfully pleochroitic. Nevertheless pleochroism is a characteristic for certain minerals, as andalusite, cordierite, tourmaline, hypersthene, hornblende, biotite, and others, and thus lends its aid to their determination.

## B. Chemical Methods of Investigation.

The chemical examination of rocks should go hand in hand with the microscopical investigation; a quantitative analysis will always give a welcome explanation of the mineralogical composition, or at least will confirm the microscopical examination to a greater or lesser degree. It is, however, impossible to determine the component minerals or to give their individual chemical composition from such a rock-analysis *alone*. In order that the rock-forming minerals may be separately analyzed and their chemical composition correctly determined it is necessary to separate them from each other. Such a mechanical separation can be simply effected with a needle beneath a microscope, when only a small fragment may be needed for a qualitative chemical test of the minerals; or it may be effected by solutions of high specific gravity, thus taking advantage of the differing specific gravities of the minerals for obtaining larger quantities of mineral for the quantitative chemical investigation. There is also another advantage in this latter method, as the specific gravities of the separate mineral components are thus known.

If the rock under examination is coarsely granular, the separate components often can be distinguished with the naked eye and the different cleavage-leaflets be examined optically as well as by chemical qualitative and quantitative analysis. In this separation it is, e.g., impossible to separate several feldspars from each other in case they occur in the same rock. Such a separation of the components is also impossible in the fine-grained rocks. In order to examine chemically the rock-constituents in such cases and thus obtain a clue in the determination, the microchemical reactions are applied; the component under examination beneath the microscope is dissolved either directly on the rock-section or on detached granules, and treated with such reagents as give exceptionally characteristic precipitates. Sometimes a more exact and careful mechanical separation of the mineral components is attempted by treating the powdered rocks with solutions of high specific gravity.

A partial analysis of the portion of rock soluble or insoluble in hydrochloric acid in many cases gives valuable conclusions and simplifies the determination of the constituents.

### MICROCHEMICAL METHODS.

H. ROSENBUSCH, l. c., p. 107, und N. Jahrb. für Min. und Geol. 1871, p. 914.
F. ZIRKEL. Basaltgesteine und Lehrb. d. Petrographie.
A. STRENG. Ueber die mikroskopische Unterscheidung von Nephelin und Apatit. Tschermak's Miner. Mitth. 1876, p. 167.
E. BOŘICKY. Elemente einer neuen chemisch-mikroskopischen Mineral- und Gesteinsanalyse. Archiv d. naturw. Landesdurchforsch. Böhmens. III. Bd., V. Abthlg., Prag, 1877.
SZABÓ. Ueber eine neue Methode, die Feldspäthe auch in Gesteinen zu bestimmen. Budapest, 1876.
TH. H. BEHRENS. Mikrochemische Methoden zur Mineralanalyse. Verslagen en Medendeelingen der k. Academie v. Wetenschappen. Amsterdam, 1881.—Afdeeling Natuurkunde. 2. Reeks, XVII. Deel. p. 27—73.
A. STRENG. XXII. Ber. der oberhesisschen Ges. f. Nat. u. Heilkunde. 1883, p. 258 u. 260.
E. BOŘICKY. N. Jahrb. f. Min. u. Geol. 1879. p. 564.
MICHEL LÉVY et L. BOURGEOIS. Compt. rendus 1882, 20 mars, and Bull. Soc. miner. 1882, V. p. 136 (Reaction auf Zirkonerde).
SCHÖNN. Zeitschr. für analyt. Chemie. 1870. IX. p. 41 (Reaction auf Titansäure).
A. KNOP. N. Jahr. f. Min. u. Geol. 1875, p. 74.

Hydrochloric acid has been applied for a long period as a microscopical reagent in investigations of rocks. Zirkel (comp. Petrogaphie, II. p. 293, 1870) applied it most advantageously in discriminating between the varieties of plagioclase allied to anorthite and those related to albite, and between magnetite and ilmenite. The application of hydrochloric acid for the determination of calcite in rocks has been known for a much longer period; also in the recognition of silicates soluble in this acid, as nepheline, members of the meionite group, etc. Thus Roth (1865) rightly conjectured the presence of melilite in the basaltic lavas from Eifel because of the large amount of calcium dissolved in the acid.

In such a testing of the rock-constituents regard is had first of all for the solubility, and secondly for the products of the decomposition effected by the acid; as the evolution of $CO_2$ from calcite, the deposition of the NaCl-cubes on evaporating a drop of the test for nepheline, the appearance of the gelatinous $SiO_2$ on treating olivine with hydrochloric acid, etc.

In such examinations the testing is made with powdered rock by examining microscopically the rock-section or powder both before treatment with acid and also afterward if a residue remains. In the second case the testing is undertaken directly on the slide without a glass cover. There are great evils in either case; in the one in that it is difficult to recognize the minerals in powdered condition and thus determine what has been dissolved away, and in the other in that in treating the section with acids the whole section crumbles away and is destroyed.

A. Streng has recommended a method of isolating the minerals of a thin section for microchemical study which is to be recommended in many cases. If a mineral granule in a thin section is treated with acid, it is almost always unavoidable that the drop of solvent may touch also the other neighboring particles, react on them, and thus render the chemical reactions questionable. This evil can be remedied by first covering the section with a perforated covering-glass which is coated on the under side with fluid boiled Canada balsam, so that the opening of about $\frac{1}{2}$–1 millimetre in diameter is opposite the mineral particle to be tested. The Canada balsam filling the opening may be easily removed by alcohol. Such perforated covering-glasses can be easily prepared by treatment with hydrofluoric acid. An ordinary covering-glass is first dipped in melted wax and allowed to cool; a hole $\frac{1}{2}$–1 mm. diameter is then made through the wax, and concentrated hydrofluoric acid dropped on the bared opening until a hole is eaten through the glass at this point. The wax is then removed from the covering-glass.

The reaction for distinguishing between nepheline and apatite, first proposed by Streng (1876), deserves special mention as one nearly always accomplishing its purpose. Both minerals occur in rocks very commonly, and are remarkably similar—hexagonal ($\infty P. oP. P$), optically negative, and colorless.

The microchemical reactions for apatite are:

(*a*) Reaction for phosphoric acid. A drop of concentrated nitric-acid solution of ammonium molybdate is transferred with a glass rod to the apatite crystal lying exposed, i.e., not covered by other minerals of the section; the whole of the thin section within the field of the microscope not protected by glass is thus covered. A muscovite or glass leaflet is often cemented with glycerine to the objective to protect the lens, which in such experiments is easily attacked by the acid vapors. The apatite dissolves slowly in the nitric acid of the reagent, forming beautiful yellow grains and small octahedra of the ammonium phospho-molybdate ($10MoO_3 + PO_4(NH_4)_3 + 1\frac{1}{2}H_2O$). These yellow crystals are wreathed about the apatite and not in the former position of the apatite crystal, as here the excess of phosphoric acid prevents the formation of a precipitate.

(*b*) Reaction for lime. A crystal of apatite in the thin section is dissolved in hydrochloric or nitric acid and a drop of sulphuric acid added: fine white feathery aggregates of gypsum are formed round about the point previously occupied by the apatite. If a crystal of apatite is treated with sulphuric acid alone it is not dissolved, as a thin coating of gypsum is formed which prevents the further action of the acid on the apatite.

The reaction of Streng for phosphoric acid is the surest and most exact if it is carried out, not on the thin section directly, but on an isolated granule; or if the thin section be treated with dilute nitric acid, the solution taken up with a capillary pipette, evaporated, again dissolved in dilute nitric acid, and the reaction completed on an ordinary object-glass.

Nepheline can be recognized from the negative results to the reactions given above for apatite, as well as by a reaction with hydrochloric acid; if a drop of the acid be deposited on a crystal under examination it is easily decomposed, i.e., dissolved. After some time numbers of minute colorless cubes of sodium chloride, easily recognized, are formed in the cavity formerly occupied by the crystal. They are formed by the action of the hydrochloric acid on sodium silicate, and are difficultly soluble in the concentrated acid.

A. Streng has recently found acetate of uranium to be an excellent reagent for sodium. If a drop of concentrated solution of acetate of uranium be added to the residue from the solution of a silicate in hydrochloric acid, clearly defined, bright yellow tetrahedra $\left(\dfrac{O}{2} \cdot -\dfrac{O}{2} \text{ or } \dfrac{O}{2} \cdot \infty O\right)$ of sodium uranate, difficultly soluble in water, are formed. More rarely penetration-twins after a tetrahedral face occur, and in polarized light can be easily distinguished from the double-refracting, rhombic, nearly cubical crystals of the acetate of uranium.

A. Knop has recommended a reaction for the recognition of members of the hauyn group, which when colorless are difficultly distinguishable from apatite or nepheline sections. The thin section of the rock bearing the hauyn is carefully loosened from the object-glass by warming, and is washed clean with alcohol. The clean section is introduced into a platinum crucible, and as much flowers of sulphur as can be taken up on the point of a knife added.  If now the crucible is heated to glowing for some minutes, whereby the sulphur vaporizes and fills the crucible, and then, still covered, is allowed to cool, all ferrous compounds appear blackened, while the hauyn is conspicuous among the rock-components by the beautiful azure-blue color.  The other rock-forming minerals do not become blue on heating in sulphur-vapor.  Knop does not state, however, whether sodalite, like hauyn, becomes blue.

These few characteristic microreactions have reference, however, to an extremely limited number of the rock-forming minerals—nepheline, apatite, and hauyn.  The necessity for a method of complete microchemical qualitative analysis of the rock-constituents has been remedied by Bořicky and Behrens.

## Bořicky's Microchemical Method.

Chemically pure hydrofluosilicic acid is the only reagent required.  It should contain 13 per cent acid, and must be absolutely pure; i.e., when allowed to dry on a layer of balsam on an object-glass it must leave no residue of silico-fluoride crystals.  It cannot, therefore, be prepared or stored in glass bottles.  Almost all of the rock-forming minerals are attacked more or less by strong hydrofluosilicic acid.  It is therefore available for the formation of the silico-fluorides, which dissolve in the solution of hydrofluosilicic acid, and after evaporation of this solution appear as beautifully-developed crystals, characteristic for the different elements or groups of elements.

The microchemical tests with this acid can be carried out either directly on the rock-section without a glass cover, or, better yet, on minute particles of the minerals of about the size of a pin's head, on an object-glass coated with Canada balsam. One or two drops of the hydrofluosilicic acid are transferred with a caoutchouc rod to the mineral granule under examination, and the preparation is allowed to rest quietly in a place free from dust, preferably at a temperature of about 18° C., until the drop has dried away.

If the mineral is easily attacked by the acid, all of the metals are generally found after evaporating the solution in their several peculiar crystalline forms, and in about the same proportion as in the mineral. If the mineral is but slightly attacked, only those metals most easily soluble can be proven, and the same mineral fragment must be treated again with the acid; in the latter case it is often of advantage to treat, in a small platinum dish, first with hydrofluoric acid and then with hydrofluosilicic acid, evaporate to dryness, redissolve in water, and allow a drop to evaporate on an object-glass.

Thin sections are more easily attacked than granules or cleavage-pieces, and must be exceedingly thin. It is better if the test is taken from carefully-selected mineral particles, as sections become coated with a dull white crust. The silico-fluorides crystallize most perfectly when lixiviated with boiling water, and the solution allowed to cool on another object-glass. The silico-fluorides are always in minute crystals, and are best observed under 200–400 diameters. They are distinguished by their crystalline forms, and there appears:

1. **Potassium Silico-fluoride** in skeleton groups of small crystals of the regular system clearly defined, generally $\infty O \infty$, also often with $O$ and $\infty O$. Yet potassium silico-fluoride often crystallizes in larger, apparently rhombic crystals of the form $\infty \breve{P} n . m \breve{P} \infty$, if the acid was in excess or the evaporation occurred at lower temperatures (12° C.), or in presence of a large amount of sodium.

2. **Sodium Silico-fluoride** (Fig. 33) in short hexagonal columns with $oP . P$, also $\infty P2$; imperfect crystals are barrel-shaped. The more calcium silico-fluoride present the larger the crystals. Easily soluble in water.

3. **Calcium Silico-fluoride** (Fig. 34) in peculiar, long, pointed,

spindle-shaped crystals, often grouped in rosettes; the combination of parallel straight lines and planes is characteristic for

FIG. 33.—SODIUM SILICO-FLUORIDE.
(After Bořicky.)

FIG. 34.—CALCIUM SILICO-FLUORIDE.
(After Bořicky.)

this compound. It crystallizes in monoclinic crystals, and is easily soluble in water.

4. **Magnesium Silico-fluoride** (Fig. 35) appears in rhombohedra with polar edges truncated by $oR$ and combinations of $R . \infty P_2$ or $R . \infty P_2 . oR$; all of the crystals have well-defined edges and faces. It often appears also in rhombohedra elongated in one direction, or in cruciform, hook-shaped, or feathery figures. It is easily soluble in water.

FIG. 35.—MAGNESIUM SILICO-FLUORIDE.
(After Bořicky.)

5. **Iron Silico-fluoride** cannot be distinguished from magnesium silico-fluoride; the same with manganese silico-fluoride; while strontium silico-fluoride can scarcely be distinguished from calcium silico-fluoride.

**Lithium Silico-fluoride** appears generally in regular flat hexagonal pyramids, where one pair of faces is sometimes remarkably developed; **barium silico-fluoride** in extremely minute, short, pointed needles.

**Distinction between the Silico-fluorides of Calcium and Strontium.**—If a drop of sulphuric acid diluted with an equal bulk of water is added to the silico-fluorides, the crystals of *calcium* are *immediately* surrounded with a thick fringe of monoclinic gypsum crystals, while those of strontium change but slowly.

**Distinction between the Silico-fluorides of Iron, Manganese, and Magnesia.**—These can be distinguished either by subjecting to the action of chlorine gas for about twenty minutes, when the magnesium silico-fluoride remains colorless, the iron becomes yellow and the manganese red; or these silico-fluorides can be distinguished by the reaction with ammonium sulphide, when the silico-fluoride of magnesium remains colorless, while the iron is blackened and the manganese becomes reddish-gray and granular.

The fluorides of Fe, Mn, Co, Ni, and Cu can be distinguished also by their reaction with potassium ferrocyanide. If this solution be dropped on the silico-fluorides the corresponding ferrocyanides will be formed, which can be recognized from the characteristic color: Fe is blue, Mn brown, Cu red, Co dark green, and Ni light green.

This method has many disadvantages; e.g., it is impossible to prove by it the presence of alumina; the distinction between the silico-fluorides of iron and magnesium is difficult and detailed; the calcium silico-fluoride crystals are also insufficiently characteristic. Nevertheless it is advantageously employed, especially in testing for the alkalies.

Th. A. Behrens has proposed another complete system of microchemical methods for use in petrography. In this method also a series of new and admirable microreactions are introduced. If a combination of these two methods—that of Bořicky for the determination of the alkalies, and of Behrens

—be effected, a complete qualitative analysis in many cases can be carried out with the microscope. In this latter method, however, the operation cannot be carried out on the rock-section itself.

## *Behrens's Microchemical Method.*

**Preparation of the Mineral.**—The minerals to be examined must always be separated from the mass of the rock. In the coarse-grained rocks this is easily done by picking out the pieces from the coarse rock-powder either under the microscope or with a pocket-lens. In the fine-grained rocks, where the rock-constituents can no longer be distinguished in the powder, the mineral particle is removed from the slide by aid of the microscope and a lance-shaped needle; the section is ground until the desired mineral granule is transparent and partly polished. The isolation of the desired mineral is effected by gradually breaking away the section from the edge. The isolation of the mineral is lightened if the object-glass is first warmed, and the Canada balsam under the rock-leaflet thus softened. The isolated mineral particle, of at least 0.3 mm. diameter and 0.1 mg. in weight, is cleaned and pulverized in an agate mortar beneath a piece of filter-paper to prevent loss.

**The Testing.**—The tests are made in a hemispherical platinum dish about 1 cm. in diameter, closed by a concave platinum cover; the reagent employed is chemically pure hydrofluoric acid, or ammonium fluoride, or concentrated hydrochloric acid. Two or three drops of either acid are transferred to the small dish, and the mineral, finely powdered, added. The mixture is heated, and, if necessary, hydrofluoric acid added a second time, and the evaporation repeated. The dried fluorides are then evaporated with concentrated sulphuric acid until voluminous clouds of the gray acid-vapors appear. The sulphuric acid, however, must not be completely volatilized; it is advisable, therefore, to repeat the evaporation with a drop of sulphuric acid. The decomposed mass is then dissolved in water, the platinum capsule being about half filled, and the contents evaporated by gentle heat until each centigram of solution contains about 0.1 mg. substance.

A drop of this solution is transferred by a capillary pipette to a slide without a covering-glass to facilitate evaporation, and is placed beneath the microscope. Two hundred diameters is the best magnifying power. The objective here also must be protected by a leaf of muscovite cemented with glycerine.

This drop is examined first for

**Calcium.**—If the mineral was calciferous, free crystals of gypsum (Fig. 36) separate on evaporation; the columns are thin, of $\infty P . \infty P \infty . P$, generally lying on $\infty P \infty$ or arranged in rosettes. Often larger crystals of the well-known swallow-tail twins are discernible in the outer edge of the drop. The presence of 0.0005 mg. CaO can be demonstrated by this reaction. If a smaller amount of lime is present, or the gypsum separates too slowly, the slide with the drop is moistened with alcohol. The crystals then formed are, however, smaller and less distinct, but the sensitiveness of the reaction is quadrupled.

FIG. 36.—GYPSUM.
(After Behrens.)

The same drop is searched for

**Potassium.**—A drop of concentrated platinum chloride is added by means of a platinum wire to the drop to be tested. Crystals of the double-chloride of platinum and potassium (Fig. 37, *a*) are formed within a few minutes, and generally on the outer edge of the drop. They are sharply-defined octahedra of high refractive power and of a bright yellow color. If a concentrated solution was employed, clover-leaved trillings and fourlings also appear. The crystals are formed more rapidly in chloride solution than in sulphate solution, and are smaller. A large excess of sulphuric acid prevents their formation. 0.0006 mg. $K_2O$ can be demonstrated by this reaction.

**Sodium** is proved with cerium sulphate. A drop of the concentrated solution of this reagent, and another drop of the solution from the decomposed mineral, are placed on a slide about 5 mm. apart, and joined by a thread of glass. Tufts of cerium sulphate appear in the drop of reagent, and on the edge an opaque brown zone of the sodium double-salt, which permeates the whole drop if the percentage of sodium is large; with 600 diameters this zone is shown to be composed of minute white transparent granules. If the mineral contains potassium also, a coarsely granular gray zone of the potassium double-salt is formed in the centre of the drop, which is made up from granules and fragments similar to potato-starch. In lower percentages of the alkali metals in the mineral the phenomena are more easily observed. Lumps and short rhombs of the potassium double-salt, and acute prisms and spindle-formed crystals of the sodium double-salt, appear. A large excess of sulphuric acid retards the reaction.

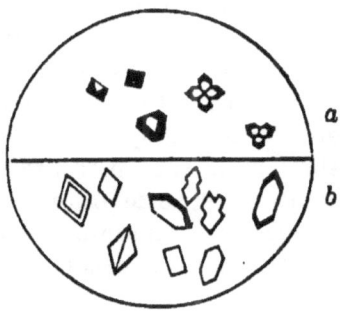

FIG. 37.
*a*. POTASSIUM-PLATINUM CHLORIDE.
*b*. POTASSIUM FLUOBORATE.
(After Behrens.)

This reaction can be first applied for both alkali-metals, and then that with platinum chloride for potassium on the same slide, and finally the test for sodium with hydrofluosilicic acid after the slide has been prepared with balsam. At any rate the Bořicky test for sodium is to be preferred, as also the test for potassium with platinum chloride.

**Magnesium** is shown by hydrogen-sodium-ammonium phosphate (microcosmic salt). The drop already searched for Al or K is saturated with ammonia, a drop of water placed at a distance of about 1 cm., a grain of microcosmic salt dissolved in it, and the two drops connected by a thread of glass. There are immediately formed either double, forked crystalloids similar to the microlites in the natural glasses, or, if the solution is quite dilute, well-defined twins of hemimorphous crystals of ammonium-magnesium phosphate (Fig. 38). The reaction for magnesium often does not appear or is ill-defined,

FIG. 38.—AMMONIUM-MAGNESIUM PHOSPHATE.
(After Behrens.)

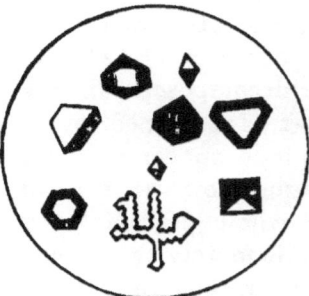

FIG. 39.—CÆSIUM ALUM.
(After Behrens.)

owing to an insufficiency of ammonium salts; it is advisable, therefore, to add a little hydrochloric acid or ammonium chloride before saturation with ammonia. 0.001 mg. MgO can be proved by this reaction.

Behrens found cæsium chloride an excellent reagent for **Aluminium.** A minute portion of the deliquescent salt is placed with the point of a platinum wire on the edge of the test-drop. Large transparent octahedra (more rarely $\infty O \infty . O$) of cæsium alum are immediately formed (Fig. 39). If the solution of the mineral is concentrated, only a dendritic mass is formed, and a small drop of water must be placed beside that of the reagent. A large amount of sulphuric acid interferes with the formation of the alum crystals. 0.01 mg. $Al_2O_3$ can be clearly proved by this reaction.

**Iron** is rarely searched for with the microscope. The color of the flocculent, fine-grained precipitate obtained with potassium ferrocyanide from iron solutions is sufficiently characteristic and intense when examined macroscopically.

**Manganese** is proved by fusing with soda. The characteristic green color is obtained with the smallest amount. A microscopical examination is therefore superfluous.

**Lithium** is precipitated by an alkaline carbonate from the solution in sulphuric acid, and gives well-developed monoclinic crystals of lithium carbonate with rectangular cross-section. These crystals can be distinguished from gypsum by their rectangular form and solubility in dilute sulphuric acid; from magnesium double-salt by the property that they are formed in every proportion of potassium carbonate and lithium sulphate, and remain constant; while the crystals of magnesium double-salt are formed only in large excess of the alkaline carbonates and in close proximity, and soon become granular. Phosphoric acid seriously retards the formation of the lithium-carbonate crystals.

**Barium and Strontium.**—These are found, together with calcium and gypsum, in the residue after lixiviation of the mass in the platinum capsule with water. This residue is dissolved in hot concentrated sulphuric acid, is allowed to cool, and is extracted with water. From a drop there is first a separation of barium sulphate in small lenticular, crossed crystals; then of strontium sulphate, at first in matted tufts and fine needles, then in larger, often rhombic, cruciform, twinned crystals; last of all gypsum separates.

**Metalloids.**—Of the remaining reactions proposed by Behrens for use with the rock-forming minerals, the following are of importance:

**Chlorine.**—The mineral granule to be examined for chlorine is fused with soda and decomposed; a large quantity of concentrated sulphuric acid is added to the fused mass in the platinum capsule, and the escaping hydrochloric-acid gas is absorbed by a drop of water adhering to the under side of a glass covering the capsule. This cover is kept cool by a few drops of water on the upper surface. At the close of the process the water is wiped from the upper surface with filter-paper, and the covering-glass inverted and placed on the stage of the microscope. A granule of thallium sulphate is then laid in the centre of the drop of adhering water. Colorless octahedra as well as $O . \infty O$ of thallium chloride are rapidly formed. These refract light powerfully, and are often combined into clover-leaf trillings and fourlings. 0.004 mg. NaCl can be thus proved.

**Phosphorus and Sulphur** can be proved by reversing the reactions already described for aluminium (for S) and for magnesium (for P). Insoluble sulphates and phosphates must be fused with soda, and the pulverized fused mass lixiviated with water. For proving the presence of sulphur a drop of this solution is placed near a drop of solution of aluminium chloride and hydrochloric acid with a little cæsium chloride. The two drops are then united by a glass thread, when the cæsium-alum octahedra are developed, as before, near the extremity. A concentrated solution of ammonium chloride and magnesium sulphate is used as a reagent for the detection of phosphorus.

**Fluorine.**—The mineral containing fluorine is dissolved in concentrated sulphuric acid, and the escaping gas is absorbed by dilute sulphuric acid. Such minerals as topaz or tourmaline must be first fused with twice their volume of soda in order to change the fluorine into hydrofluosilicic acid; powdered sand is sometimes added. A drop of the sulphuric acid is placed on the convex surface of the platinum cover, and is then laid on the platinum capsule with the drop downward; the upper surface being cooled as in the chlorine reaction. The capsule is gently warmed, and at the close of the distillation the water used for cooling is removed by filter-paper, and the drop of acid containing the fluorine is transferred to a slide coated with Canada balsam, or a leaflet of barite. (In order to avoid spurting it is advisable to heat the test, first fused with soda, with acetic acid, and evaporate before using the sulphuric acid.) A grain of sodium chloride is then added to the transferred drop. At first six-leaved rosettes, and later hexagonal tablets, $\infty P . oP$, and short columns, $\infty P . P$, of sodium silico-fluoride will appear. 0.0036 mg. fluorine can be thus detected.

**Silicon and Boron.**—Their determination is precisely the same as fluorine, except that hydrofluoric acid must be used with the sulphuric. If only one of the two elements is to be proved, sodium chloride is again used as the reagent; the hexagonal tablets already mentioned are again formed. If, however, boron as well as silicon is to be detected, potassium chloride is used. Potassium silico-fluoride crystallizes in the regular system, as $O$ and $O . \infty O \infty$; while potassium boro-fluoride (Fig. 37, *b*) appears in lance-shaped leaves and in rhombs with obtuse angles, often replaced by edges. The silico-fluorides separate first. If the mineral under examination is rich in silicon, the greater part of the silicon must be removed before the presence of boron can be accurately proved. The mineral powder mixed with hydrofluoric and sulphuric acids must be warmed until the greater part of the silico-fluoride is driven out, which is absorbed by the diluted sulphuric acid and tested for silicon with sodium chloride. Hydrofluoric acid is again added to the mineral test and again heated until the white fumes of sulphuric acid appear. The distillate is warmed to about 120° C., and a drop of water is added to the residue, which is transferred to a slide and tested for boron with potassium chloride. The rhombic crystals of potassium boro-fluoride are formed only when the drop has dried.

**Water.**—The water-determination is carried out with minute mineral particles in the same way as in blowpipe analysis. Behrens recommends the following small apparatus for this purpose: A small tube about 10 mm. long and 3 mm. in diameter is drawn out at one end to a thread about 2 cm. in length and 0.5 mm. in diameter; after a gentle heating of the whole tube and drawing through of air it is closed. While the tube is yet warm, the mineral granule is introduced and the tube drawn out to about half its length and melted at the other end also, making it blunt. The capillary end is then cooled by alcohol, or is heated to glowing if no deposition has taken place. Such a deposition of water then generally occurs, which collects in the capillary portion without artificial cooling.

By the application of the delicate method of Behrens we are in position to determine immediately with ease and perfect accuracy those most important elements of the rock-forming minerals, potassium, calcium, magnesium, and aluminium; the Bořicky method appears to be more characteristic and accurate for sodium. Rosenbusch recommends the flame-reaction when the amount of sodium is very small.

## C. Mechanical Separation of the Rock-forming Minerals.

THOULET. Bull. de la Soc. minéralog. de France, 1879, II. p. 17 and 189.
FOUQUÉ ET MICHEL LÉVY. Minéralogie micrographique, p. 114.
GOLDSCHMIDT. N. Jahrb. f. Mineralogie und Geologie. 1881, 1. Beilagebd. p. 179.
K. OEBBEKE. Ebenda. p. 454.
E. COHEN U. L. V. WERVEKE. N. Jahrb. f. min. u. Geol., 1883, II. Bd. p. 86–89.
D. KLEIN. Bull. de la Soc. minér. de France, Juin 1881, 4. p. 149, and Zeitschr. f. Krystallographie und Mineralogie v. Groth, VI. 1882, p. 306, or N. Jahrb. f. Min. u. Geol. 1882, II. Bd. Ref. p. 189.

P. Gisevius. Beiträge z. Methode d. Bestimmung d. spec. Gew. v. Min. u. d. mechanischen Trennung von Mineralgemengen. Inaug.-Diss. Univ. Bonn, 1883.

C. Rohrbach. N. Jahrb. f. Min. u. Geol. 1883, II. Bd. p. 186, and Wiedemann's Annalen f. Physik u. Chemie.

P. Mann. N. Jahrb. f. Min. u. Geol. 1884, II. p. 175.

In order to institute a quantitative chemical analysis of the several rock-forming minerals, they must be separated as perfectly as possible from each other; a partial separation of the minerals, as already stated, is possible by treatment with different acids and with the magnet; but the separation is best effected by taking advantage of the relative specific gravities of the minerals. Solutions of high specific gravities are best adapted to this purpose, as by dilution of the solution it can be lowered easily. This method of the mechanical separation of the rock-constituents has the additional advantage that their specific gravities can be exactly determined at the same time, and thus a further vantage-ground for the determination of the mineral be won.

The solutions at present known and universally applied to the mechanical separation and determination of the specific gravities are:

I. The solution of iodides of potassium and mercury with a highest specific gravity of 3.196 (Thoulet-Goldschmidt).

II. The solution of cadmium boro-tungstate with a specific gravity of 3.6 (Klein).

III. The solution of iodides of barium and mercury with a specific gravity of 3.588 (Rohrbach).

I. Separation with the Solution of the Iodides of Potassium and Mercury.

**Preparation and Properties of the Solution.**—Potassium iodide and mercuric iodide are weighed out in proportion of 1 : 1.239; both portions are thrown into a large evaporating-dish, mixed, and dissolved in as little water as possible. The solution is then evaporated on the water-bath until a piece of mineral, tourmaline e.g., sp. gr. 3.1, floats upon it; the dish is then removed from the water-bath and allowed to cool, when the mass thickens and the maximum of specific gravity is reached. Generally acicular crystals of a hydrous double iodide of potassium and mercury separate from the concentrated solution during the process of cooling; this precipitate can be dissolved in a few drops of water, or can be filtered off if there is an abundance of the solution. The salt thus removed by filtration can be redissolved in water and evaporated to the required specific gravity. If too much potassium iodide was used, crystals of the salt of the combination $\infty O \infty . O$ will separate on the surface of the liquid; if, on the other hand, there is an excess of mercuric iodide, a thick felt of yellow needles is formed which is decomposed on dissolving in water, with the deposition of a red crystalline powder $HgI_2$, but which dissolves in potassium-iodide solution without decomposition. The concentrated solution is often decomposed on adding water with deposition of the red powder, which is, however, again redissolved on agitating the solution. The specific gravity of the solution changes on long standing; this depends on the temperature and moisture of the atmosphere; the solution is also decomposed by organic substances, as filter-paper, etc. The highest attainable specific gravity of the solution is 3.196 (Goldschmidt).

**Determination of the Specific Gravity of Minerals and Rocks by the Solution.**—The specific gravity of all those minerals under 3.196 can be determined by means of this solution in the following manner: The fragments of the mineral or rock, washed in pure water and dried, are thrown into a tall slim beaker-glass filled with the solution at its maximum density; the liquid is then diluted with water, or diluted solution, until the mineral is completely suspended in the solution, i.e. neither sinks nor rises. The solution is then poured into a 25-cc. flask accurately calibrated, and filled exactly to the mark—the mark had best be on the under side of the meniscus. The excess of liquid is removed either with a capillary pipette or filter-paper. The filled flask is weighed and then emptied back into the beaker-glass and the solution tested with the fragment of mineral; the flask is refilled to the mark and weighed, and the operation repeated for a third time. A mean is taken of these three weighings. The weighings need not be perfectly exact (i.e. to a few milligrams), varying often between 10 and 20 milligrams, as the error is lessened by the triple weighing. Determinations of specific gravity by this method are carried with accuracy to the third decimal place. E.g., quartz and a 25-cc. flask gave:

$$
\begin{aligned}
\text{First weighing} &= 77.981 \text{ grams.} \\
\text{Second \phantom{weighing}} &= 77.919 \text{ "} \\
\text{Third \phantom{weighing}} &= 77.973 \text{ "} \\
\hline
\text{Mean} &= 77.957 \text{ "} \\
- \text{Flask} &= 11.682 \text{ "} \\
\hline
&\phantom{=}\, 66.275 \text{ "}
\end{aligned}
$$

$66.275 \div 25 = 2.654$ specific gravity.

Such determinations can be made much more rapidly and as accurately, according to the principle of Mohr, on a balance constructed by G. Westphal of Celle (price, 45 marks). By this method the specific gravity is read directly on the balance-beam after a single weighing and with weights in rider form.

It must be noted that specific-gravity determinations of mineral *powder* cannot be made with the solution, and, as is well known, that decompositions or inclosures may lower or raise the specific gravity of minerals.

**Separation of the Rock-components by means of the Solution.** —In order to separate the components of a rock from each other, the rock must be pulverized; this should be preceded by an orientation concerning its probable mineralogical composition by an investigation of a thin section. The powder is then passed through sieves of different mesh, and that part selected for separation which the microscopical examination has demonstrated to be homogeneous, i.e., wherein several minerals do not cohere. The very finest flour-like powder cannot be used for the separation, as it mixes with the syrupy solution to form a thin mud; the minute mineral particles, grains, and crystals, therefore, which constitute for the most part the micro-crystalline or porphyritic rocks cannot be separated by this method.

If the rock is very coarsely granular, it is often of great advantage if the minerals distinguished by the pocket-lens, broken away and dissociated, are separated by means of the solution; e.g., the white feldspars or the black bisilicates. Mica can be obtained pure by allowing the mineral powder simply to slide over rough paper.

The granular powder obtained in this manner is poured into an apparatus filled with the potassium-mercury-iodide solution at its highest specific gravity.

**Apparatus.**—As the very simplest piece of apparatus and one especially adapted to the purpose, an ordinary large glass separating-funnel, or the pear-shaped vessel described by T. Harada, is to be recommended. This latter apparatus is closed above with a ground-glass stopper, and terminates in a narrow tube below, also provided with a ground-glass stop-cock (Fig. 40). The solution after the powder is added to it is well stirred with a glass rod and allowed to settle; those minerals possessing a higher specific gravity than the solution sink to the bottom, and can be removed by carefully opening the lower glass cock after the solution has had time to clear.

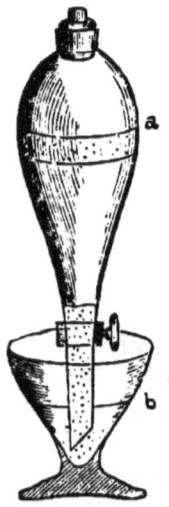

FIG. 40.
HARADA'S SEPARATING-APPARATUS.
(Copy from K. Oebbeke.)

## METHODS OF INVESTIGATION. 71

The potassium-mercury solution is then diluted by carefully dropping distilled water accompanied by constant agitation of the liquid with a stirring-rod until another portion of the powder has either settled to the bottom or is suspended in the liquid. Care must be taken that particles of the powder do not cling to the rod itself or the walls of the funnel.

In order to establish the specific gravity of the solution, and consequently of the precipitated mineral granules, either a direct specific-gravity determination is made with the Mohr-Westphal balance, whereby a short and broad glass tube is thrust into the solution and the plunger of the balance sunk inside of it (a device preventing a large loss of mineral by adhesion), or the so-called indicators are employed. A series of larger mineral fragments of a known specific gravity and varying from 1 to 3.2 is used for this purpose. A large number of such minerals, especially of those with a specific gravity 2–3.2, should be at hand. By the use of several of these indicators, selected according to the mineral composition of the rock as established by the microscope, the specific gravity of the solution can be determined easily.

After removing the powder which has fallen to the bottom, the solution is again diluted, and the operation repeated. The separated powder is well washed with water. The washings can be evaporated with the diluted solution on the water-bath until the maximum density is again reached.

The rock-powder can thus be divided into portions of different known specific gravity which are partly pure, i.e., contain fragments made up of one and the same mineral, or, if the rock was too coarsely pulverized, show the so-called intermediary products, impurities resulting from the interpenetrations of several minerals. In the latter case these portions must be more finely pulverized and again separated.

**Example.**—*Tonalite.*—The microscopical examination of this coarse-grained rock developed as components: plagioclase predominating, orthoclase subordinate, much quartz, green hornblende, brown biotite, and magnetite, ilmenite, and garnet as accessory.

The biotite is first of all slid off on rough paper, and thus obtained quite pure. The magnetite can be withdrawn by a magnet. The residual powder is then thrown into the solution, when the garnets and titanic iron sink to the bottom. Hornblende, orthoclase, and quartz fragments are selected as indicators, as the specific gravities of the minerals to be separated lie between them. By slow dilution of the potassium-mercury solution the hornblende will be first precipitated, and only a white powder will remain. The plagioclase will first precipitate from this white powder, then quartz, and finally the orthoclase.

If the specific gravity of the solution was determined while the plagioclase was suspended, and it was found to be 2.67, the value shows that the plagioclase is an andesine.

Finally, optical investigations can be instituted on cleavage-fragments of andesine and hornblende selected from the separated mineral particles. The plagioclase also can be subjected to a quantitative chemical analysis after the purity of the powder is established.

**Precautionary Rules in Working with the Potassium-Mercury Solution.**—1. A large loss of the solution should be guarded against, because of the cost of preparation. All scattered drops, residues, and washings from the apparatus should therefore be gathered, and this dilute solution again evaporated on the water-bath. 2. *The solution is very poisonous and attacks the skin.*

**Regeneration of the Solution.**—The solution changes to a dark or reddish brown after long usage, owing to the separation of free iodine. The iodine is removed, as L. v. Werveke has recommended, by addition of mercury and agitation of the cold solution; or, better, by concentrating the solution on the water-bath with constant agitation, and consequent division of the mercury. The solution again assumes a honey-yellow color, and can be raised to its highest specific gravity without injury. The free iodine combines with the mercury to form the sub-iodide, which precipitates as a dirty-green dust on the mercury. This is again changed to metallic mercury and mercuric iodide on concentrating the solution, and is dissolved by the excess of potassium iodide which caused the separation of the free iodine.

## II. Klein's Solution.

D. Klein has recommended a solution[*] of boro-tungstate of cadmium ($9WO_3 . B_2O_3 . 2CdO, 2H_2O + 16$ aq.) for the separation of the rock-forming minerals. Although the preparation of this solution is far more complicated than that of the potassium-mercury iodides, yet it is to be preferred, as nearly all of the rock-forming minerals can be separated by it, owing to its high specific gravity—3.6; while many minerals, and the most important, as augite, hornblende, olivine, etc., whose specific gravity lies above 3.19, cannot be separated by the solution of the iodides.

The process of separation with Klein's solution is exactly analogous to that with the iodide solution. It must be remembered, however, to dissolve out with acids all carbonates, such as calcite, etc., from the rock-powder, as they decompose the solution. The apparatus, either separating-funnel or Harada's vessel, must be surrounded by hot water or otherwise warmed, as the salt must be melted at 75° if a solution with a specific gravity of 3.5–3.6 is desired.

**The Preparation** of the solution is as follows: A solution of $Na_2WO_4$ in five parts water is first prepared and then boiled

---

[*] According to the author's experience, Klein's solution is the best and the most durable of all the solutions of high specific gravity used for the mechanical separation of the rock-components.

with 1.5 parts $B(OH)_3$ until the whole is dissolved. On cooling and agitating the solution, crystals of borax and sodium polyborates separate, which must be removed. The decanted liquid is again evaporated, and the newly-formed crystals removed, and this process is repeated until glass floats on the surface. A boiling solution of $BaCl_2$ is then added ($1 BaCl_2 : 3 Na_2WO_4$). A thick white precipitate is formed, which is filtered off, well washed with water, and finally dissolved in dilute HCl ($1 HCl$ sp. gr. 1.18 : $10 H_2O$). Hydrochloric acid is added in excess to the solution, and the whole evaporated to dryness, when $H_2WO_4$ separates. The dried mass is again dissolved in hot water, boiled for about two hours, water being added from time to time, and the $H_2WO_4$ filtered off. Tetragonal crystals of the compound $9WO_3 . B_2O_3 . 2BaO, 2H_2O + 19$ aq. separate from the solution, and these are purified by recrystallization. Finally, $CdSO_4$ is added to a boiling solution of these crystals, when the soluble cadmium boro-tungstate $9WO_3 . B_2O_3 . 2CdO, 2H_2O + 16$ aq. is formed and filtered from the insoluble $BaSO_4$.

Cadmium boro-tungstate dissolves in less than $\frac{1}{10}$ of its weight of water; it crystallizes on evaporation on the water-bath and cooling. The solution of these crystals has a specific gravity of 3.28 at 15° C.

Evaporation of the solution must be done always on the water-bath; if a specific gravity of 3.6 is desired, the solution is evaporated until olivine floats, and is then allowed to stand 24 hours. Crystalline masses are deposited which are removed from the solution, purified and melted at 75° in the separating-apparatus, placed either over the water-bath or in a jacket filled with hot water. Spinel floats on this fused mass.

Cadmium boro-tungstate solution can be obtained from chemical depots ready for use.

In addition to its higher specific gravity this solution has these further advantages over the potassium-mercury solution: it is non-poisonous, does not attack the skin, and remains at a constant specific gravity; carbonates and metallic iron, however, decompose it.


III. ROHRBACH'S SOLUTION OF THE IODIDES OF BARIUM AND MERCURY.

This is even more valuable than Klein's solution for the separations. The specific gravity of the concentrated barium-mercury solution is nearly the same as Klein's, but the preparation is not so complicated; moreover no decomposition is effected by the carbonates.

The solution of the **Iodides of Mercury and Barium** is prepared in the following manner: 100 parts of barium iodide and 130 parts of mercuric iodide are weighed as rapidly as possible; both in powdered form are transferred to a dry kolben over an oil-bath heated to about 200° C., are well shaken together, and dissolved in about 20 kcm. of water. The solution is hastened by whirling the contents with a glass rod bent at the lower extremity. If all is dissolved, the solution is allowed to boil a little, and is then transferred to a water-bath, where it is evaporated until a fragment of epidote floats. On allowing the solution to cool, the specific gravity increases until olivine floats; a double-salt, however, is deposited, which is allowed to settle at the bottom of a tall beaker-glass, and is removed by careful decantation of the clear solution. Filtration is not advisable, as filter-paper cannot be used. The solution thus prepared attains a specific gravity of 3.575–3.588.

The method of operation with this solution is exactly the same as with the potassium-mercury solution, except that the barium-mercury solution must not be diluted with water, but always with dilute solution. This latter solution can be obtained easily by allowing a layer of water to stand for about 24 hours on the concentrated solution in a beaker-glass, when the mixing will follow by diffusion. Red mercuric iodide generally deposits on diluting with water. The powder to be separated must be perfectly dry; iodide of potassium must be used at first in washing, which redissolves any precipitated mercuric iodide.

Rohrbach recommended also that the separation of all minerals below 3.1 should be carried out with the potassium-mercury solution, and that the further separation of the heavier minerals of sp. gr. 3.1–3.58 should be prosecuted with the *barium-mercury* solution; closed apparatus for separation, as Harada's, is also advisable. On continued standing (i.e., for several months) the solution becomes specifically lighter, owing to the deposition of mercuric iodide; it cannot, therefore, be employed in separating minerals of sp. gr. 3.2–3.6.

## IV. Methods of Separation based on the Different Action of Acids on Minerals.

Zirkel und Rosenbusch, l. c.
F. Fouqué et Michel Lévy. Minéralogie micrographique. Paris, 1879, p. 116.
F. Fouqué. Nouveaux procédés d'analyse médiate des roches et leur application aux laves de la dernière éruption de Santorin. Mém. savants étrangères de l'Académie des sciences. Paris, XXII. p. 11, and Compt. rend. 1874. p. 869.
K. Oebbeke. N. Jahrb. f. Min. u. Geol. 1881, I. Beilagebd. p. 455.
A. Cathrein. Ebenda, 1881. I. Bd. p. 172.

It has been hinted already that a basis for the more exact determination of many minerals can be obtained in many cases by simple treatment of the powdered rock with various acids. With this in view, a thin section of the rock is first examined in order to gain some idea of its mineralogical composition. Small fragments of the rock are then finely powdered and treated with concentrated hot hydrochloric acid in a beaker-glass. Any evolution of gas must be carefully noted, or formation of any precipitate, especially separation of sulphur or silicic acid. The acid is generally allowed to act on the powder for some hours, and is then filtered. The sulphur is then dissolved from the dried powder on the paper with carbon disulphide or ether, and the silicic acid by boiling in sodium carbonate. The powder is then thoroughly washed, dried, mixed with Canada balsam, and suitably prepared on a slide for a microscopical examination. If it is evident that one or more of the rock-forming minerals has dissolved, the ordinary qualitative chemical analysis of the filtrate is set in course.

The following rock-forming minerals are soluble in hydrochloric acid:

I. Soluble *without* evolution of gas or separation of a precipitate:
    *Magnetite*, *Hematite*, *Apatite* ($P_2O_5$), *Titaniferous Magnetite* (difficultly soluble).

II. Soluble with evolution of $CO_2$:
    *Calcite*, *Aragonite* (Ca), *Dolomite* (CaMg), *Magnesite* (difficultly soluble), *Siderite* (Fe).

III. Soluble with separation of S:
    *Pyrrhotite*, *Pyrite* (difficultly soluble).

IV. Soluble with separation of pulverulent $SiO_2$:
    *Leucite* (K), *Meionite* (Ca), *Scapolite* (Ca, Na), *Labradorite* and *Bytownite* (more difficultly soluble, Ca, Na), *Anorthite* (Ca).

V. Soluble with separation of gelatinous $SiO_2$:
    *Sodalite* (Cl), *Hauyn* and *Nosean* ($SO_3$), *Nepheline* (Na), *Wollastonite* (Ca), *Olivine* (Mg), *Melilite* (Ca), nearly all *Zeolites*, *Serpentine*, then *Chlorite* and *Epidote* (difficultly soluble).

Exact determinations cannot be carried out by this method, and all the less because many minerals, and those too the most commonly-occurring silicates, possess a similar chemical composition; e.g., scapolite or meionite, with the species of plagioclase closely related to anorthite. Such minerals as the carbonates, apatite or sodalite, can be more easily demonstrated, as they give characteristic reactions. If hydrochloric acid of different degrees of concentration be used, more exact results are obtained, as the solubility of the minerals depends upon the size of the granule, temperature, duration of action, and degree of concentration of the acid. Unfortunately no careful, systematic investigations have been made in this direction; e.g., nepheline and olivine occurring together in a nepheline basalt can be separated by treatment with hydrochloric acid.

Fouqué has proposed another method of separation which depends upon the application of hydrofluoric acid of different degrees of strength.

Pure concentrated hydrofluoric acid is poured into a platinum dish, and about 30 grams of the powdered rock is slowly added and stirred with a platinum spatula. Nearly all minerals except those containing *Fe and Mg* are dissolved, forming fluorides and silico-fluorides and a thick jelly of silicic acid and alumina. The different minerals can be separated according to the duration of the reaction; the amorphous minerals being decomposed first, then the feldspars, then quartz, and finally the iron silicates and magnetite. If the action of the acid on a mineral has been studied sufficiently and its arrest is desired, a strong fine stream of water may be directed into the dish, and the acid thus be diluted until it ceases to act on the powder. The gelatinous mass is pressed together, and washed with water; the unattacked mineral remaining at the bottom of the dish.

In this manner feldspar, e.g., can be separated from a vitreous mass, or augite and hornblende from other components.

## V. Separation of the Rock-constituents by Means of the Electro-magnet.

F. Fouque. Santorin. Paris, 1879.
F. Fouque. Mém. Acad. des sciences, 1874, XXII, No. 11.
C. Doelter. Sitzungsb. d. k. Akad. d. Wiss. in Wien. LXXXV. Bd. I. Abth. 1882. p. 47 and 442.
C. Doelter. Die Vulcane der Capverden. Graz, 1882.
P. Mann. N. Jahrb. f. Min. u. Geol. 1884. II. p. 181.

It has been noted already that for a long period the extraction of magnetite from the rock-powder has been effected by means of an ordinary powerful magnet; more recently the electro-magnet has been applied to the separation of the ferriferous minerals from those containing no iron.

The credit for its application to petrographical investigations is due to Fouqué, and especially that he called attention to its value in the mechanical analysis of rocks.

It is impossible to separate the components of a rock by use of the electro-magnet alone; several methods must always be combined in order that the minerals may be separated as pure as possible. Therefore the solution of the iodides of potassium and mercury is first advantageously employed, then Klein's or Rohrbach's solution, and finally the mineral portions separated by means of these solutions are completely purified with the electro-magnet. E.g., it is required to separate the components of a phonolite—magnetite, sanidine, nepheline, and augite. The magnetite is removed with the magnetic needle. In the residue, sanidine and nepheline are separated from the augite by means of the potassium-mercury solution of specific gravity about 3, when the augite is obtained very pure. The sanidine and nepheline can be purified by means of the electro-magnet, and the nepheline separated from the sanidine (and augite accidentally present) again by means of the potassium-mercury solution; or the nepheline can be dissolved in hydrochloric acid.

If, on the other hand, the components of a vitreous augite-andesite are to be separated, the vitreous base may be removed by means of hydrofluoric acid, the augite separated from the plagioclase by the electro-magnet, and the varieties of plagioclase, in case several species are present, isolated by the potassium-mercury solution.

The powder must be dry and free from the very finest dust when the electro-magnet is used. The size of the grains depends upon the density of the rock.

If several ferriferous mineral species occur in the rock to be examined, e.g., magnetite, ilmenite, augite, biotite, olivine, etc., they can be separated from each other by varying the strength of current passing through the electro-magnet. At first two elements are used, then four, six, eight, and finally ten. Doelter has shown that the minerals can be arranged in the following series according to their different powers of being attracted:

*Magnetite,*
*Hematite, Ilmenite,*
*Chromite, Siderite, Almandine,*
*Hedenbergite, Ankerite, Limonite,*
*Augite* (rich in iron), *Pleonaste, Arfvedsonite,*
*Hornblende, Augite* (light-colored), *Epidote, Pyrope,*
*Tourmaline, Bronzite, Idocrase,*
*Staurolite, Actinolite,*
*Olivine, Pyrite, Chalcopyrite,*
*Biotite, Chlorite, Rutile,*
*Hauyn, Diopside, Muscovite,*
*Nepheline, Leucite, Dolomite.*

Doelter has also described a piece of apparatus suitable for such separations. In this the distance between the powder lying on a glass plate and the hook-shaped poles of the horse-shoe magnet can be measured. He also advised the preparation of a scale of minerals for each apparatus with its varying power of the current, analogous to the indicators used in the separation by solutions of high specific gravity, in order to determine the individual power of attraction with the different strength of current. The mineral granules to be separated should be from 0.14 to 0.18 mm. in diameter. v. Pebal states that powder suspended in water is preferable to the dry.

## D. Explanations of the Tables relating to the Morphological Properties of the Rock-forming Minerals.

ZIRKEL. Mikr. Beschaff. d. Min. u. Gesteine. Leipzig, 1873.
ROSENBUSCH. Mikr. Physiogr. d. petrogr. wicht. Miner. Stuttgart, 1873.
E. COHEN. Sammlung von Mikrophotographien zur Veranschaulichung der mikroskopischen Structur von Mineralien und Gesteinen. Stuttgart, 1883.
FOUQUÉ ET MICHEL LÉVY. Minéralogie micrographique. Paris, 1879.
THOULET. Contributions à l'étude des propriétés physiques et chimiques des minéraux microscopiques. Paris, 1880.
v. PEBAL. Sitzungsber. d. k. k. Akad. der Wiss. math. nat. Cl. 1882. p. 193.

### I. MODE OF OCCURRENCE OF THE ROCK-CONSTITUENTS.

The mineral constituents of a rock occur either in perfectly-developed crystals, often sharply defined, in crystalline grains, or as microlites or crystallites.

It is seldom, however, that the crystals appearing in the rocks are so large that the system of crystallization can be determined by the macroscopical examination or measurement of the angles alone. In order, therefore, to determine the mineralogical composition of a rock, a thin section must be prepared wherein the constituents, appearing in the forms just mentioned, are in sections in every possible direction. In this case the determination of the crystalline form is rendered much more difficult, and is impossible simply from the form of the cross-section. By suitable combination of the form of cross-section, optical properties, cleavage, and finally by measurement of the angles, it can be determined in most cases to which system of crystallization the mineral belongs. E.g., a mineral appears whose cross-sections are octagonal, with cleavage at nearly right angles; or are elongated, rectangular, or hexagonal, with cleavage-fissures parallel to the longest axis. The mineral could belong to the tetragonal as well as the rhombic or monoclinic system. The section must be examined, therefore, in parallel and convergent polarized light. The form of the cross-sections shows that the mineral is developed in long eight-sided prisms with prismatic cleavage; the octagonal sections are the transverse sections at right angles to the $c$-axis. If they appear as isotrope in parallel polarized light and show in convergent polarized light a fixed axial cross, the mineral is tetragonal, possibly belonging to the meionite group. If, on the contrary, the transverse sections as well as the longitudinal are anisotrope and develop a middle line in converging polarized light, it is rhombic; and if, finally, one optic axis is visible, it is monoclinic and the mineral may be, e.g., from the augite group.

By measurement of the angles it can, in the latter case, still be determined which faces belong to the prism $\infty P$ and the pinacoids, and to which faces the cleavage-fissures are parallel.

In measuring the angle of cleavage the direction of the section must always be carefully noted, as the value of the angle of cleavage varies within wide limits, according to the inclination of the section to the chief or vertical axis. E.g., augite cannot be distinguished from hornblende by the angle of cleavage alone, as augite prisms cut at an angle of 40° to the vertical axis, following $-2P\infty$ in the zone $oP : \infty P\infty$, will show a cleavage-angle of 124° 2′, which lies very near the angle of a section of hornblende cut perpendicularly to the vertical axis.

Thoulet (l. c., p. 28) has determined the value of the cleavage-angle of augite, hornblende, orthoclase, and labradorite for the different directions of the sections and according to the amplitude of its inclination to the vertical axis. The determination for the first two of these minerals is given in the table on the following page.

It is therefore impossible by observation of a single cross-section with nearly rectangular cleavage to determine with accuracy, for example, whether the observed monoclinic green or brown mineral is augite or hornblende. Nor less by simply proving the presence or absence of pleochroism. It is therefore necessary to examine a series of cross-sections of the particular mineral, and it can only be settled with any great accuracy whether a mineral is augite or hornblende when several transverse sections show a cleavage-angle approaching 87° or 124°.

Often the shape of the crystal outline shows that the plane of the section is inclined to the vertical axis, and gives approximately its angle of inclination; if the constituents are in a granular condition, this mark of recognition is wanting, and hence complicates the determination. The direction of the section can also be approximately determined by comparison of the optical relations (according to examinations in convergent polarized light).

The simple proof of parallel extinction on one or a few sections can give no safe conclusions as to whether the mineral is rhombic or monoclinic; e.g., the determination of $c : c$ to about 20° in augite and hornblende. As many observations as possible, therefore, must be made on sections optically oriented. In the cases mentioned this is done most easily on prismatic cleavage-leaflets.

**Microscopical Measurements of Angles** are made with the polarization-microscope in the same manner as the determina-

## THE PRISMATIC CLEAVAGE-ANGLE OF

| By an Inclination of the Section to $oP$ of | AUGITE | | | HORNBLENDE | | |
|---|---|---|---|---|---|---|
| | Zone $oP : \infty P\infty$. Section in sense of $mP\infty$. | Zone $oP : \infty P\infty$. Section in sense of | | Zone $oP : \infty P\infty$. Section in sense of $mP\infty$. | Zone $oP : \infty P\infty$. Section in sense of | |
| | | $+ mP\infty$ | $- mP\infty$ | | $+ mP\infty$ | $- mP\infty$ |
| 0° 0′ | 84° 40′ 18″; ‖ $oP$ | 95° 11′; ‖ $oP$ | 95° 11′; ‖ $oP$ | 122° 32′ 20″; ‖ $oP$ | 57° 27′ 40″; ‖ $oP$ | 57° 27′ 40″; ‖ $oP$ |
| 5 | 85 3 | 94 0 | 96 50 | 122 45 | 56 32 | 58 48 |
| 10 | 85 45 | 92 46 | 99 0 | 123 21 | 56 0 | 60 36 |
| 15 | 85 59 | 92 56 | 101 40 | 124 22; ‖ $P\infty$ | 56 48 | 62 52 |
| 20 | 88 38 | 93 4 | 104 54 | 125 48 | 56 0 | 65 44 |
| 25 | 90 51 | 93 38; ‖ $P\infty$ | 108 42; ‖ $-P\infty$ | 127 37 | 56 32 | 66 18; ‖ $-P\infty$ |
| 30 | 93 40 | 94 8 | 113 8 | 129 51 | 57 28; ‖ $P\infty$ | 69 38 |
| 35 | 97 5 | 96 4 | 118 14 | 133 28 | 58 48 | 73 55 |
| 40 | 101 9 | 98 4 | 124 2 | 135 27 | 60 36 | 78 24 |
| 45 | 105 55 | 100 32 | 130 32 | 138 48 | 62 54 | 85 24 |
| 50 | 111 27 | 103 32 | 137 44 | 142 29 | 65 46 | 93 14 |
| 55 | 117 45 | 105 50 | 145 38 | 146 23 | 69 22 | 102 46 |
| 60 | 124 59 | 111 18 | 154 6 | 150 44 | 73 40 | 114 14 |
| 65 | 133 41 | 116 6 | 163 6 | 155 1 | 79 0 | 127 14 |
| 70 | 144 14 | 121 38 | 172 24 | 159 58 | 85 28 | 143 50 |
| 73 59 | | | 180; ‖ $\infty P\infty$ | | | 161 66 |
| 75 2 | 150 22 | 127 50 | | 164 50 | 93 20 | 179 54 |
| 80 | 159 59 | 134 46 | | 169 49 | 102 52 | 180 ; ‖ $\infty P\infty$ |
| 85 | 165 55 | 142 24 | | 174 53 ; ‖ $\infty P\infty$ | 114 20 | |
| 90 | 180 ; ‖ $\infty P\infty$ | 150 38 | | 180 ; ‖ $\infty P\infty$ | 127 58 | |
| 95 | | 159 26 | | | 143 46 | |
| 100 | | 168 40 | | | 161 24 | |
| 104 58 | | 178 6 | | | 180 ; ‖ $\infty P\infty$ | |
| 105 | | | | | | |
| 106 1 | | 180 ; ‖ $\infty P\infty$ | | | | |

tion of the direction of extinction. The instrument is accurately centred, one leg of the angle to be measured so disposed that it coincides exactly with one arm of the cross-threads, the apex of the angle reaching exactly to the junction of the cross-threads of the ocular. The position of the stage is read and the stage revolved until the other leg of the angle coincides with the same arm of the cross-threads, and its position again read : the difference of the two readings gives the magnitude of the angle measured.

If the rock-components are granular, their determinations are greatly complicated, as one can neither draw any satisfactory conclusion as to the crystalline form from the character of the outline merely, nor can it be determined to which faces the cleavage-fissures are parallel; one is therefore restricted to the determination of the color, direction of cleavage, magnitude of the cleavage-angle, and especially to the optical properties of the mineral granules.

The **Microlite** is another form of development of the rock-forming minerals. E. Cohen has designated as "microlites" all those crystals which cannot be prepared in sections in suitable positions, generally horizontal, the micas, however, vertical, appearing in the thin section as perfectly developed individuals; it makes no difference whether the mineral species can be determined or not. Vogelsang (Phil. d. Geol. 1867, p. 139) has recommended that the term "microlite" be used only with the acicular microscopical mineral forms without any regard as to whether it can or cannot be determined to which mineral the microlite belongs. Many rock forming minerals, as augite, hornblende, and the feldspars, appear as microlites; in the porphyritic rocks these occur with larger crystals or grains, and thus chronicle their different stages of formation or separation. The large crystals and grains—the so-called "springlings" (*Einsprenglinge*) (components of the first class)—were formed sooner than the microlites (components of the second class)

## 86 DETERMINATION OF ROCK-FORMING MINERALS.

of the same mineral species forming the principal ground-mass of the porphyritic rocks.

As microlites, and nearly always as such, appear sillimanite (comp. Fig. 71), rutile, zircon, commonly tourmaline, etc.; while other minerals, as olivine, titanite, etc., never or rarely thus appear.

The **Crystallites** (see Fig. 41) form a transition-stage to the microlites, i.e., lie between the amorphous and crystalline condition. Vogelsang designates by this term "all inorganic products which show some systematic arrangement, but not the general character of crystallized bodies, i.e., no polyhedral outline." The crystallites exert no influence on polarized light.

FIG. 41.
CRYSTALLITES AND MICROLITES.

Crystallites occur frequently in vitreous or semi-vitreous rocks. The simplest forms are the **Globulites**, as those exceedingly minute, isotrope, for the most part globular, forms which have separated in the vitreous ground-mass of such rocks are designated. If several such globulites are chained together, the **Margarites** are formed. If the members of this chain-like aggregate of globulites are fused together into a long needle, the **Longulites** are formed.

The **Crystalloids** form yet another stage of transition to the microlites; "these are more of a unit, act also on polarized light, but do not yet show the polyhedral outline of the microlite."

FIG. 42.
MICRO-FLUCTUATION STRUCTURE.
BELONITES AND TRICHITES.

The genesis of the rock-forming minerals is therefore

briefly as follows: The *crystallites* are the primitive form, —the *globulites* being first in order; the *crystalloids* mark a further progress in development; these form a transition to the *microlites*, which in turn only differ in size from the *crystals*.

Vogelsang has proposed a further subdivision of the crystallites and crystalloids, resting upon their pellucidity. A pellucid species may be called a **Belonite**; a non-pellucid, a **Trichite**. (Fig. 42.)

## II. STRUCTURE OF THE ROCK-FORMING MINERALS.

The following should be especially noted concerning the microscopical relations of the rock-components:
1. The disturbances in crystallization.
2. The destruction of crystals already formed.
3. The concentric structure of crystals.

*Disturbances in Crystalization* are not common, and are manifested in the imperfect development of the crystal at one end or in the sunken faces whereby the crystals take on an "etched appearance;" the phenomenon so often noticed in magnetite is also to be mentioned—the regular grouping of several small crystals in three directions at right angles to each other corresponding to the axes, thus forming the outline to a larger crystal.

Imperfectly-developed crystals occur on one termination; e.g., on hematite, where hexagonal tablets are notched and lapped on one or two sides, or on the crystals of hornblende, augite, etc., which are often covered at one end with several sub-individuals and thus acquire an appearance resembling a ruin:

On olivine, leucite, etc., often occur crystals with faces depressed in consequence of the interrupted development. In a word, exactly the same phenomena of growth and disturbance are noticed in the crystals separated from the molten rock-magma as can be perceived on crystals formed from a solution. The destruction, fracture, and bruising of crystals already fully formed can be commonly observed on the microscopic constituents of the more recent and vitreous rocks, just as the same phenomena are observed on the macroscopic individuals; e.g., of tourmaline, epidote, etc. The larger mineral components which first separated show such fractures especially. These are a direct consequence of the pressure which the molten, fluctuating rock-magma exerted on the crystals already formed, if any change in the rapidity of fluctuation was induced by any obstruction; e.g., another opposing large crystal lying in the immediate vicinity. The corresponding fragments of the crystal, as well as the crystal or other matter causing the fracture, can be observed very often lying close together. Such fractures are for the most part restricted to the thin tabular or long acicular crystal individuals; they are observed, therefore, most commonly on the feldspars, augite or hornblende crystals, while the micas because of their elasticity show only a bending or exfoliation. However, quartz grains and crystals often appear shattered into small splinters and plates.

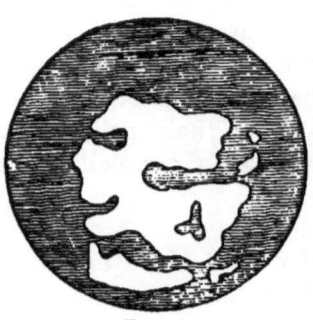

FIG. 43.
CORRODED QUARTZ CRYSTAL.
(After Fouqué.)

### *The Destruction of Crystals already Formed.*

The larger crystalline components undergo further changes through the caustic action of the liquid magma, as manifested in the corrosion, partial fusion, and even total destruction of the crystal. Thus quartz occurring in the porphyritic eruptive rocks often shows a sinus-like penetration of the ground-mass. (Fig. 43.) Leucite and olivine as well as augite crystals or grains often show an etched surface, sometimes covered with regular depressions, probably caused by the caustic action of the magma on the crystals for a long period, similar to the figures and depressions often formed on artificial crystals by action of the mother-liquor.

If action of magma on the crystals already formed was more powerful, a partial fusion ensued, as may be observed very often on crystals of feldspar or augite of the eruptive rocks, where some faces are yet more or less evident.

The resolution of the edges into minute crystals and grains as is often observed on the larger olivine, augite, and feldspar crystals is another remarkable corrosion-phenomenon, depending upon this action of the magma. The minute crystals are to be regarded as newly-deposited crystals of the same mineral, and the grains as separated particles. The diopside, bronzite, and olivine grains of the so-called "olivine lumps" in the basalts often show such changes. More remarkable yet is that on the omphacite of eclogite, a rock classed, however, according to its formation with the crystalline schists.

Another change also ascribed to the action of the molten magma, and commonly observed on hornblende and **biotite** crystals of the more recent eruptive rocks richer in iron, consists of the appearance of an *opaque margin* (Fig. 44). The crystals are surrounded by a border, or narrow, dense, opaque black hem, formed from exceedingly minute granules of an unknown iron compound — the so-called "opacite." Often the whole crystal has undergone such an igneous metamorphosis and only remnants of the fresh, brown, original mineral are to be found.

FIG. 44. OPACITIC-BORDERED HORNBLENDE.

This opaque bounding of hornblende and biotite must not be confounded with the decompositions effected by water, whereby such a marginal hem is formed, proved to be of magnetite. In this case the hornblende is not perfectly fresh, but is partially changed to chlorite, and the opaque hem is not so dense as those crystals metamorphosed by fire.

Finally, the occurrence of the so-called "**Pseudo-crystals**" of hornblende, augite, and biotite must be briefly noticed. In the younger eruptive rocks bearing these minerals, aggregates of minute augitic granules, feldspathic grains, and especially magnetite or hematite leaflets often occur, which assume their crystalline forms; often a fresh, irregular, partially-fused kernel of hornblende or biotite or augite is seen within. It is very probable that these aggregates occurring in the eruptive rocks have been formed by the action of the liquid rock-magma on the unchanged hornblende, biotite, or augite crystals, the form of the crystal being meanwhile preserved. These pseudo-crystals can be formed experimentally by dipping hornblende, etc., crystals in fused rock-magma and allowing to cool.

### The Shell-formed Structure of Crystals.

A macroscopical examination of many crystals shows a zonal structure, e.g. barite, tourmaline, epidote, garnet, etc.; the shell-structure proves a repeated interrupted growth of the crystal, each layer or coat corresponding to a period of growth. This shell-structure may be easily shown in artificial crystals by suspending a crystal successively in different mother-liquors; e.g., an octahedron of alum in a solution of chrome-alum.

In the same way an exceedingly detailed laminated formation may be observed often in the microscopical crystal individuals occurring as rock-constituents. Among these, the feldspars, augite, hornblende, melanite, tourmaline, more rarely epidote, titanite, disthene, andalusite, corundum, hauyn, nepheline, etc., must be mentioned particularly.

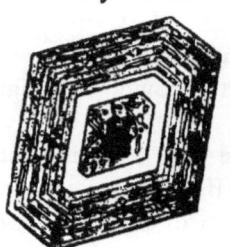

FIG. 45.
ZONALLY-DEVELOPED AUGITE.
Section $\parallel \infty P \infty$.

The different layers are often very numerous and exceedingly thin, and can be distinguished from each other easily, especially if multicolored, as is so commonly the case with augite (Fig. 45) or hornblende, where a green centre is surrounded by a brown layer, or green and brown or nearly colorless layers alternate. In melanite dark-brown layers alternate with lighter; in andalusite often a red centre, in disthene and corundum a blue centre, is enveloped by a colorless coating.

In many cases the shell-formed structure of crystals, as in the feldspars, augite, and hornblende, is first evident in polarized light; the different layers thus show different polarization-colors, and also the direction of extinction varies somewhat in them, due, it appears, to the slight variation in chemical constitution of the successive layers. These lines of growth run undisturbed through the twinnings of the feldspars, etc.; this would indicate that the laminated development was synchronous with the formation of the twins.

The single layers often can be distinguished from each other more sharply by the inclosures of fluids, glass, or microlites lying between them; the successive layers have a course nearly parallel with the central crystal (see Fig. 45). Now and then, however, crystals are observed, especially of feldspar and augite, where the edges and angles of the kernel-crystal are replaced by faces of the enveloping layers.

As already mentioned, a very common and prominent development of crystals from two zones of different optical orientation is noticed in the feldspars, in sanidine, as well as in some species of plagioclase. In these latter species it can be proved often that the kernel-crystal is a plagioclase of more basic composition; but the envelopes, on the other hand, belong to a plagioclase richer in silicic acid and sodium. Hoepfner (N. Jahrb. f. Min. u. Geol., 1881, II. p. 883) first called attention to these relations by showing that the plagioclase of andesite from Monte Tajumbina often has an anorthite centre surrounded by an envelope of oligoclase. Becke confirmed these observations on the feldspars in kersantite from the lower Austrian forest (Tscher. Min. Mitth., 1882, V. p. 161).

The change from kernel to envelope is quite gradual, as each successive layer deposits a feldspar richer in sodium. The observation of Rosenbusch that the decomposition of a feldspar is generally from the centre outward is quite in harmony. The hypothesis already proposed by the same investigator, that the kernel of these species of plagioclase possesses a more basic constitution, and therefore undergoes an alteration first, is confirmed by the observations of Hoepfner and Becke.

A peculiar structure of crystal is the so-called "hour-glass structure" as seen not rarely in monoclinic augite of many basaltic rocks (Figs. 46 and 47), especially of limburgite,

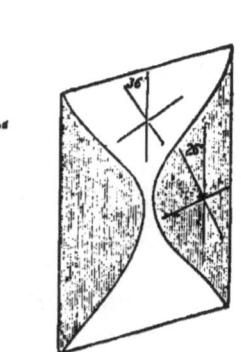

Fig. 46.—Augite with "Hour-glass Structure." Section ∥ ∞P∞. (After L. v. Werveke.)

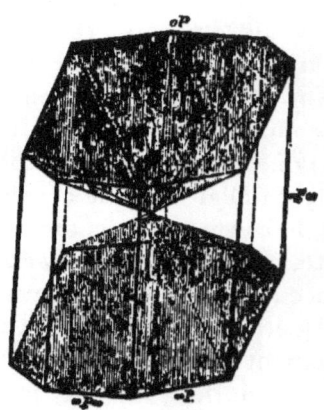

Fig. 47.—Schematic Representation of the "Hour-glass Augite."

more rarely in hornblende, and also in andalusite and staurolite. Sections parallel to the plane of symmetry divide into four fields in polarized light, any two of which lying opposite each other show the same colors and the same optical orientation. The deviation in optical orientation is generally slight. The sections parallel $\infty P\infty$ are similar.

While sections perpendicular to the vertical axis show the

ordinary zonal structure. At first a crystal-skeleton shaped like an hour-glass appears to have been formed, both of whose conical spaces were filled subsequently with an augitic substance varying somewhat in chemical composition.

## *Interpenetration of the Rock-constituents.*

Graphic granite or pegmatyte serves as one of the best-known examples of a regular interpenetration of two rock-constituents. In pegmatyte numberless macroscopic quartz individuals all showing the same optical orientation are formed within large orthoclase individuals. The same penetration precisely is found commonly among the microscopic individuals of the rock-constituents, and is called the " micro-pegmatitic structure." This proves a nearly simultaneous formation of both mutually-developed individuals, and occurs very commonly in the granites and crystalline schists. In the latter case, however, not only is the orthoclase regularly developed with quartz, but also other constituents, as garnet or augite with quartz, plagioclase with augite, etc. Their development is often irregular, in that the augite grains penetrating the plagioclase individuals, e.g., do not show throughout the same optical orientation. Regular interpenetrations commonly occur also between the augites and hornblendes, where either monoclinic augite, especially diallage or omphacite, also possessing the brachy-pinacoidal separation (*Absonderung*), is grown into the monoclinic hornblende so that the ortho-pinacoidal faces of both lie parallel; or rhombic and monoclinic augite are interpenetrated so that both lie with the ortho- or macro-pinacoids adjoining.

## III. INCLOSURES OF THE ROCK-FORMING MINERALS.

Macroscopical inclosures have been observed in many crystalline minerals for a long period; quartz is especially rich in them. The microscopic constituents of the rocks also contain inclosures many of which may be regarded as characteristic for certain minerals. Among these inclosures of the rock-components are gas-pores, fluids, vitreous particles (of the rock-mass), and, finally, inclosures of other minerals also sharing in the composition of the rock.

### Gas-pores (Fig. 48).

During the development of a crystal minute bubbles of air often cling fast to the faces, which afterward are surrounded and finally inclosed by the crystalline material during the succeeding growth; this phenomenon can be best observed with artificial crystals on removal from the solution. In exactly the same manner bubbles of gas which were absorbed by the mother-liquor and are of such common occurrence in the vitreous ground-mass of rocks were inclosed by the rock-forming minerals during their separation from the molten magma: these are the so-called **Gas-pores.** It is difficult to determine what gases are inclosed within the minute, generally egg-shaped or irregularly-defined spaces; it is very probable that gaseous (i.e. condensed) carbon dioxide is of common occurrence. The gas-pores are often regularly distributed through the crystals; being sometimes zonal, parallel to the crystal faces if they are inclosed between two successive concentric layers, or forming an elongated series.

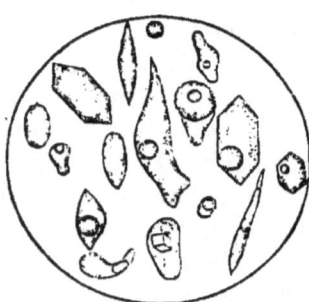

FIG. 48.
GAS-PORES AND FLUID INCLOSURES.

The minerals of the hauyn group among the rock-constituents are especially rich in inclosures of gas-pores; apatite, the feldspars, augite, etc., also contain them. Cavities empty, or filled with gas, often occur, especially in quartz, which exhibit the form of the mineral in which they occur—the so-called "negative crystals." Such regular pores filled with air occur in artificial crystals; e.g., the cube-shaped cavities in rock-salt. During the development of this mineral regular cubical depressions are formed; an air-bubble forces its way into the depression, which becomes covered afterward by succeeding depositions of the crystalline material.

### *Fluid Inclosures* (Fig. 48).

If the mother-liquor is forced into the irregular or cubical cavity mentioned in the last example, instead of air or other gases absorbed by the mother-liquor, fluid inclosures are formed which contain a small air- or gas-bubble, sometimes called the "libella," which by turning the piece of salt vibrates along the sides of the cavity.

In just the same way the fluid inclosures commonly occurring, especially in quartz, are formed in the rock-forming minerals. The fluid inclosures occur more rarely in the younger and recent eruptive rocks, and are for the most part inclosures of liquid carbon dioxide—a proof that these rocks were formed under immense pressure. Inclosures of aqueous solutions also occur in the constituents of the volcanic rocks; it is probable that these liquids were inclosed in a fluid condition. The formation of the bubble within the fluid inclosures can be accounted for most easily by supposing that the crystals separated at a high temperature and under heavy pressure; on subsequent cooling the inclosed liquid contracted and thus left an empty space—the bubble. The bubble in the microscopic fluid inclosures commonly shows a perfect freedom of motion, at one time slow and again exceedingly rapid.

If the inclosed liquid was a concentrated salt solution, minute crystals have been deposited since the cooling, and liquid, crystals, and bubble can be distinguished within the cavity. The form of the fluid inclosure is generally an irregu-

lar one ; the egg-shaped and spherical are more rare ; and more
rare yet those assuming the form of the inclosing mineral, as
occasionally in quartz, gypsum, etc. The inclosure is commonly very small and does not generally exceed some hundredths or thousandths of a millimetre. What has been said
already concerning the distribution of the gas-pores is equally
applicable to these fluid inclosures.

As regards the chemical constitution of the inclosed liquids,
all determinations up to the present time have shown them to
be either water, liquid carbon dioxide, or some salt solution, especially of sodium chloride. The majority of the simply
aqueous inclosures have a quiescent or feebly-vibrating bubble,
which does not disappear on heating to about 100° C. The inclosures of liquid carbon dioxide, on the other hand, have generally a very mobile bubble which disappears on heating to
about 32° C. If the bubble in such an inclosure is very large,
i.e. but little liquid is present, the liquid $CO_2$ is changed into
the gaseous condition when the bubble disappears; if, on the
other hand, the bubble is so minute that the whole space is filled
through the expansion of the liquid carbon dioxide, the gaseous
bubble disappears.

Inclosures of liquids of two kinds commonly occur where
liquid carbon dioxide is present together with a purely aqueous
inclosure in one and the same mineral grain ; also, but rarely
in quartz, two different liquids are inclosed in one and the
same cavity, without commingling ; in this case the inner liquid,
generally carbon dioxide, possesses a bubble.

Inclosures of concentrated salt solutions have, for the most
part, an immovable bubble, or at least one moving but slowly or
after warming, and minute crystals deposited from the inclosed
mother-liquor; sodium-chloride crystals are the most common.
The bubble, as well as the minute cube, does not disappear on
warming the preparation, or disappears first at higher temperatures.

# METHODS OF INVESTIGATION. 97

The bubble is wanting in many fluid inclosures, as the cavities are completely filled with liquid. Such microscopic cavities can be distinguished from gas-pores only with great difficulty. They are surrounded in transmitted light with a broad dark border, in consequence partly of a total reflection of the rays; the two can be distinguished only by the presence of the bubble. This dark border of the gas and fluid inclosures will be the stronger the greater the indices of refraction of the inclosed gas and the inclosing mineral. For this reason the gas-pores have always a darker border than the fluid inclosures.

## *Inclosures of Vitreous Particles.*

Particles of the ground-mass, either purely vitreous or semi-individualized, become inclosed during the process of crystallization from the fused magma, just as fluids are inclosed within crystals deposited from solution. These very minute and irregular, egg-shaped, or spherical glassy particles, the vitreous inclosures (Fig. 49), solidified during or after their inclosure, generally have one or several gas-bubbles inclosed with them. This gas-bubble is of course immovable, and, unlike the bubble of the fluid inclosures, cannot be moved by heating.

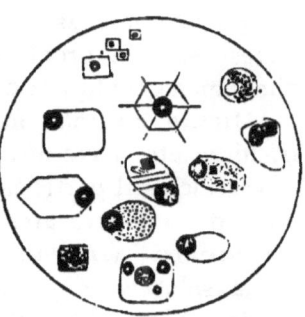

FIG. 49.—VITREOUS INCLOSURES.

The vitreous inclosures in minerals are colorless or brown according as the vitreous matrix of the rock is light or dark colored (the acidic lavas have generally only a colorless, basic, light-colored or brown glass); both varieties very commonly occur together, the coloration of the glass depending merely on the amount of iron present.

The distribution of the vitreous inclosures is either an irregular one or is in zones corresponding to the shell-formed structure of the crystal. Sometimes the kernel of the crystal is filled with these inclosures, and the enveloping layers poor in them, or the reverse.

The vitreous inclosures are especially common in the feldspars of the younger and recent eruptive rocks, common also in quartz and augite.

Vitreous inclosures of dihexahedral form are occasionally found in quartz, corresponding to its crystalline form. Such regular inclosures are formed in the same manner as the dihexahedral gaseous or fluid inclosures in quartz, with this difference, that the substance filling the regular cavities is in this case a vitreous mass. A jagged bubble is often seen in such vitreous inclosures, or a gas-bubble partially freed from the inclosure, which was prevented from escaping by rapid deposition of crystalline matter. The presence of such an escaping bubble, as well as that of several bubbles within the inclosures, is a proof of their solid vitreous character: such phenomena could not occur in fluid inclosures.

Minute crystals, magnetite octahedra, augite microlites, trichites, etc., have often separated during solidification of vitreous, inclosed particles in the same manner as crystals are deposited from inclosures of saturated solutions; i.e., the glass is "devitrified" (*entglast*). The magnitude of the gas-bubble has absolutely no genetic connection with the magnitude of the inclosure. The vitreous inclosures will show in transmitted light no such dark border as the gas-pores and fluid inclosures, as the index of refraction of the glass is rather high and differs less than air or water from that of the mineral. The vitreous portion of the inclosure has consequently a less marked border, although the gas-bubble shows all the darker broad band.

The presence of a gas-bubble in the vitreous inclosure cut

through in the process of grinding the mineral section is an additional means of discriminating between a vitreous and a fluid inclosure. As the gas-bubble is an empty cavity, fixed in the solid vitreous body, it is cut through during the process of preparation, becomes filled with Canada balsam, and the vitreous inclosure appears in the preparation as only a feebly outlined circle; a fluid inclosure, on the other hand, thus cut through would become completely filled with Canada balsam, as the liquid escapes during the process of cutting and the bubble in this case is completely dissipated.

Often large, irregular particles of non- or but poorly-individualized vitreous masses with no inclosed gas-bubbles occur in the rock-forming minerals; as, e.g., between the layers or in the kernel of feldspar, olivine, etc. They, as well as the vitreous inclosures containing gas-bubbles, are a proof of the formation of the rock (i.e. the minerals) from a molten magma.

In the quartz grains of rock of undoubted sedimentary origin which were solidified from confined and metamorphosed eruptive rocks, vitreous inclosures are also discovered, but of a secondary character, being first formed through the action of eruptive magma heated to redness on the inclosed rock; this can be proved by experiment. The way, however, in which such secondary vitreous inclosures could be made is at present unexplained. (See Chrustschoff, Tschermak's Min. Mitth. 1882, IV. p. 473.)

### *Inclosures of Foreign Minerals.*

Macroscopical inclosures of other minerals have been observed commonly in quartz (prase, etc.). Among the microscopical constituents also, quartz, as well as many other minerals, as staurolite, etc., is especially rich in inclosures. The granules or crystals thus inclosed within the rock-constituents are of those minerals making up the composition of the particular rock, and are for the most part very minute and often regularly distributed through the inclosing mineral. In augite, e.g., long, narrow indeterminable microlites (augite?) together with vitreous inclosures are commonly arranged in zones these were inclosed in the same manner as the vitreous particles, during separation of the crystal from the vitreous, semi individualized magma. In other minerals the mineral inclos-

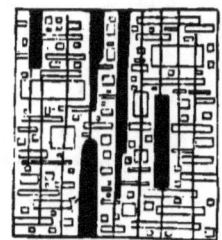

FIG. 50.
INCLOSURES OF BROOKITE (?) TABLETS IN HYPERSTHENE.

ures are regularly distributed parallel to certain faces, as the opaque to brownish translucent rectangular tablets parallel to $\infty \bar{P} \infty$ in hypersthene and bronzite (Fig. 50), or the opaque microlites and tablets parallel to the $c'$-axis in labradorite.

The zonally arranged inclosures of small quartz granules in the garnet and staurolite of the crystalline schists; the inclosures of minute elongated needles of rutile, regular and crossed at an angle of 60°, occurring in some species of magnesian micas in certain eruptive rocks; and, finally, the inclosures of sillimanite microlites in cordierite and quartz of crystalline schists, etc., are also especially worthy of mention.

Comparison of the inclosures of rock-constituents often proves of importance in determining the order of separation, i.e. the formation; thus magnetite, menaccanite, spinel, rutile, zirconite, are generally the minerals first formed in the crystalline rocks, as they are always found included within all the minerals occurring in one and the same rock.

In the eruptive rocks the magnesian silicates generally followed these in order of separation (augite, hornblende, biotite, and olivine), then the feldspars, and finally quartz. Nevertheless no universal law can be formulated. Still less possible is it to formulate a law for the crystalline schists. Quartz, and also orthoclase, are found included within hornblende and garnet—i.e., they were first formed; or quartz and orthoclase are interpenetrated (micro-pegmatitic, graphic-granitic)—i.e., both were developed at the same time.

The chemical and physical properties of minerals are of course changed by these inclosures. Specimens as free as possible from inclosures must therefore be selected for examination.

## IV. Decomposition of the Rock-constituents.

J. Roth. Allgemeine und chemische Geologie. Berlin, 1879. I. Bd.

The rock-forming minerals are far more exposed to the decomposing and solvent influences of filtrating waters than the larger developed minerals. In the volcanic rocks a further change of the rock-constituents is induced by the action of the gaseous emanations accompanying the eruptions. For these reasons, therefore, different minerals are found in the rock-preparations in different stages of decomposition. The metamorphosis in most cases can be studied and followed on the thin sections. It begins almost always from without and advances inwards, especially on the cleavage-fissures of crystals or grains; the crystal-kernel, as in the feldspars, though rarely, first undergoes decomposition.

Olivine, orthoclase, and magnetite, of the rock-forming minerals, most commonly occur thus metamorphosed.

In the metamorphosis of olivine into serpentine, fine greenish or brown thread-like aggregates appear along the fissures. These gradually broaden, whereby the cross-section of olivine on the slide seems drawn into a net of serpentine, in whose meshes lie the fresh olivine residues. These also finally undergo decomposition, and a complete pseudomorphosis of **serpentine** after olivine results.

Serpentine is generally tinged red by freshly-formed iron

hydroxide. Clino-chlore is deposited in many cases in olivine-fels by the metamorphosis of magnetite. In these cases water is taken up and magnetite and iron silicates are deposited. If the silicates are removed so that only the ferrous oxide separated from olivine remains as ferric oxide and hydroxide, pure pseudomorphs of ferric oxide and hydroxide after olivine are often formed.

Grayish to brownish opaque pseudomorphoses after olivine are often found in the picrites, consisting principally of calcite and showing a mesh-like structure. The meshes themselves are formed from calcium silicate, while the spaces between are filled with calcite. In this case silicic acid and magnesia are removed, and alumina, lime, carbon dioxide, and alkalies are taken up. Similar pseudomorphs of calcite after augite also occur.

In the metamorphosis of feldspar into kaolin no such regular progress of decomposition beginning with the cleavage-fissures, as a rule, can be determined; they become spotted and opaque, and metamorphosed into an aggregate of minute gray or white grains. The alumina remains constant, silicic acid is partially removed, water and potassium are taken up. In the zonally-developed feldspars the layers rich in inclosures first undergo decomposition.

Potassium micas, in minute brilliantly-polarizing tablets, are also commonly formed by the decomposition of the feldspars; quite perfect pseudomorphs of muscovite, after orthoclase, are often found. In this case the greater part of the alkali remains; the rest is removed together with silicic acid, which often separates as quartz ($SiO_2$).

Menaccanite becomes coated with a gray opaque coating (leucoxene), and is finally metamorphosed into transparent titanite; lime must be added. More rarely menaccanite metamorphoses into rutile with separation of ferric oxide, which deposits as a reddish border about the decomposed mineral.

Finally, mention must be made of the metamorphosis of minerals of the hauyn group, and of nepheline into the zeolites, especially natrolite, wherein calcite often separates; the metamorphosis of garnet into chlorite ; of biotite, hornblende, and augite into chlorite and epidote, with elimination of quartz, ferric hydroxide, and calcite ; the decomposition of rhombic augite in bastite, etc.

END OF PART I.

# PART II.

## TABLES FOR DETERMINING MINERALS.

### ABBREVIATIONS USED IN THE TABLES.

**Under the heading "Optical Properties:"**

$AP$ = Plane of the optic axes.
1 M. = First middle line.
2 M. = Second middle line.
$\mathfrak{a}$ = Axis of greatest elasticity.
$\mathfrak{b}$ = Axis of middle elasticity = optic normal.
$\mathfrak{c}$ = Axis of least elasticity.
$\|$ = Parallel.
$\perp$ = At right angles.
$n$ = Index of refraction.

For optically-uniaxial minerals.
 $\omega$ = Index of refraction for the ordinary ray.
 $\varepsilon$ = Index of refraction for the extraordinary ray.

For optically-biaxial minerals.
 $\beta$ = Index of refraction of middle value.
 $\rho$ = For red light.

i. c. p. l. = In convergent polarized light.
i. p. p. l. = In parallel polarized light.

**For the crystallographic axes:**

c = Chief, i.e. vertical, axis.

In rhombic or triclinic minerals.
 $\check{a}$ = Brachydiagonal axis.
 $\bar{b}$ = Macrodiagonal axis.

In monoclinic minerals.
 $\check{a}$ = Clinodiagonal axis.
 $b'$ = Orthodiagonal axis.

**Under the heading "Structure:"**

I. O. = Components first in order of separation.
II. O. = Components second in order of separation.

# Table for Determining the System of Crystallization of the Rock-forming Minerals.

| | ISOTROPE. | ANISOTROPE. | |
|---|---|---|---|
| | | A part of the cross-section becomes colored and dark between crossed nicols during a complete revolution. | |
| | | Optically-Uniaxial. | Optically-Biaxial. |
| | All cross-sections remain dark between crossed nicols throughout a complete revolution. | Isotropic sections show a fixed axial cross in converging polarized light. | Isotropic sections show a black cloud in converging polarized light which during revolution of the microscope-stage moves in the opposite direction. |
| **Division of the Minerals according to their Optical Properties.** | | | |
| **Relations between the Axes of Elasticity and the Crystallographic Axes** | Equal optical elasticity in all directions. | The optical elasticity in the direction of the chief axis different from that at right angles to it. The chief axis coincides with the optic axis and corresponds with the axis of either the greatest or least elasticity. | The three axes of elasticity correspond to the crystallographic axes. Both optic axes lie in a plane parallel to a pinacoid. | One axis of elasticity coincides with one of the crystallographic axes, the orthodiagonal; the other two, together with the optic axes, lie either in the plane of symmetry ∞P∞, or in a plane at right angles to it, and inclined according to oP or +P∞, and form an angle with the crystallographic axes. | No axis of elasticity coincides with a crystallographic axis. Plane of the optic axes neither perpendicular nor parallel to a pinacoidal face, but inclined to them. |

## Examination in Parallel Polarized Light.

### Sections at right angles to the chief or vertical axis.

| ISOTROPE | Optically-Uniaxial | Optically-Biaxial | | |
|---|---|---|---|---|
| All cross-sections remain perfectly darkened during a complete revolution. | The *quadratic* or *octagonal transverse* sections remain perfectly dark throughout a complete revolution. | The *hexagonal* or 12- (3- or 9-) sided *transverse sections* remain dark throughout a complete revolution. | Rectangular, extinguishing parallel and at right angles to the sides, i.e., the pinacoids. | Extinguish parallel, i.e., parallel and at right angles to the pinacoidal faces. | |

### Sections parallel to the chief or vertical axis.

| | | | |
|---|---|---|---|
| | Rectangular or hexagonal elongated longitudinal sections have parallel extinction, i.e., parallel and at right angles to the chief axis or the pair of sides parallel to it. | Rectangular, *all with parallel extinction*, i.e., parallel and at right angles to the sides parallel to the vertical axis. | Sections from the zone oP : ∞P∞ extinguish parallel; *sections parallel* ∞P∞, on the other hand, show an *extinction oblique* to the edge oP : ∞P∞ or ∞P∞ : ∞P∞. | *No pinacoidal section extinguishes parallel*, the obliqueness of extinction on oP and ∞P∞ known and characteristic. |

# TABLES FOR DETERMINING MINERALS.

| | | | | | | | |
|---|---|---|---|---|---|---|---|
| **Examination in Converging Polarized Light.** | **Random Sections** | Sections parallel to the chief or vertical axis. | No interference-figure visible in any cross-section. Total darkness throughout a complete revolution. Rarely optical anomalies in connection with concentric structure, e.g., opal. | As before. Rarely optical anomalies in connection with concentric structure, e.g., garnet, analcime, perowskite. | Transverse sections show a fixed black axial cross, with or without colored rings, according to the power of double-refraction and the thickness of the mineral leaflet. | Perpendicular appearances of 1 M. in one pinacoidal section and of 2 M. in another depending on the position of the plane of the optic axes; i.e., a symmetrical interference-figure of an optically-biaxial body is visible, with or without lemniscates, according to the power of double-refraction and thinness of the mineral leaflet. No interference-figure in the third pinacoidal section. | If the plane of the optic axis is parallel $\infty P\infty$, none of the pinacoidal sections shows a perpendicular appearance of a middle line, but an interference-figure distorted in the direction of the vertical axis or appearance of one of the optic axes. If the plane of the optic axes is at right angles to $\infty P\infty$, then perpendicular appearance of the 1 M. or 2 M. on $\infty P\infty$. | None of the pinacoidal sections shows perpendicular appearance of a middle line; but either a side distorted axial picture or appearance of one of the optic axes. |
| | | Sections at right angles to the chief or vertical axis. | Cross-sections show no polygonal regular outline, and especially no crystalline structure. | Cross-sections show polygonal regular outline and cleavage. | Longitudinal sections show no interference-figures and become four times bright and dark during a complete revolution, as in parallel polarized light. | Sections inclined to the chief axis show a side appearance of the optic axis in convergent polarized light, the axial point lying either within or without the field according to the obliquity of the section; the fixed axial cross moves in the direction the stage is turned. | Isotropic sections at right angles to one of the optic axes show in converging polarized light a black cloud with or without colored rings, according to the power of double-refraction. According as the section is more or less perpendicular to the middle line, the axial point appears without or within the field. On revolving the stage this cloud revolves in a contrary direction. If this cloud, i.e., hyperbola, is red on the convex side and blue on the concave, then the dispersion of the axes is $\rho > v$; if the reverse, $v > \rho$. The angle of inclination of the axes of elasticity to the crystallographic axes in sections parallel $\infty P\infty$ in monoclinic minerals, and parallel $\rho P$ and $\infty P\infty$ in the triclinic, gives an admirable means of determining them. | | |
| | **System of Crystallization.** | | AMORPHOUS. | REGULAR. | TETRAGONAL. | HEXAGONAL. | RHOMBIC. | MONOCLINIC. | TRICLINIC. |

## A. Even in the thinnest Sections

| Name. | Chemical composition and reactions. | Specific gravity. | System of crystallization. | Cleavage. | Ordinary combinations and form of the cross-section. | Twins. |
|---|---|---|---|---|---|---|
| 1. Magnetite. (*Magneteisen.*) | $Fe_3O_4$ ($FeO + Fe_2O_3$). Easily soluble in HCl. | 4.9–5.2. | Regular. | According to O. | Grains and octahedra. Squares and equilateral triangles. | According to O. |
| 2. Titaniferous Magnetite. (*Titanmagneteisen.*) | $FeO + \dfrac{Fe_2O_3}{FeTiO_3}$ *Distinguished from magnetite only by chemical analysis.* (*Reaction for titanium.*) | 4.8–5.1. | | | Octahedra and grains. | |
| 3. Pyrite. | $FeS_2$. Easily soluble in $HNO_3$, with separation of S. | 4.9–5.2. | | According to $\infty O \infty$. | $\dfrac{\infty O_2}{2}$. Regular hexagons and pentagons. | Penetration-twins of $\dfrac{\infty O_2}{2}$. |

## of Opaque Minerals.

| Color and lustre. | Structure. | Association. | Decomposition. | Occurrence. | Remarks. |
|---|---|---|---|---|---|
| Iron-black; in reflected light *bluish-black metallic* lustre. | Often in beautiful cruciform aggregates; or as product of decomposition wreathed about the minerals; also deposited upon the cleavage-fissures. | With nearly all of the rock-forming minerals; especially with augite, olivine, plagioclase, nepheline, and leucite. | Commonly into *iron hydroxide*. A *reddish-brown circle* about the *magnetite crystals*. | 1. As primary essential constituent of the basic eruptive rocks; accessory in nearly all of the crystalline rocks. 2. As decomposition-product of olivine, augite, hornblende, and biotite. | |
| Ditto. | | | Into *titanite*, *leucoxene*, and *iron hydroxide*. | Primary; in basaltic rocks and crystalline schists. | Forms at the same time the transition-products to ilmenite. |
| In reflected light *brass-yellow*. Metallic lustre. | | | Into iron hydroxide. | Rarely as accessory secondary constituents in decomposed basic eruptive rocks, and (also primary) in crystalline schists. | |

| Name. | Chemical composition and reactions. | Specific gravity. | System of crystallization. | Cleavage. | Ordinary combinations and form of the cross-section. | Twins. |
|---|---|---|---|---|---|---|
| 4. Ilmenite. (Titan-eisen.) | $FeTiO_3 +$ $\chi(Fe_2O_3)$. Difficultly soluble in HCl. *Ti-reaction* with microcosmic salt. | 4.56–5.21. | Hexagonal. | $R$ and $oR$; conchoidal separation (absonderung). | Tabular $R \cdot oR$; also $-\tfrac{1}{2}R, -2R$, and *grains* which are not spherical but for the most part long rods. Cross-sections generally hexagonal, *long threadlike, jagged*, or netted forms. | With parallel axial systems. Polysynthetic twins after $R$. |
| 5. Graphite (and *bitumen*). | C. Bituminous black rocks, becoming grayish-white on heating. | 1.9–2.3. | Hexagonal. | $oP$. | Rarely in thin hexagonal tablets and *irregular leaves*. | |
| 6. Pyrrhotite. (Magnet kies.) | $Fe_nS_{n+1}$. | 4.54–4.64. | | | *Irregular grains*. | |

## MINERALS RENDERED TRANSPARENT

| | | | | | | |
|---|---|---|---|---|---|---|
| 1. Chromite. | See page 14. | | Regular. | | Grains and octahedra. | |
| 2. Pleonaste. | | | | | | |
| 3. Hæmatite. | See page 32. | | Hexagonal. | | Tablets. | |

| Color and lustre. | Structure. | Association. | Decomposition. | Occurrence. | Remarks. |
|---|---|---|---|---|---|
| Black-brown; *metallic lustre.* In reflected light *gray*, *if decomposed.* | | With plagioclase, augite, hornblende, and olivine. | *Into titanite (leucoxene) and rutile with hæmatite.* Ilmenite is metamorphosed by decomposition first into a grayish, opaque, pulverulent mineral (leucoxene), changing gradually into one brown and transparent, which can be determined as titanite; often thin decomposed threads of ilmenite remain. (Comp. Fig. 51.) | In basic eruptive rocks (especially the granular diabases, gabbros, basalts, picrites); also in crystalline schists. | Can be distinguished from magnetite by the form of the cross-section, and especially by the phenomena attending decomposition. |
| Iron-black; metallic lustre. | | | | Rare, in crystalline schists, clay and clay-mica schists, gneiss, limestone, and as an inclosure in staurolite, andalusite, chiastolite, dipyre, and couzeranite. | Distinguished from hæmatite by its opacity or decoloration by heating. |
| Bronze-yellow and copper-red. | | | | Rarely in crystalline schists, contact-schists. | Can be distinguished from pyrite easily by the lustre in reflected light. |

## ONLY WITH DIFFICULTY.

| Color and lustre. | Structure. | Association. | Decomposition. | Occurrence. | Remarks. |
|---|---|---|---|---|---|
| Black; metallic lustre; if transparent, *brown.* | | | | Rare in olivine rocks. Contact rocks and schistose rocks. | Similarity with magnetite. |
| *Green.* | | | | | |
| *Red.* | | | | Generally as accessory constituent and product of decomposition. | Similar to graphite, etc. |

## B. Minerals Transparent
### I. SINGLE-REFRACTING MINERALS.
#### a. Amorphous

| Name. | Chemical composition and reactions. | Specific gravity. | Color. | Structure. |
|---|---|---|---|---|
| 1. Opal. (Porodinamorph.) | Essentially $SiO_2$ ($H_2O$, traces of Fe, Ca, Al, Mg, and the alkaloids). Soluble in KOH. | 1.9–2.3. | Colorless (white, yellowish), often colored red and brown by ferric oxide and hydroxide. $n = 1.455$. | a. Homogeneous and devoid of structure. b. *Concentric-conchoidal*, and then showing often in parallel polarized light feeble double-refraction (interference-cross). *In clusters*, crust-like. (See Fig. 52.) |
| 2. Hyalite. (Glasmasse.) | Always a complicated silicate (Si, Al, Fe, Ca, Mg, alkalies). Acid vitreous mass containing about 70 per cent $SiO_2$ insoluble in HCl. Basic vitreous mass with about 40 per cent $SiO_2$, for the most part soluble in HCl. | Acidic = 2.2–2.4 (obsidian). Basic = 2.5t (trachylyte). | Colorless, or colored gray, brown, or red. The basic hyalite is generally dark, the acidic light. $n$ (for obsidian) = 1.488. | a. Obsidians absolutely devoid of structure, with separation of free glasses. b. Pitchstone, with macroscopic separations. c. Pumice-stone, fibrous and filled with gas-pores. d. Perlite, spherical with concentric-conchoidal structure. |

## TABLES FOR DETERMINING MINERALS.

### in Thin Sections.

(Isotropic in all cross-sections.)

*Minerals.*

| Inclosures. | Decomposition. | Occurrence. | Remarks. |
|---|---|---|---|
| a. Brownish-red, dust-like inclosures of ferric hydrate. b. Aggregates of hexagonal tablets of tridymite. c. Fluid inclosures and gas-pores. | | Always secondary; decomposition-product of the rock-constituents feldspar, augite, hornblende, biotite, and then deposited either in the primary position, i.e., as pseudomorphs after these minerals, or in some secondary position lining the walls of cavities; especially in the acidic younger eruptive rocks, the rhyolites and andesites, but also in the basic basalts. | The ground-mass of many decomposed eruptive rocks is almost completely metamorphosed into opal (semi-opal). |
| *Inclosures*, i.e., separations, are *gas-pores*, *crystallites*, and *microliths* very commonly; also *crystals* and *sphæroliths*. (Compare Figs. 41 and 42.) | Into viridite in the basic rocks, basalt; into opal in the acidic, rhyolite. Basic glasses are often decomposed into a yellowish, double-refracting, fibrous substance (pelagonite). | The *natural glasses* are only *one method of solidification of the eruptive rocks.* Hyalite occurs more or less commonly in often apparently purely crystalline eruptive rocks, and only in them. | Rock glasses (vitrophyre) are known in the following eruptive rocks: a. Acidic = vitreous rhyolith, trachyte, dacite, andesite, porphyries; rarely porphyrites and phonoliths. b. Basic = vitreous diabase, melaphyr, augite-andesite, and basalts (trachylyte, hyalomelane, sidero-melane, palagonite, hydrotachylyte). Frequently pure hyalite can be distinguished from opal only with difficulty; the only surety lies in the *micro-chemical analysis* (preferably *corrosion* with *hydrofluosilicic acid*). The glasses are mentioned here only because of their differences from opal. |

## DETERMINATION OF ROCK-FORMING MINERALS.

### b. Minerals Crystallizing

| Name. | Chemical composition and reactions. | Specific gravity. | Cleavage. | Ordinary combinations and form of the cross-section. | Twins. | Color and power of refracting light. |
|---|---|---|---|---|---|---|
| 1. Hauyn Group. *a.* Sodalite. | $3(Na_2Al_2Si_2O_8) + 2\,NaCl$. *Cl-reaction*; easily soluble in HCl; gelatinous $SiO_2$; *NaCl-cubes* on evaporation. | 2.13–2.29. | ∞O. | *Grains and* ∞O (rarely O.∞O∞); cross-sections rectangular and hexagonal. | Penetration twins after a trigonal secondary axis. | *Colorless;* colored by $Fe_2O_3$ red, green, and blue— mostly blue. |
| β. Hauyn | $2Na_2CaAl_2Si_2O_8 + Na_2(CaH)SO_4$. Reaction for Ca and $H_2SO_4$. | 2.4–2.5. | | Crystals ∞O and O, like sodalite. | Twins after O and like sodalite. | *Colorless, blue* or *black.* |
| and | | | | | | |
| γ. Nosean. | $3Na_2Al_2Si_2O_8 + Na_2SO_4$ Reaction for $H_2SO_4$. Both soluble in HCl with separation of *gelatinous* $SiO_2$. | 2.279–2.399 | ∞O. | Commonly distorted or corroded crystals. | | *Colorless, brown* or *black.* |

## in the Regular System.

| Structure. | Association. | Inclosures. | Decomposition. | Occurrence. | Remarks. |
|---|---|---|---|---|---|
| Interpenetrated with feldspar and hornblende; the centre often colorless, and outer layers blue or colored red by ferric oxide. | With microcline, augite, and mica in *syenites*. With sanidine and augite in trachytes. | Fluid inclosures and gas-pores. Vitreous inclosures and augite needles. | Becomes opaque by decomposition into zeolites. | As primary constituent in syenites (elæolith-syenite), and rarely in augitic trachytes. Secondary in cavities of the latter. | The three minerals can be accurately distinguished only by the *micro-chemical qualitative analysis*. |
| The outer coats colored, with opaque or dark core; often colored red by iron oxide at the cleavage-fissures. Regularly disposed inclosures, and systems of dark streaks at right angles to each other. (See Fig. 53.) | Generally with *leucite*, *nepheline*, and *augite*. | Numberless gas pores and vitreous inclosures arranged in streamers. Black minute grains and needles, like dust, often at regular spaces. Pyrite tablets. | Into a felt-like aggregate of colorless, double-refracting needles and filaments of zeolites and calcite. A decoloration of the hauyn thus occurs; a yellowish, secondary coloration of the decomposition-product by ferric hydroxide. | Primary constituent. In the *younger* eruptive rocks and the sanidine and plagioclase rocks, as trachyte (rarely), phonolite, leucitophyr, tephrites, nepheline and leucite basalts. Very common in the trachytic volcanic lavas. | Hauyn is distinguished from sodalite by presence of the characteristic gypsum needles on evaporating a drop of the hydrochloric acid solution (on account of the calcium present in hauyn); sodalite is characterized by the chlorine. It is difficult also to distinguish hauyn from nosean chemically. Mineralogically they are one. |

| Name. | Chemical composition and reactions. | Specific gravity. | Cleavage. | Ordinary combinations and form of the cross-section. | Twins. | Color and power of refracting light. |
|---|---|---|---|---|---|---|
| 2. Garnet Group. α. Almandine. | $Fe_3Al_2Si_3O_{12}$. | 3.78 (3.1–4.2). | Imperfect $\infty O$. | $\infty O.2O2$ and *grains*. Cross-sections quadratic, hexagonal, or octagonal. | | Red, in very thin sections nearly colorless. $n\rho = 1.772$. |
| β. Pyrope. | (CaO, MgO, FeO, MnO) $Al_2O_3 3SiO_2$. Contains Cr. | 3.7–3.8. | Imperfect $\infty O$. | *Grains.* | | *Blood-red.* |
| γ. Melanite. | $Ca_3Fe_2Si_3O_{12}$. | 3.6–4.3. | Imperfect $\infty O$. | *Crystals* $\infty O$. | | *Black; dark brown* in sections. Transparent only with difficulty. |
| | All garnets are insoluble in acids. | | | | | |

| Structure. | Association. | Inclosures. | Decomposition. | Occurrence. | Remarks. |
|---|---|---|---|---|---|
| *Commonly* disseminated through micro-pegmatic quartz and feldspar. | Generally with *quartz, orthoclase, biotite,* and hornblende. | Cavities of the form of garnet (= negative crystals). Fluid inclosures, quartz-granules. Rutile; often zonally disposed. (See Fig. 54.) | Commonly metamorphosed into *chlorite tablets* on the upper surfaces and cleavage-fissures. More rarely, as in pyrope, metamorphosed about the edges into a *fibrous* hornblende, or augite-zone. | Primary constituent; in many crystalline schists, common in granite, rare in trachytic rocks. | |
| | With olivine and augite. | Very poor. | Augitic fibrous tufts shooting out in marginal zones, perpendicular to the surface of the grains are very common and characteristic. (See Fig. 55.) | Primary constituent. In serpentines. | The garnets can be easily distinguished from the hauyn by the color and insolubility in acids. |
| Very commonly beautiful *zonal structure,* then generally showing double refraction. (See Fig. 54.) | With *augite, sanidine, nepheline, hauyn,* and *leucite.* | Very poor. Augite and apatite needles; vitreous inclosures. | | Primary constituent. In phonoliths, leucitophyr, and volcanic lavas. | Compare with chromite. |

## DETERMINATION OF ROCK-FORMING MINERALS.

| Name. | Chemical composition and reactions. | Specific gravity. | Cleavage. | Ordinary combinations and form of the cross-section. | Twins. | Color and power of refracting light. |
|---|---|---|---|---|---|---|
| 3. Spinel Group. <br> α. Chromite. | $FeO, Cr_2O_3$. | 4.4–4.6. | Imperfect O. | *Grains* and octahedra. | | Becomes *translucent only with difficulty*; *dark brown*, reddish brown, metallic lustre. |
| β. Picotite. | $MgO \brace FeO$ $Al_2O_3 \brace Fe_2O_3$ | 4.08. | | Octahedra. Very minute grains. | Twins according to O. | ditto. |
| γ. Pleonaste. | $FeO \brace MgO$ $Al_2O_3 \brace Fe_2O_3$ | Above 3.65. (3.8–4.1). | | ditto. | | *Dark green*. |
| δ. Hercynite. | $FeO, Al_2O_3$. <br><br> Insoluble in acids; unattacked by HFl. | 3.91–3.95. | | Octahedra. | | ditto. |
| 4. Analcime. | $Na_2Al_2Si_4O_{12}$ $+ 2H_2O$. Soluble in HCl with separation of gelatinous $SiO_2$. | 2.1–2.28. | (Imperfect); according to Tschermak, clearly $\infty O \infty$. | *Generally compact grains;* in cavities 2O2. | | *Colorless, white.* $n\rho = 1.4874$. |

| Structure. | Association. | Inclosures. | Decomposition. | Occurrence. | Remarks. |
|---|---|---|---|---|---|
| Many individual grains occurring in basalts show a broad, opaque border. | With *olivine* and *augite*. | | | Primary accessory constituent. In *olivine* rocks, serpentines, and in *basalts*. Picotite commonly *inclosed in olivine*. | Great similarity with *melanite*; if in *grains*, can be distinguished only by chemical tests. Melanite is attacked by concentrated HFl, and is free from chromium. Melanite is almost always crystallized, and hence can be easily distinguished from chromite. Chromite and picotite can be distinguished *only by chemical means*. The spinels are distinguished from magnetite by their transparency (in very thin sections) and insolubility in acids. Pleonaste and hercynite can be distinguished *only by chemical analysis*. |
| | Rarely with olivine and augite. | | | The same, but rare. More common in *granulites* and in *metamorphic* (contact) *rocks*. | |
| | Common with *quartz, orthoclase,* and *mica*. | | | | |
| Often showing double-refraction and remarkable zonal structure; generally *opaque;* interpenetrated with plagioclase. | With plagioclase, augite, or hornblende. | Poor in inclosures. Fluid inclosures. Apatite needles. | | Either primary (?) or decomposition product of nepheline (?) Rare in the *younger basic eruptive* rocks, the teschenites. As decomposition-products in cavities (secondary) in phonoliths, trachytes, andesites, basalts. | Can be determined accurately *only by chemical tests*. |

| Name. | Chemical composition and reactions. | Specific gravity. | Cleavage. | Ordinary combinations and form of the cross-section. | Twins. | Color and power of refracting light. |
|---|---|---|---|---|---|---|
| 5 Fluorite. | $CaFl_2$. Decomposed by concentrated $H_2SO_4$ with evolution of HFl. | 3.1–3.2. | Perfect after O. | In rocks only in form of minute angular granules. | | Blue, transparent. $n = 1.435$. |
| 6. Perowskite. | $CaTiO_3$, not attacked by HCl; decomposed by concen. $H_2SO_4$. | 4.0–4.1. | ∞O∞. | In *irregular, arborescent,* and *jagged forms,* often in sharp octahedra. (See Fig. 56.) | Rare; penetration-twins. | *Grayish-violet; grayish-reddish brown.* Relief *well marked.* |

MINERALS APPARENTLY CRYSTALLIZING

| Leucite. | | | | Apparently 2O2. Compare with minerals of the *tetragonal* system. | | |
|---|---|---|---|---|---|---|

| Structure. | Association. | Inclosures. | Decomposition. | Occurrence. | Remarks. |
|---|---|---|---|---|---|
| Developed in feldspar and irregularly distributed through the ground-mass. | With quartz, orthoclase, biotite. | Fluid inclosures. | | Very rare; secondary in quartzose porphyries. | |
| The rough surface of the slide very characteristic. Grouped as inclosure in melilite and also in olivine, often showing double refraction. *Polarisation-colors very faint.* | With *nepheline, melilite, augite,* and *olivine.* | Very poor. | | In nepheline, leucite, and melilite basalts. | Can be distinguished from spinel by its color and optical anomalies; and from garnet by the crystalline form. |

IN THE REGULAR SYSTEM.

| | | | | | |
|---|---|---|---|---|---|
| *Twinning striations, double-refracting.* | | | | | |

## II. DOUBLE-REFRACTING
### a. Optically-Uniaxial
#### 1. MINERALS CRYSTALLIZING IN
##### A. DOUBLE-REFRACTION

| NAME. | Chemical composition and reactions. | Specific gravity. | Cleavage. | Ordinary combinations and form of the cross-section. | Twins. | Character and strength of double-refraction. | Polarization-color. |
|---|---|---|---|---|---|---|---|
| 1. Leucite. | $K_2Al_2Si_4O_{12}$. *Soluble in HCl.* Separation of pulverulent $SiO_2$. K-reaction with hydro-fluosilicic acid. | 2.45–2.5. | Imperfectly prismatic, $\infty P\infty$ and $oP$. | Grains, but (mostly) crystals $P$, $4P2$. Apparently a *regular* form, 202. Crystal cross-section generally octagonal, often nearly circular, more rarely rectangular or hexagonal. | After $2P\infty$; polysynthetic twinning-striations after these faces, crossing at right or oblique angles. (See Fig. 57.) | The *small* individuals, without twinning-striations, *apparently isotrope.* No clear axial picture evident in c. p. l. Double-refraction positive; very weak. | Not very brilliant bluish-gray. |
| 2. Rutile. (Nigrine, Sagenite.) | $TiO_2$. Ti-reaction with microcosmic bead. | 4.2–4.3 (4.277). | $\infty P$ and $\infty P\infty$. | $\infty P$, $\infty P\infty$. $P$. Grains; often, however, in minute, very long and narrow needles and crystals. The prisms show a striation parallel to the $c$-axis. | Very common and characteristic after $P\infty$. Bent at an angle of 114° 25'. Also, a web of needles which cut each other at an angle of about 60°. *Sagenite.* Heart-shaped *twins* according to $3P\infty$ are very common. (Comp. Figs. 20 and 59.) | The crystals are generally too minute to examine with the condenser. Double-refraction strongly positive. | None especially bright. |

# MINERALS.
## Minerals.
### THE TETRAGONAL SYSTEM.
### POSITIVE.

| Color and power of refracting light. | Pleochroism. | Structure. | Association. | Inclosures. | Decomposition. | Occurrence. | Remarks. |
|---|---|---|---|---|---|---|---|
| Colorless, clear as water. $\omega = 1.508$. $\epsilon = 1.509$. | | Aggregates of spherical crystals into a large crystal. Zonal and radial disposition of the inclosures. (See Fig. 58.) Large corroded crystals I. O. and minute often sharply formed II. O., the latter also developed in augite. | With augite, olivine, nepheline, plagioclase, and sanidine. | Inclosures of minute vitreous particles, gas-pores, needles of augite, etc., arranged in zones and rays, or gathered together at the centre, are characteristic. Also rich in inclosures of other minerals, as hauyn, augite, apatite, melanite. | Into an aggregate of colorless or yellowish, fine radial filaments or grains of zeolites. Rarely pseudomorphs of analcime after leucite. | Primary essential constituent. With sanidine, etc., in the leucitophyrs, leucite-tephrites, and basalts; also with nepheline and plagioclase. Especially only in the *younger basic eruptive rocks*. | Easily distinguished from other minerals by crystalline form, twinning-striations, and inclosures, i. e., their regular arrangement. If the leucite occurs in very minute grains through the ground-mass, it is often difficult to distinguish from the colorless vitreous base lying between; in such cases recognized only by micro-chemical reactions. |
| *Honey-yellow* to *reddish brown*. In grains often opaque or only translucent (nigrine), then with metallic lustre; occurring in this form but rarely. | Not especially noticeable. | Rutile, as sagenite, often occurs regularly developed in biotite; also interpenetrated with ilmenite. Very common as inclosure in the minerals accompanying it, especially in garnet and omphacite. | With quartz, *potassium feldspar, garnet, hornblende, omphacite.* | Very poor | | As primary accessory constituent very common in nearly all crystalline schists, especially those containing hornblende and augite, as the hornblendites and eclogites. As *decomposition-product of ilmenite* secondary. Very common in aluminious schists, as "aluminous-schist needles." | Easily distinguished from zircon by polarization-colors, color, and common twinned formation. |

| Name. | Chemical composition and reactions. | Specific gravity. | Cleavage. | Ordinary combinations and form of the cross-section. | Twins. | Character and strength of double refraction. | Polarisation-colors. |
|---|---|---|---|---|---|---|---|
| 3. Zircon. | $ZrO_2 + SiO_2$. Acids have no action, except $H_2SO_4$, which decomposes it. | 4.4–4.7. | Imperfect, $P$ and $\infty P$. | $P. \infty P\infty$, also $3P3$; rich in combinations; nearly always in *minute* but sharply-defined crystals. (See Fig. 60.) | Rarely after $P\infty$. | Double-refraction; very strongly positive. | *Exceedingly brilliant*, emerald-green, hyacinth-red, and iridescent. |

B. DOUBLE-REFRACTION

| | | | | | | | |
|---|---|---|---|---|---|---|---|
| 4. Anatase. | Like rutile. | 3.83–3.93. | $oP$ and $P$. | Sharp $P$. | | Like rutile. | Like rutile. |
| 5. Meionite Group. <br> α. Meionite. | $Ca_6(Al_2)Si_6O_{26}$ | 2.734–2.737 | | | | | |
| β. Scapolite. | $R_3Al._2Si_6O_{24}$ R = predominating Ca, some Mg, Na; soluble in HCl, with separation of pulverulent $SiO_2$. | 2.63–2.79. | Perfect $\infty P\infty$. (See Fig. 61.) | Crystals after $\infty P, \infty P\infty, P$ and larger *grains*, or *elongated prismatic* individuals. | | Double-refraction; *rather strongly negative*. | Brilliant like quartz. |

| Color and power of refracting light. | Pleochroism. | Structure. | Association. | Inclosures. | Decomposition. | Occurrence. | Remarks. |
|---|---|---|---|---|---|---|---|
| Colorless, wine-yellow; very strong refraction; therefore the contours have black borders (by the total reflection of the incident light). $\omega = 1.92$ $\epsilon = 1.97$. | Not noticeable. | Like rutile, one of the first-formed rock constituents; therefore common as inclosure in the others. | With quartz, orthoclase, plagioclase, biotite, hornblende, augite. | Fluid inclosures, acicular cavities, and elongated undeterminable needles. | | Primary accessory constituent in *garnet*, *syenite*, quartz, *porphyry*, *trachytes*, and many other eruptive rocks, but rare; more commonly accompanying rutile in chrystalline schists. | Well characterized by crystalline form, polarization-colors, and powerful refraction of light. |

NEGATIVE.

| Color and power of refracting light. | Pleochroism. | Structure. | Association. | Inclosures. | Decomposition. | Occurrence. | Remarks. |
|---|---|---|---|---|---|---|---|
| Dark lavender-blue. | Like rutile. | | With quartz. orthoclase, and biotite. | | | Very rare in granite, quartzose porphyries, and crystalline schists. | |
| $\omega = 1.594 - 1.597$ $\epsilon = 1.558 - 1.561$ Colorless. White. $\omega = 1.566$ $\epsilon = 1.545$. | | Scapolite appears often to replace plagioclase and to be a decomposition-product from it. | With sanidine, sodalite, augite. With quartz, plagioclase, calcite, augite, garnet, rutile, and titanite. | Poor; fluid inclosures; rutile in scapolite. | Opaque, fibrous; decomposed into calcite. | Primary accessory constituent; *very rare in trachytic rocks.* *Rare in crystalline schists*, with plagioclase secondary accessory constituent. | Scapolite can be easily distinguished from orthoclase and calcite by the optical properties and cleavage; meionite is recognizable by the crystalline form. |

| Name. | Chemical composition and reactions. | Specific gravity. | Cleavage. | Ordinary combinations and form of the cross-section. | Twins. | Character and strength of double-refraction. | Polarization-colors. |
|---|---|---|---|---|---|---|---|
| γ. Couseranite and Dipyr. | Similar to scapolite; rich in the alkalies, $H_2O$. Not attacked by acids (HCl), or at least only with difficulty. | 2.69–2.76 (2.613). 2.62–2.68. | According to $\infty P\infty$. According to $oP$. | *Long prisms* $\infty P . \infty P \infty$; with terminations either rounded or fibrous. | | As in scapolite. Rather energetic. | Rather brilliant. |
| δ. Melilite. (Humboldtite.) | $(Ca,Mg,Na_2)_{12}, (Al_2Fe_2)_2, Si_9O_{36}$. Easily soluble in HCl with separation of gelatinous $SiO_2$. | 2.90–2.95. | Parallel to $oP$ and $\infty P$. | Nearly always in crystals; *thin tablets* predominating, $oP . \infty P . \infty P\infty$. Irregular grains. Cross-sections for the most part rectangular, more rarely circular. | Rarely penetration twins, with chief axes at right angles to each other. | Double-refraction feebly negative. | Not very brilliant; if yellow and fibrous, shows aggregate polarization-colors; if colorless, bluish-gray polarization-colors. |

# TABLES FOR DETERMINING MINERALS.

| Color and power of refracting light. | Pleochroism. | Structure. | Association. | Inclosures. | Decomposition. | Occurrence. | Remarks. |
|---|---|---|---|---|---|---|---|
| Bluish, colorless in thin section, *clear as water*, black from inclosures. $\omega = 1.558$. $\epsilon = 1.543$. | | Crystals developed in *limestone, often rich in inclosures*. | With calcite, actinolite, and mica. | Very rich; particles of carbon, quartz-grains, and leaflets of muscovite distributed at random. | Fibrous decomposition, with formation of calcite on the crevices. | As *contact-mineral* in metamorphosed limestone. Very rare. | Can be distinguished from chiastolite by the structure; from andalusite by the optical properties. |
| Generally lemon-yellow, *honey-yellow*, colorless to yellowish white. | Longitudinal sections; rectangles show a very feeble dichroism. | Rectangular longitudinal sections show a striation and fibrous tendency parallel to the short sides, i.e., the chief axis $c$; there are also very fine spindle-shaped cavities which appear as minute circles within the rounded sections cut at right angles to the chief axis — the so-called "*Pflock-structure.*" (See Fig. 62.) Developed with leucite, i.e., interpenetrated with its crystal. | With nepheline, leucite, augite, and olivine. | Poor. | The formation of fibres is a result of the decomposition into zeolitic substances. (Compare with "structure.") | As *primary* constituent often *replacing nepheline in the nepholine and leucite basalts* and lavas. | Easily recognizable by the crystalline form, color, and fibrous tendency. If colorless, easily confounded with nepheline, although the hexagonal isotropic sections are wanting in melilite. Can be distinguished from serpentine often only by the paler color and the interlacing of olivine particles; from biotite leaflets by the paler color and the want of dichroitic longitudinal sections. |

2. *MINERALS CRYSTALLIZING IN*

A. DOUBLE-REFRACTION

| Name. | Chemical composition and reaction. | Specific gravity. | Cleavage. | Ordinary combinations and form of the cross-section. | Twins. | Character and strength of double-refraction. | Polarization-colors. |
|---|---|---|---|---|---|---|---|
| 1 Quartz. | $SiO_2$. Unattacked by HCl and $H_2SO_4$; dissolved by HFl. | 2.65 average (2.651). | Imperfect according to $R$. The sections uneven owing to the conchoidal fracture. | Grains or crystals $R.-R$ or $\infty R.R.-R$. Generally in large individuals; regular hexagons, rhombs, and hexagons with two parallel longer sides. *Never as microlites.* | With parallel axial-systems. As a rock-constituent never or rarely twinned. | Double-refraction positive. Strong. | Brilliant yet weak in very thin sections; bluish-gray, like feldspar. |

## TABLES FOR DETERMINING MINERALS.

### THE HEXAGONAL SYSTEM.

#### POSITIVE.

| Color and power of refracting light. | Pleochroism. | Structure. | Association. | Inclosures. | Decomposition. | Occurrence. | Remarks. |
|---|---|---|---|---|---|---|---|
| Colorless; clear as water; vitreous lustre. $\omega = 1.548$. $\epsilon = 1.558$. | | Often colored by $Fe_2O_3$ entering fissures; *cloudy from numberless inclosures*, as in the granites and the clastic rocks. Grains and crystals. Quartz from the eruptive rocks give evidence of *corrosion*, being rounded and shattered; the groundmass is forced between as leaves of a book (see Fig. 43). In granites commonly developed with orthoclase, as graphic-granite = *micropegmatite*. (Comp. Fig. 63.) In the porphyritic eruptive rocks also with radial structure as spherulites. | With orthoclase (and sanidine), more rarely plagioclase, biotite, and augite. *Never as primary component in augite-olivine rocks*; as also in nepheline or leucite rocks. | Poor in mineral inclosures. Apatite prisms. In clastic schists and granites very rich in fluid inclosures and long brown or black, often bent, needles. In the porphyries, trachytes, dacites, and other eruptive rocks rich in primary *glassy inclosures* and gas-pores. | None. Changes resulting from the action of melted magma are not uncommon among the quartz of the eruptive rocks, or from the rocks contained in it as inclosures. Compare corrosion-phenomena and secondary glassy inclosures. (See Fig. 43.) | I. As primary component: (a) In eruptive rocks as component I. O. As macroscopic constituent in grains and crystals with fluid inclosures in granites, quartz-porphyries, quartz-trachytes, and their glasses; in dacite with vitreous inclosures as an essential constituent, and accessory in many other eruptive rocks; as component of the II. O. in the ground-mass of those rocks in minute irregular grains, never as crystals. (b) In nearly all crystalline schists in irregular grains with fluid inclosures, as with the feldspars; especially in gneiss, mica-schist; in minute grains in clay schists. II. As secondary product through decomposition of silicates, especially of augite, hornblende, and biotite; in diabases, as granular aggregates; on fissures in lines and filaments in many rocks. III. In clastic rocks as flattened grains; fluid inclosures, joined together, reaching to the very edges. IV. As simple rock, building quartzite and quartz schists. | In grains often similar to sanidine, but can be easily distinguished optically from it. Distinguished from nepheline and apatite by insolubility in HCl; from corundum by the character of double-refraction; from calcite by cleavage and twinning. |
| | | | With muscovite and biotite. | Intertwined fluid inclosures. | | | |

| Name. | Chemical composition and reactions. | Specific gravity. | Cleavage. | Ordinary combinations and form of cross-section. | Twins. | Character and strength of double-refraction. | Polarization-colors. |
|---|---|---|---|---|---|---|---|
| 2. Tridymite. | Like quartz. | 2.282–2.326. | Imperfectly ‖ *oP*. | In *very minute thin tablets*, pred. *oP* and ∞*P*. | Very common. Twinning-plane a face of ½*P* and ⅔*P*. <br><br> (According to v. Lasaulx and Schuster, twins according to a plane of ∞*P*.) | Positive. Very feeble. <br><br>—<br><br> According to v. Lasaulx and Schuster, *tridymite crystallizes in the triclinic system.* <br><br> A.P. differing but little from the normals to *oP*. 1.M. = c nearly ⊥ *oP*. Axial angle 65–70°. | Not very brilliant. Gray. |

*A more exact crystallographical and optical determination of tridymite is generally impossible*, owing to the minuteness of the crystals occurring in the rocks. Microscopical tridymite behaves like an hexagonal mineral in p.p.l.

| Color and power of refracting light. | Pleochroism. | Structure. | Association. | Inclosures. | Decomposition. | Occurrence. | Remarks. |
|---|---|---|---|---|---|---|---|
| *Colorless*, clear as water. $n$, i.e. $\beta = 1.4285$. | | Generally in *aggregates of minute thin tablets;* either *hexagonal or irregular tablets, lapping over each other like shingles.* Often in the neighborhood of feldspars, or in large groups in the groundmass. (See Fig. 64.) | With quartz, sanidine, plagioclase, augite, biotite, and hornblende. *Secondary* with opal and chalcedony. | Fluid inclosures. | | Primary as accessory constituent, and secondary as decomposition-product in rhyolites, trachytes, hornblende- and augite-andesites. Exceedingly common in the younger acidic rocks; rare in the basic older rocks. Secondary in cavities of these rocks, and then generally in larger tablets. | The tendency to form aggregates is very characteristic for microscopic tridymite; the optical properties and the twinnings for the larger crystals and those suitable for optical investigations. |

## B. DOUBLE-REFRACTION

| Name. | Chemical composition and reactions. | Specific gravity. | Cleavage. | Ordinary combinations and form of cross-section. | Twins. | Character and strength of double-refraction. | Polarization-colors. |
|---|---|---|---|---|---|---|---|
| 1. Calcite. | $CaCO_3$. Easily soluble in HCl, with rapid evolution of $CO_2$. Easily soluble in acetic acid. | 2.6–2.8 (2.72). | Perfect $R$. (See Fig. 65.) | Only in regular *grains* and crystalline aggregates. | Polysynthetic twinning-striation after $-\tfrac{1}{2}R$. (See Figs. 21 and 65.) | Double-refraction very strongly negative. | Generally weak; gray; yet often brilliantly iridescent like talc, especially in those cases where the calcite occurs in minute granules. |
| 2. Dolomite. | $(Ca)(Mg)CO_3$. More difficultly soluble in acids than calcite. | 2.85–2.95. | ditto. | Grains and $R$. | See "Remarks." | | ditto. |
| 3. Magnesite. | $MgCO_3$. More difficultly soluble in HCl. | 2.9–3.1. | ditto. | ditto. | | | ditto. |
| 4. Siderite. | $FeCO_3$. Soluble in HCl with evolution of gas. | 3.7–3.9. | ditto. | ditto. | | | ditto. |

# TABLES FOR DETERMINING MINERALS.

**NEGATIVE.**

| Color and power of refracting light. | Pleochroism. | Structure. | Association. | Inclosures. | Decomposition. | Occurrence. | Remarks. |
|---|---|---|---|---|---|---|---|
| Colorless, white, grayish. $\omega = 1.6543$ $\epsilon = 1.4833$ | Feeble absorption. | Generally in granular aggregates, in cavities; in threads and fibres. In irregular grains, single individuals, between the other constituents. | In nearly all rocks bearing hornblende, augite, biotite, and plagioclase. | Fluid inclosures; very poor in mineral inclosures. | None. | As *primary* constituent, building by itself a *simple* rock, limestone; not yet assuredly proved as such in eruptive rocks. Here as *decomposition product*, especially of the bisilicates and of mica, where it occurs in lenticular forms between the laminæ. Primary and secondary in crystalline schists. | Well characterized by the rhombohedral cleavage and twinning-striation. If occurring in minute granules, often difficult to accurately determine; the solubility and polarization colors remain as means of recognition. |
| ditto. | | ditto. | | | | | The polysynthetic twinning-striations after $-\tfrac{1}{2}R$ are wanting on dolomite. |
| ditto. | | ditto. | With serpentine. | | | With *olivine* and *serpentine* as decomposition-product. | Magnesite and siderite can be distinguished from calcite only by chemical means. |
| Yellowish to brown. | | ditto. | See Calcite. | | | As *decomposition-product* in small balls of *concentrically-arranged layers* and with radial fibres; in andesites, etc. | |

| Name. | Chemical composition and reactions. | Specific gravity. | Cleavage. | Ordinary combinations and form of the cross-section. | Twins. | Character and strength of double-refraction. | Polarization-color. |
|---|---|---|---|---|---|---|---|
| 5. Nepheline Group. α. Elæolite. | | 2.65 (2.591). | *Imperfect;* coarse fissures. | Only in larger *grains.* | | | Generally bluish gray, not very brilliant. |
| β. Nepheline. | $(Na, K)_2 Al_2Si_2 O_8$. Easily soluble in HCl with separation of gelatinous $SiO_2$; on evaporation cubes of NaCl. | (2.58–2.65) 2.56. | *Imperfect* $oP$ and $\infty P$. | Hexagons and rectangles; in *minute* crystals $\infty P$, $oP$, *in short prisms,* and in minute irregular granules. (See Fig. 66.) | | Double-refraction negative, not energetic. | Similar to the feldspar in very thin sections. |

| Color and power of refracting light. | Pleochroism. | Structure. | Association. | Inclosures. | Decomposition. | Occurrence. | Remarks. |
|---|---|---|---|---|---|---|---|
| Gray, reddish brown, fatty lustre; colorless in thin section. | | Irregular grains interpenetrated with other constituents. | With sodalite, microline, hornblende, titanite. | Poor; often colored green by hornblende. | Fibrous, zeolitic metamorphosis. | As primary essential constituent in the older eruptive rocks; in the elæolite-syenites. | Well recognizable macroscopically. The solubility and Na-reaction are characteristic. |
| Colorless, clear as water. $\omega = 1.539$ — $1.542$ $\epsilon = 1.534$ — $1.537$ | | In crystals or in aggregates of minute irregular granules. | With leucite, augite, olivine, or with sanidine and augite, or with hornblende and titanite. | Inclosures of augite very commonly arranged parallel to the faces. (See Fig. 66.) | Generally fresh, in phonolites more often opaque and metamorphosed into zeolites; then polarizing like an aggregate. | As primary essential constituent in the younger eruptive rocks: nephelinites, nepheline- and leucite-basalts, phonolites and tephrites. | Distinguished from: *apatite* by the imperfect cleavage, microchemical reactions, and crystalline forms, as apatite commonly shows $P$, besides $\infty P$, $oP$, and occurs in long prisms; *quartz* never occurs in such minute crystals as nepheline; *feldspar-threads* are long and twinned; *melilite* has no hexagonal transverse sections; *zeolites* generally evidence their secondary character. The short rectangular longitudinal sections are wanting in *tridymite*. If nepheline occurs in aggregates of minute granules, then it is similar to a colorless vitreous mass or quartz and orthoclase aggregates, and can be proven only by microchemical tests. |

# 136  DETERMINATION OF ROCK-FORMING MINERALS.

| Name. | Chemical composition and reactions. | Specific gravity. | Cleavage. | Ordinary combinations and form of the cross-section. | Twins. | Character and strength of double-refraction. | Polarization-colors. |
|---|---|---|---|---|---|---|---|
| γ. Cancrinite. | Composition like a nepheline, poor in potassium, together with CaO, CO$_2$, and H$_2$O. Soluble in HCl with effervescence, with separation of gelatinous SiO$_2$. | 2.448–2.454. | *Imperfect* ∞$P$. | Larger irregular *grains*. | | Double-refraction negative. | Rather brilliant; aggregate polarization. |
| δ. Liebenerite. | Potassium-aluminium silicate, H$_2$O, traces of Fe, Mg. *Similar to pinite*, incompletely decomposed by HCl. | 2.799–2.814. | Very imperfect ∞$P$. | Only larger crystals ∞$P$. $oP$. | | Double-refraction negative (?) Cannot be confirmed, as the crystals are always completely decomposed. | Remarkable aggregate *polarization*, very *brilliant*. |
| 6. Apatite. | Ca$_5$P$_3$O$_{12}$Cl. Ca$_5$P$_3$O$_{12}$Fl. Soluble in acids. *Reaction for phosphoric acid.* | 3.16–3.22. | *Crystals*, more rarely grains. Imperfect cleavage parallel $oP$ and ∞$P$. Remarkable "*separation*" (*absonderung*) ‖ $oP$, the acicular crystals thereby separating into several members. | ∞$P$. $P$ and more rarely $oP$. Generally *long prisms*. (See Fig. 67.) | | Double-refraction negative, feeble. | Generally not very brilliant, as with nepheline. |

# TABLES FOR DETERMINING MINERALS.

| Color and power of refracting light. | Pleochroism. | Structure. | Association. | Inclosures. | Decomposition. | Occurrence. | Remarks. |
|---|---|---|---|---|---|---|---|
| *Lemon-yellow*, nearly colorless, in sections. | | *Fibrous*, inter-penetrated with nepheline and orthoclase. | Like elæolite. | Poor. Leaflets of ferric oxide, etc., like elæolite. | Fibrous decomposition with formation of calcite. (Cancrinite appears to be only a *decomposed nepheline*.) | Like elæolite; rare. | Can be distinguished from elæolite only macroscopically and by the content of $CaCO_3$. |
| Oil-green; in sections colorless; white. | | *Only as* "springling" *in macroscopic crystals*. | With flesh-red orthoclase and mica. | | It is probably a *completely decomposed nepheline*(?) or *cordierite* (?); consists principally of minute *muscovite leaflets*, which i.p.l. appear very clearly. | Rare. In orthoclase-porphyry. | Easily recognizable by the crystalline form and decomposition. |
| Colorless, white; colored reddish, brown, black, from numberless inclosures; not water-clear like nepheline; more prominent among the rock-constituents. $n = 1.657$. | If colored, plainly dichroitic. | In irregular grains, or in elongated often very narrow columns, broken as a consequence of the *basic separation*. *Inclosures!* (See Fig. 67.) Only accessory constituent. As inclosure especially common in the bisilicates hornblende and biotite. | Proven in nearly all rocks. | Vitreous inclosures, gas-pores. Very characteristic are *inclosures* of black or brown needles, or minute dust-like granules, which permeate the whole crystal; in this respect, in the transverse sections especially, showing a great similarity to many hauyns also rich in inclosures. Central inclosures of glass, etc., often with the form of apatite. | Always fresh. | As accessory constituent in *nearly all* eruptive rocks and crystalline schists. One of the minerals first eliminated in formation of the rocks. | Distinguished from: *nepheline* especially by the microchemical reactions (comp. nepheline), inclosures very characteristic; *hauyn* in the longitudinal sections and basic separations; *olivine* by the optical properties and the separation. |

| Name. | Chemical composition and reactions. | Specific gravity. | Cleavage. | Ordinary combinations and form of the cross-section. | Twins. | Character and strength of double-refraction. | Polarization-colors. |
|---|---|---|---|---|---|---|---|
| 7. Corundum. | $Al_2O_3$. Insoluble in acids. | 3.9–4. | $R$ and $oR$. | $\infty P_2 . oR$. $R$ and grains. Hexagons and rectangles whose angles are truncated by $R$. | In rocks seldom (?) | Double-refraction strongly negative. | Very brilliant. |
| 8. Tourmaline. (Schörl.) | Very complicated. $\overset{I}{R_6}Al_2B_2Si_4O_{20}$ $+\overset{II}{R_3}(Al_2)_3 . B_2Si_4O_{20}$ $\overset{I}{R} = Na$ predominating and $\overset{II}{R} = Mg, Fe$. Contains boric acid. Not attacked by acids. | 3.059. | Imperfect $R$ and $\infty R_2$. Separation $\parallel oR$. Very perfect. | Almost *only* in *crystals*. $R . \infty P_2 . \frac{\infty R}{2}$, Transverse sections *three-, six-,* and *nine-sided* when observed parallel to the chief axis; often showing good *hemimorphism*, $oR$ below, $R$ above. (Comp. Figs. 68 and 69.) | | Double-refraction negative, energetic. | Rather brilliant; between brown and red. |
| 9. Hæmatite. (Eisenglanz.) | $Fe_2O_3$. Easily soluble in HCl. | 5.19–5.28. | $R . oR$. Not characteristic in microscopic individuals. | Mostly tabular *thin* leaflets, $oR . \infty P_2$, and irregular leaflets. | With parallel axial systems. Penetration twins with re-entrant angles. | Indeterminable, as occurring always in exceedingly thin leaflets in crevices in minerals. | Not very brilliant. |

| Color and power of refracting light. | Pleochroism. | Structure. | Association. | Inclosures. | Decomposition. | Occurrence. | Remarks. |
|---|---|---|---|---|---|---|---|
| Colorless, *azure-blue*, spotted, also *brown* from inclosures; *powerfully refracting light*, appearing well in sections. $\omega = 1.768$ $\epsilon = 1.760$. | If colored, *very strong*. $\omega$ = azure-blue. $\epsilon$ = sea-green. | *Rough section-surface.* In rounded grains or short prisms. One of the minerals first separated. Zonal structure, blue core, and colorless layers. | With quartz, orthoclase, and biotite; pleonaste, andalusite. | Very poor; fluid and vitreous inclosures; zircon. Brown dust-like inclosures (so-called ordinary corundum). | | Very rare. *Contact-mineral*, in metamorphic schists and in trachytes. | When in grains similar to apatite, yet recognizable by the brilliant polarization-colors, distinguished from: *quartz* by the rough surface and character of the double-refraction, also not so clear as quartz; *olivine* by the optical properties. |
| Mostly *grayish blue, brown*. $\omega = 1.64$ $\epsilon = 1.62$. | *Very marked dichroism*. $\omega$ = dark blue, brown to black. $\epsilon$ = light blue to light gray and brown. | In macroscopic and in *exceedingly minute crystals*, rarely in granules, as in certain metamorphic rocks. In granites in grains interpenetrating quartz. The larger individuals often in radial fibres at the terminations. | With quartz, orthoclase, and muscovite in granite. With quartz, orthoclase, mica, and other accessory minerals, as staurolite and garnet. | Very poor. Fluid inclosures. | | Common as primary constituent. In certain granites in grains. Accessory in many crystalline schists, especially clay-schists, also in clastic rocks. Finally, common and characteristic in schists metamorphosed by *contact* with eruptive rocks, especially granite. | Easily recognizable by crystalline form and pleochroism. Distinguished from: *hornblende* by the optical properties; *biotite* by the repeated formation of laminæ. |
| Iron-black with metallic lustre; in thin leaves *blood-red*, also yellowish red to brownish violet. | | Occurring only in leaves infiltrated on the fissure of minerals. Is always a *secondary mineral*. Only in some basalts also appearing as primary. | In *nearly all rocks* especially with decomposed biotite, hornblende, augite, magnetite, as decomposition-product. | | Into brownish-red and brown pulverulent ferric hydroxide. | Compare association. *Accessory secondary mineral.* | Easily recognizable by the form of occurrence and blood-red color. |

# 140  DETERMINATION OF ROCK-FORMING MINERALS.

C. MINERALS APPARENTLY

1. **Biotite**; in brown, apparently isotrope (optically-uniaxial),
2. **Chlorite**; in green, apparently isotrope (optically-uniaxial),

## II. b. Optically-Biaxial

### 1. MINERALS CRYSTALLIZING IN

#### α. NO INTERFERENCE-FIGURE VISIBLE

| Name. | Chemical composition and reactions. | Specific gravity. | Cleavage. | Ordinary combinations and form of the cross-section. | Twins. | Optical orientation. | Character and strength of double-refraction. | Direction of extinction. |
|---|---|---|---|---|---|---|---|---|
| 1. Olivine. (Chrysolite.) | $n\,Mg_2SiO_4 + FeSiO_4$. Rather easily soluble in HCl, with *separation of gelatinous* $SiO_2$. | 3.2–3.4. | Perfect ‖ ∞$\check{P}$∞, imperfect ∞$\bar{P}$∞. Conchoidal fracture *not so evident in sections.* Generally twisted crevices. | *Tabular crystals,* ∞$P$, $\check{P}$∞, ∞$\bar{P}$∞. Hexagonal cross-sections ∞$P$=130°2′, $\bar{P}$∞=76°54′ or large rounded grains. (See Fig. 71.) | Very rare according to $\bar{P}$∞; also penetration-twins. | 1. M. ⊥ ∞$\check{P}$∞ $\mathfrak{a}=\mathfrak{c}$. $\mathfrak{b}=\mathfrak{a}$. $\mathfrak{c}'=\mathfrak{b}$. Feeble dispersion of the axes. ρ < ν, large axial angle. | Double-refraction very strongly *positive.* | |

## HEXAGONAL.

hexagonal leaflets; small axial angle. See *Monoclinic System*.
hexagonal or irregular leaflets; small axial angle. See *Monoclinic System*.

## Minerals.

### THE RHOMBIC SYSTEM.

(opt. $A.P. \parallel oP$) in Sections $\parallel oP$.

| Polarization-colors. | Color and power of refracting light. | Pleochroism. | Structure. | Association. | Inclosures. | Decomposition. | Occurrence. | Remarks. |
|---|---|---|---|---|---|---|---|---|
| Exceedingly brilliant, stronger than in augite. | *Colorless;* in sections rarely greenish; *rough section-surfaces*. Relief marked. $\beta = 1.678$. | | Possesses a rough section-surface; the manner of *decomposition* into yellowish-red, brown or greenish *serpentine*, beginning at the crevices, is characteristic; also the *inclosures of picotite* (see Fig. 70). Partly in sharp *crystals*, partly in *fragments* of them, or in irregular grains. Constituent I. O. in vitreous eruptive rocks; also in minute crystals, otherwise only as "springling." | Principally with augite, plagioclase, nepheline, leucite. Also with hornblende and biotite. Almost never with primary quartz or orthoclase. | Rather poor; besides the minute brown picotite octahedra, vitreous and rarely fluid inclosures, magnetite. Very rarely other mineral inclosures. | Most commonly into serpentine (compare aggregates), whereby the picotite inclosures remain. Also into a brown fibrous aggregate; into picrites and pseudomorphs of calcite after olivine. By the decomposition, elimination of ferric hydroxide, and magnetite in the crevices. Totally decomposed olivine, very rich in iron, always in sharp tabular crystals in limburgite from Sasbach, was called hyalosiderite. | As primary essential constituent in *all basaltic rocks*. in olivinefels and picrite, melaphyr, olivine-gabbro, olivine-norite, olivine-diabase. (In crystalline schists?) Also in certain mica-porphyries. | Distinguished from: *quartz* in isotrope sections easily; *zoisite* by the crystalline form (never in long needles) and polarization-colors; *colorless augite* by the cleavage in sections at right angles to the *c*-axis; *sanidine* by the rough surface and the exceedingly brilliant polarization-colors. |

β. Axial Picture Visible in Sections ∥ $oP$.

aa. *Appearance of the* I (+)

| Name. | Chemical composition and reactions. | Specific gravity. | Cleavage. | Ordinary combinations and form of the cross-section. | Twins. | Optical orientation. | Character and st. ength of double-refraction. | Direction of extinction. |
|---|---|---|---|---|---|---|---|---|
| 1. Silli-manite. | $Al_2SiO_5$. Not attacked by acids. | 3.23–3.24. | ∥ $\infty P \infty$ Separation of the thin needles ∥ $oP$. | Prismatic individuals without defined terminations $\infty P = 111°$. (See Fig. 72.) | | A.P. ∥ $\infty P \infty$ I.M. ⊥ $oP$. $c' = c$. $b = a$. $d = b$. Small axial angle $\rho = 44°$. Strong dispersion. | Double-refraction *positive*. | |
| 2. Stau-rolite. | $H_2R_2(Al_2)_6 Si_4O_{24}$. $R = 3Fe + 1Mg$. Insoluble in acids. | 3.34–3.77. | *Perfect* $\infty \check{P} \infty$, *imperfect* $\infty \check{P}$. Separation ∥ $oP$. | Rarely irregular grains. *Crystals* $\infty \check{P}. \infty \check{P} \infty$ $oP$. $\infty P = 128° 42'$. | Penetration-twins, wherein the c-axes cut each other at right or nearly right angles; rarely microscopic. (See Figs. 22 and 73.) | A.P. ∥ $\infty \check{P} \infty$ I.M. ⊥ $oP$. $c' = c$. $b = a$. $d = b$. (Dispersion feeble $\rho > v$.) | Double-refraction *positive*, strong. | |

## TABLES FOR DETERMINING MINERALS. 143

**DOUBLE-REFRACTION IN THEM POSITIVE.**

*Middle Line on oP.*

| Polarization-colors. | Color and power of refracting light. | Pleochroism. | Structure. | Association. | Inclosures. | Decomposition. | Occurrence. | Remarks. |
|---|---|---|---|---|---|---|---|---|
| *Very brilliant*, somewhat like muscovite. | *Colorless*, often colored red by $Fe_2O_3$ on fractures. | | In *exceedingly long, thin needles*, generally in large numbers, often *finely fibrous* and arranged parallel; developed in *quartz*, *cordierite*, and other minerals. (See Fig. 77.) | With quartz, orthoclase, biotite, and muscovite. | Very poor. Fluid inclosures. | | As primary accessory constituent *in crystalline schists*; rare. | Distinguished from: *zoisite* by the character of the double-refraction and polarization-colors; *andalusite* by the character of the double-refraction and cleavage. |
| *Very brilliant*. | Light or *deep yellowish brown*. Relief very *marked*. $\beta\rho = 1.7526$ | Easily recognizable, especially in the longitudinal sections. $c$ = dark brown. $a = b$ with slight difference = light yellow. | In large and *small crystals* the numberless inclosures are characteristic. | With quartz, orthoclase, mica, and garnet. | Inclosures of *minute quartz grains*, bitumen, hematite, are common. | | As primary accessory constituent in *crystalline schists*, especially mica-schists. | Well characterized by the color and pleochroism. |

| Name. | Chemical composition and reactions. | Specific gravity. | Cleavage. | Ordinary combinations and form of the cross-section. | Twins. | Optical orientation. | Character and strength of double-refraction. | Direction of extinction. |
|---|---|---|---|---|---|---|---|---|
| 3. Enstatite. | $MgSiO_3$. Only with difficulty *attacked* by acids. | 3.1–3.29 (3.153). | Perfect $\parallel \infty P$; $\infty \bar{P}\infty$, $\infty \check{P}\infty$. Longitudinal sections inclining to fibrous. $\infty P$ about $92°$. Separation $\parallel oP$. | *Long prismatic* $\infty P . \infty \bar{P}\infty$ $\infty \check{P}\infty . mP\infty$. Octagonal transverse sections with *two controlling pairs of faces*, similar to *monoclinic augite*. |  | N.B That position is selected where $\infty P = 92°$ lies *to the front*: A.P. $\parallel \infty \check{P}\infty$ 1. M. $\perp oP$ $c' = c$. $\bar{b} = b$. $\check{a} = a$. (See Fig. 7.) Like bronzite. The positive axial angle increasing with iron present. Dispersion not strong. $\rho > v$, and clear. [Comp. Zirkel, Min. p. 597. According to Tschermak's position the optical orientation in enstatite and bronzite is the following: A.P. $\parallel \infty \bar{P}\infty$ $c' = c$. 1. M. $\bar{b} = a$. $\check{a} = b$.] (See Fig. 74.) | Double-refraction *positive*, rather strong. *Weaker (f)* than in monoclinic augite. |  |

| Polarization-colors. | Color and power of refracting light. | Pleochroism. | Structure. | Association. | Inclosures. | Decomposition. | Occurrence. | Remarks. |
|---|---|---|---|---|---|---|---|---|
| Very brilliant. | *Colorless* to greenish. Relief marked. | | In irregular elongated prismatic individuals which show ∥ *c* a *longitudinal striation* like *fibres*. (See Fig. 75.) More rarely in crystals, generally decomposed. More often interpenetrated ∥ *c* with monoclinic augite. | With plagioclase, olivine, and monoclinic augite. | Very poor. | Into serpentine with formation of talc. *Into bastite* (compare). Decomposition resembles the metamorphosis of olivine into serpentine, yet mostly crystalline outlines obtained. | As essential and accessory constituent in *basic porphyritic eruptive rocks*. With olivine in *olivine-fels*. Rare in quartzose rocks as quartz-porphyrites; in porphyrites, diabase-porphyrites, melaphyrs; also in gabbro and norite. | Distinguished from: *olivine* by the fibrous tendency ∥ *c*; *zoisite* by the character of the double-refraction and polarization-colors; *sillimanite* by the form (never in so minute needles) and cleavage; the following minerals only by the variation of the contained iron. |

# DETERMINATION OF ROCK-FORMING MINERALS.

| Name. | Chemical composition and reactions. | Specific gravity. | Cleavage. | Ordinary combinations and form of the cross-section. | Twins. | Optical orientation. | Character and strength of double-refraction. | Direction of extinction. |
|---|---|---|---|---|---|---|---|---|
| 4. Bronzite. | $m$ (MgSiO$_3$) + $n$ (FeSiO$_3$). Not attacked by acids. | 3–3.5 (3.12–3.25). | Perfect $\infty P$, and separates according to $\infty \breve{P}\infty$. | Elongated acicular. $\infty P \cdot \infty \bar{P}\infty \cdot \infty \breve{P}\infty$ predominating; $\frac{2}{3}P \cdot \frac{2}{3}\breve{P}\infty$, very *similar* to the *monoclinic* augite. | Not rarely the large bronzite cleavage-leaves $\| \infty \breve{P}\infty$ bent, wavy, through repeated *twinning* after $\frac{1}{4}\breve{P}\infty$. Rarely in porphyritic eruptive rocks knee-shaped twins after $m \breve{P}\infty$ in asteroid crystalline groups. | Like enstatite. [According to Tschermak $c = c +$ or $c = a -$] Large axial angle, 69°–90°. Intermediary product between enstatite and hypersthene. | Double-refraction positive, like *enstatite*. In sections at right angles to the middle lines (i.e., $\| oP$ and $\infty \breve{P}\infty$) only an opening cross, with traces of the lemniscates, is visible. In sections at right angles to an optic axis one or no ring is visible. | |
| 5. Anthophyllite. | $n$ (MgSiO$_3$) + FeSiO$_3$. Not attacked by acids. | 3.187–3.225. | $\| \infty \breve{P}\infty$ $\infty P$, $\infty \bar{P}\infty$ *imperfect* [According to Tschermak imperfect $\| \infty \bar{P}\infty$, conchoidal separation after $\infty \breve{P}\infty$.] $\infty P$ = about 125° or 55°. | In leaf-like masses, very rarely in crystals. *Transverse sections* like those of *monoclinic hornblende*. | | $A. P. = \infty \breve{P}\infty$ $1.M \perp oP$ $c' = c$ $\bar{b} = b$ $\bar{a} = a$. Dispersion clear about $c = v > \rho$; large axial angle. (See Fig. 8.) | Double-refraction strongly *positive*. | |

| Polarization-colors. | Color and power of refracting light. | Pleochroism. | Structure. | Association. | Inclosures. | Decomposition. | Occurrence. | Remarks. |
|---|---|---|---|---|---|---|---|---|
| Interference-figures *less brilliant by far* than in *monoclinic* augite. | $\beta = 1.639$ Dark brown. | Very slight. | Partly in *large irregular grains* in coarsely-granular rocks; partly in sharply-defined *crystals* in the porphyritic eruptive rocks. | With olivine, plagioclase, monoclinic augite, magnetite; like enstatite. | Inclosures of brown rectangular leaflets, or opaque needles distributed $\|\infty\bar{P}\infty$ (or, after Tschermak, $\|\infty\bar{P}\infty$). Vitreous inclosures. | Similar to bastite, into a green fibrous aggregate, with elimination of $Fe_3O_4$ or $Fe_2O_3$. | Like *enstatite*, accessory primary constituent. Often replacing monoclinic augite as essential constituent. Also in the *younger basic eruptive rocks* and the coarse-grained older ones. | Can be distinguished from: *monoclinic augite* only by examining the transverse sections and the exactly parallel direction of extinction of the longitudinal sections; *hypersthene* by pleochroism and character of the double-refraction; *hornblende* and *biotite* by the want of powerful pleochroism. |
| Brilliant. | Dark brown. $\beta\rho = 1.636$. Relief not marked. | Strong pleochroism. Greenish yellow parallel to the striations ($\|c$). reddish brown at right angles to them. | Inclosures similar to bronzite. The longitudinal sections generally fibrous as a consequence of cleavage. | With olivine, plagioclase, augite, and hornblende. | Inclosures of minute brown and greenish mica-like leaves, often regularly arranged; otherwise very poor in inclosures. Magnetite. | | Very rarely accessory as secondary constituent. Decomposition-product of olivine in gabbro and olivine-fels. | Distinguished from: *biotite* by cleavage, strength of pleochroism, and magnitude of axial angle; *hornblende* by the optical orientation; *bronzite* and *hypersthene* by the pleochroism (axial colors) and cleavage. |

148  DETERMINATION OF ROCK-FORMING MINERALS.

*rance of the*

| Name. | Chemical composition and reactions. | Specific gravity. | Cleavage. | Ordinary combinations and form of the cross-section. | Twins. | Optical orientation. | Character and strength of double-refraction. | Direction of extinction. |
|---|---|---|---|---|---|---|---|---|
| 1. Hypersthene. | Like bronzite, yet far richer in iron. | 3.3–3.4. (3.34.) | $\infty P$ perfect. $\infty \check{P} \infty$ conchoidal separation. $\infty \bar{P} \infty$ imperfect. $\infty P =$ about 92°. | Large irregular *grains* and minute *columns* of $\infty P . \infty \check{P} \infty$ $\infty \bar{P} \infty$, also: $\tfrac{1}{2}\check{P}\infty$ $2\check{P}\infty . \tfrac{3}{2}\check{P}\tfrac{3}{2}$. | Knee-shaped twins in the crystals as in bronzite. | A.P. $= \infty \check{P}\infty$ 2.M. $\perp oP$. 1.M. $\perp \infty \check{P}\infty$ $c' = c$ $\mathfrak{b} = b$ $\mathfrak{a} = a$ (See Fig. 5.) Large axial angle. Dispersion about $a$ $\rho > \nu$, feeble. [According to Tschermak the acute $\infty \check{P}$-angle lies to the front, then A.P. $= \infty \bar{P}\infty$ $c' = c$. $\mathfrak{b} = a$. $\mathfrak{a} = b$.] (See Fig. 74.) | $1\,oP$ positive. $1\,\infty \check{P}\infty$ negative. Feebler than in the monoclinic augites. (Compare bronzite.) | |

# TABLES FOR DETERMINING MINERALS.

*Second Middle Line* (+) *on oP.*

| Polarization-colors. | Color and power of refracting light. | Pleochroism. | Structure. | Association. | Inclosures. | Decomposition. | Occurrence. | Remarks. |
|---|---|---|---|---|---|---|---|---|
| Rather brilliant. Compare bronzite. | Light to dark brown. Black from iron inclosures $\beta = 1.639$. | *Strong*, especially in the longitudinal sections and the thicker sections. Axial colors: $\mathfrak{a}=$ hyacinth red, $\mathfrak{b}=$ reddish brown, $\mathfrak{c}=$ grayish green. Absorption $c'>\mathfrak{a}>\mathfrak{b}$. | In large irregular *grains* in the granular *older*, and in small, augite-like crystals in the *younger* porphyritic eruptive rocks. Primary constituent I. O. | With plagioclase, olivine, and monoclinic augite. | *Numberless inclosures* of brown or violet rectangular leaflets often in the large grains with marked *separation* $\frac{1}{3} \infty \check{P} \infty$, whereby they appear striated. (See Fig. 50.) Inclosures of opaque needles regularly distributed often occur in the crystals. Otherwise *poor* in inclosures. Vitreous particles. | Hypersthene often decomposes into a dirty-brown or greenish *fibrous aggregate* parallel to the $c'$-axis and similar to that of enstatite; the decomposition begins here also, first on the fissures and especially on those at right angles to the $c'$-axis. It is a "*bastite-like*" *decomposition*. | In *grains* in *gabbro*, *norites* in *younger* eruptive rocks; especially in augite-*andesites*, and feldspathic basalts poor in olivine. As primary essential constituent and together with monoclinic augite. | Distinguished from: *bronzite* by the character of the double-refraction and powerful pleochroism; *monoclinic augite* often only by examination with the condenser, especially in transverse sections, and by the feebler double-refraction; *biotite* by absence of the marked cleavage; *hornblende* by optical orientation and prismatic angle. |

| Name. | Chemical composition and reactions. | Specific gravity. | Cleavage. | Ordinary combinations and form of the cross-section. | Twins. | Optical orientation. | Character and strength of double-refraction. | Direction of extinction. |
|---|---|---|---|---|---|---|---|---|
| 2. a. Protobastite. (Diaclasite.) | | 3.054. | | | | | | |
| β. Bastite. | Like bronzite. Contains $H_2O$. | 2.6–2.8. | $\infty \bar{P}\infty$, $\infty P$. | Partly in rather *sharply-defined crystals*, partly in *grains* of columnar form, and in *irregular leafy individuals*. $\infty P = 93°$. | Very rare. Penetration-twins. | A. P. = $\parallel \infty \bar{P}\infty$. 2. M. $\perp oP$. 1. M. $\perp \infty \bar{P}\infty$. | In sections $\perp oP$ positive; consequently *negative* $\bar{c} = \mathfrak{c}$ $\bar{b} = \mathfrak{a}$ $\bar{a} = \mathfrak{b}$ Dispersion $\rho > v$ about a. Rather strongly doubly-refracting, like hypersthene. | |

## DISTINGUISHING OF THE RHOMBIC AUGITES

The three rhombic augites, enstatite, bronzite, and hypersthene, are in general distinguished only by the amount of iron present, together with the magnitude of the optic axial angle lying in the plane $\parallel \infty \bar{P}\infty$; in those poor in iron, 1. M. ($= \mathfrak{c}'$) $\perp oP$; in those rich in iron is $\mathfrak{c}'$ to 2. M. ($\perp oP$). A positive double-refraction is observable in the transverse sections of *both* varieties, only the magnitude of the axial angle determining whether the acute angle is visible $\parallel oP$ or $\parallel \infty \bar{P}\infty$.

Pleochroism also, in general, allows no conclusion, as only hypersthenes which are very rich in iron seem to show the mentioned powerful pleochroism. Protobastite and its decomposition product, bastite, however, have the optic axial plane $\parallel \infty \bar{P}\infty$. The rhombic augites mentioned above also show a tendency to metamorphose into bastite.

The rhombic augites, as regards optical orientation, are distinguished from the monoclinic by the much feebler double-refraction and inferior brilliancy of the polarization-colors. The isotrope

# TABLES FOR DETERMINING MINERALS.

| Polarization-colors. | Color and power of refracting light. | Pleochroism. | Structure. | Association. | Inclosures. | Decomposition. | Occurrence. | Remarks. |
|---|---|---|---|---|---|---|---|---|
| Rather brilliant. | Light yellowish. | | Protobastite, *fresh* and free from inclosures, often shows the *beginning of a fibrous decomposition into bastite*, in that the formation is of fibres ‖ *c'*. | | | Into bastite. | As primary essential or accessory mineral in certain gabbros and porphyritic augite-plagioclase rocks. | Distinguishable from *enstatite* and *bronzite* only by the optical orientation (position of 1. M.). |
| Not very brilliant. | Dirty pale green. | Very weak. Absorption *c* > *a* and *b*. | Commonly interpenetrated with olivine. A metallic lustre on ∞*P*∞. Finely striated *parallel* to the *vertical axis*. Often shows a remnant of fresh enstatite or protobastite mineral. | With plagioclase, olivine, monoclinic augite, magnetite. | Many times inclosures like hypersthene and bronzite. Inclosures of picotite and chromite. | Bastite itself is always a decomposition-product of rhombic augite. | As secondary decomposition-product of rhombic augite in olivine-fels, gabbro, norite, andesites, rarely in melaphyrs, and diabase-porphyries. | Distinguished from: *serpentine* by the striation parallel to the vertical axis; *chlorite* by less perfect cleavage, and not running ‖ *oP*, by the feebler pleochroism, and, finally, almost always by the pseudomorphs after augite crystals. |

## FROM EACH OTHER AND FROM THE MONOCLINIC.

sections of *monoclinic augite*, cut at right angles to one of the optic axes, show two to three rings and clouds; those of *rhombic augite* of the same thickness, none or at most one ring.

The polarization colors of *rhombic augite* in very thin sections are generally yellowish white I. O., ‖ *oP* and ∞*P*∞ (in bronzite and hypersthene, enstatite shows more brilliant polarization-colors); in these sections also a biaxial interference-figure is discernible; if *monoclinic* augite, a blue to red, green, and side appearance of one of the optic axes.

Finally, all sections of *rhombic augites* parallel to the *c'*-axis have a parallel extinction i. p. p. l.; of *monoclinic* augites, an extinction with a varying obliquity (to 45°) to the *c*-axis. The common polysynthetic twins of monoclinic augites ‖ ∞*P*∞ are wanting in the rhombic (seen especially well on transverse sections).

## DETERMINATION OF ROCK-FORMING MINERALS.

γ. AXIAL PICTURE VISIBLE IN SECTIONS $\parallel oP.$;
aa. *Appearance of the* I. *M.*

| Name. | Chemical composition and reactions. | Specific gravity. | Cleavage. | Ordinary combinations and form of the cross-section. | Twins. | Optical orientation. | Character and strength of double-refraction. | Direction of extinction. |
|---|---|---|---|---|---|---|---|---|
| 1 α. Andalusite. | $Al_2SiO_5$. Not acted on by acids. | 3.10–3.17. | Prismatic $\infty P$. Imperfect after $\infty \check{P}\infty$, $\infty \bar{P}\infty$, and $\bar{P}\infty$ = $\infty P =$ 90° 50'. Separation $\parallel oP$. | Rarely grains; *long columns* $\infty P.oP.\bar{P}\infty$. Quadratic transverse sections, longitudinal sections, elongated rectangles. | | A.P. $\parallel \infty \bar{P}\infty$ I.M. $\perp oP$. $c' = a$ $b = b$ $a = c$. Large axial angle. | Double-refraction strongly *negative*. | |
| β. Variety of andalusite: Chiastolite. | ditto. | 2.9–3.1. | Perfect $\infty P$. $\infty P =$ 91° 40'. | *Long columns* $\infty P.oP$; not in form of microlites. | | | | |

## TABLES FOR DETERMINING MINERALS.

IN THESE DOUBLE-REFRACTION NEGATIVE.

on oP Negative.

| Polarization-colors. | Color and power of refracting light. | Pleochroism. | Structure. | Association. | Inclosures. | Decomposition. | Occurrence. | Remarks. |
|---|---|---|---|---|---|---|---|---|
| Very brilliant. | *Colorless;* tinged *flesh-red.* Relief very marked. $\beta\rho = 1.638$. | *Very strong;* $\mathfrak{a} =$ dark blood-red, $\mathfrak{b} =$ oil-green, $\mathfrak{c} =$ olive-green. absorption $\mathfrak{c}' > \mathfrak{b} > \mathfrak{a}$ | Rarely in grains, almost always in columnar individuals. Like staurolite, often so filled with inclosures that but little of the andalusite substance is to be seen. Often in long thin needles in radial aggregates. | With quartz orthoclase, biotite, and muscovite. | Sometimes very poor, and again in the metamorphic schists very rich granules, in quartz granules, bituminous inclosures, and leaves of biotite. | Commonly decomposed into a *greenish fibrous aggregate,* which has a certain similarity to the decomposition-product of cordierite. | As primary accessory constituent in *granite* and in *crystalline schists,* as mica schist, granulite. As *metamorphic* mineral in the contact-schists, hornfels. | Distinguished from: colorless *augite* by the commonly occurring pleochroism (reddish green), and by the always parallel extinction; *enstatite* by the character of the double-refraction; *hypersthene* by the color and character of double refraction; *zoisite* by the pleochroism, form of cross-section, prismatic angle, and position of the t.M.; *sillimanite* only with difficulty if occurring in minute needles. Sillimanite generally occurs in minute needles, andalusite in large columns or grains. They differ, moreover, in pleochroism, prismatic angle, and cleavage. |
| ∴ | ∴′ | | The transverse sections present a peculiar structure. *Quadratic cores,* inclosures of a bituminous substance, are arranged at the centre and on the four corners; very common are the remarkable regularly-disposed inclosures of carbonaceous particles. (See Fig. 76.) | | Bitumen. Leaves of muscovite and biotite. | Similar to andalusite; whole pseudomorphs of quartz, muscovite, and chloritic substance after chiastolite. | Rarely in *metamorphic schists* (contact on granite). | Characterized by the regular inclosures. |

| Name. | Chemical composition and reactions. | Specific gravity. | Cleavage. | Ordinary combinations and form of the cross-section. | Twins. | Optical orientation. | Character and strength of double-refraction. | Direction of extinction. |
|---|---|---|---|---|---|---|---|---|
| Cordierite. (Dichroite.) | $Mg_2R_2$ $Si_5O_{18}$ $R_2 =$ $Al_2, Fe_2$. Scarcely attacked by acids. | 2.59–2.66. | $\infty \bar{P} \infty$, imperfect $\bar{P} \infty$, $\infty P =$ 119° 10'. | In large grains and small crystals. $\infty P . \infty \bar{P} \infty$ . $oP$. Hexagonal transverse sections and rectangular longitudinal sections. | If in crystals so often *penetration twins* and fourlings after $\infty \check{P}$, rarely after $\infty \bar{P} 3$. (See Figs. 23 and 78.) | A. P. $\parallel$ $\infty \bar{P} \infty$. 1. M. $\perp oP$. $c' = a$ $\bar{b} = c$ $d = b$. Axial angle rather large. Dispersion feeble $\rho < v$. | *Negative*, not very energetic. | |
| Pinite. (Decomposition-product of cordierite.) | | | | *Large crystals* $=$ $\infty \check{P} . \infty \bar{P} \infty$ . $\infty \bar{P} \infty . oP$. | | | | |

*bb. Appearance of 2 M.*

| Zoizite. | $H_2Ca_4$ $(Al_2)_3$ $Si_6O_{26}$. Attacked by acids only with difficulty; after ignition, however, soluble with separation of amorphous $SiO_2$. | 3.22–3.36. | $\infty \bar{P} \infty$ very perfect. Separation $\parallel oP$. | Elongated grains and long *transverse-limbed columns*. $\infty P . \infty \bar{P} \infty$ (see Fig. 79). Hexagonal transverse sections. $\infty P =$ 116° 26'. | | A. P. $\parallel$ $\infty \bar{P} \infty$ always $d = c =$ $b = b$ $c' = a$. Or if A. P. $\parallel oP$, $b = a$ $c' = b$; very powerful dispersion $\rho < v$. About $a$! (if A. P. $\parallel oP$, then dispersion $\rho > v$.) | In $oP$ appearance of 2. negative M. *positive*. Feeble double-refraction. | |

# TABLES FOR DETERMINING MINERALS.

| Polarisation-colors. | Color and power of refracting light. | Pleochroism. | Structure. | Association. | Inclosures. | Decomposition. | Occurrence. | Remarks. |
|---|---|---|---|---|---|---|---|---|
| Rather brilliant, like quartz. | Violet-blue. In very thin sections, *colorless.* $\beta = 1.54–1.56$. | *Very marked.* In thicker sections well recognizable. $\mathfrak{a}$ = yellowish white. $\mathfrak{b}$ = pale to prussian blue. $\mathfrak{c}$ = dark prussian blue. Absorption | Always in larger individuals; never in microlites. In rounded larger *grains,* or in small *crystals;* the latter in eruptive rocks. Metamorphic mineral. | With quartz, orthoclase, and biotite. With plagioclase, quartz, sanidine, augite, pleonaste, corundum. | Fluid inclosures, sillimanite needles, pleonaste crystals, zircon, vitreous inclosures. | Very common, especially if occurring in grains or large crystals, on the crevices, or completely decomposed (*pinite*) into a greenish fibrous aggregate, similar to andalusite. (See Fig. 77.) | Rare, as accessory primary constituent in *granite,* quartz-porphyry (pinite), and in grains in *gneiss.* Rarely in crystals in *trachytes* (twins!), and in the trachytic volcanic overflows. | In thin sections and in grains often very similar to quartz, yet easily distinguished by the phenomena of decomposition on the crevices in c. p. l. If in crystals, recognized by the color and pleochroism. |
| Aggregate polarization. | Green. Colorless. | $\mathfrak{b} > \mathfrak{a} > \mathfrak{c}'$. | Wholly composed of *minute threads and leaflets.* | With quartz, orthoclase, and biotite. | | | | Easily recognized macroscopically by the crystalline form, and from the decomposition. |

*(negative) on oP.*

| | | | | | | | | |
|---|---|---|---|---|---|---|---|---|
| Generally feebly brilliant blue-green. | Colorless —white. $\beta\rho = 1.70$. Relief very marked. | | The *transverse crevices* on the *long columns* and the inclosures are characteristic. (See Fig. 79.) | With quartz, omphacite, garnet, mica, hornblende. | *Fluid inclosures* are very common. | Often opaque on the border. | Common in *crystalline schists* as eclogites and especially amphibolites. | Distinguished from: *apatite* easily by the optical properties; *andalusite* by the cleavage in sections parallel *oP,* moreover by the pleochroism and polarization-colors; *sillimanite* by the polarization-colors and the optical orientation (never sinks, like sillimanite, to the microlitic form); *olivine* by the crystalline form and polarization-colors (optical investigation, power of dispersion); *enstatite* by the optical orientation, the polarization-colors, cleavage, and the $\infty \breve{P}$-angle. |

156  DETERMINATION OF ROCK-FORMING MINERALS.

## II. b. 2. Minerals Crystallizing
### a. MINERALS APPARENTLY CRYSTALLIZING
#### CLEAVAGE MOST

| Name. | Chemical composition and reactions. | Specific gravity. | Cleavage. | Ordinary combinations and form of the cross-section. | Twins. | Optical orientation. | Character and strength of double-refraction. | Direction of extinction. |
|---|---|---|---|---|---|---|---|---|
| 1. Mica Group. a. Meroxene (Biotite). | $m\ R_4SiO_4$ <br> $n\ R_2SiO_4$ <br> $v\ R_2Si_3O_{12}$ <br> $R = K, Na, H,$ <br> $R = Fe, Mg,$ <br> $R_2 = Al_2, Fe_2.$ <br> Slightly attacked by HCl, but completely decomposed by $H_2SO_4$ with separation of a silica-skeleton. <br><br> According to Tschermak mixtures of $H_2K_2(Al_2)_2Si_5O_{24}$ and $Mg_{12}Si_8O_{24}$ in proportion of 1:1 or 2:1. | 2.8–3.2. | Highly eminent $\|oP.$ Separations corresponding to the pressure-surfaces or "sliding-planes" (gleitfläche) $-P_2$ and $\tfrac{1}{2}P\infty.$ | $\infty P\ quite\ 120°.$ <br> $\infty P.\ \infty P\infty.$ <br> $oP.$ Thin *tablets* or *short columns*. Transverse sections ($\|oP$) *hexagonal tablets* without cleavage-cracks. More often with "sliding plane" (gleitfläche), three line-systems crossing each other at an angle of 60°, and rectangular *longitudinal sections* (∥ to the $c'$-axis), with numberless cleavage-lines parallel to the longer sides. (See Figs. 80 and 81.) | Rare. Twinning-plane, $\infty P$; both individuals, however, forced over each other in a plane quite $\|oP$; also with several lamellæ interpolated. Only the latter recognizable i. p. l. | A.P. $\|\infty P\infty$ (mica second class). A.P. parallel to two opposite sides($\infty P\infty$) of a hexagon coinciding with a "fracture-line" (schlaglinie). $1, M = a$ vary but little from the normal to $oP.$ Axial angle generally very small $= 5°-13°,$ but variable, being sometimes very large. *Dispersion* $\rho < v.$ (See Fig. 19.) <br><br> The axial angle lessens with decrease of iron present. | As *hexagonal* as a consequence of the apparently constant parallel extinction and of the small axial angle, or, as the 1. M. differs but little from the normal to $oP,$ *apparently rhombic*. Negative. | The transverse sections generally apparently isotrope; the longitudinal sections with parallel extinction. therefore cannot be studied in c. p. l. Apparently hexagonal. |

## in the Monoclinic System.
### IN THE HEXAGONAL (OR RHOMBIC) SYSTEM.
### PERFECT ∥ oP.

| Polarization-colors. | Color and power of refracting light. | Pleochroism. | Structure. | Association. | Inclosures. | Decomposition. | Occurrence. | Remarks. |
|---|---|---|---|---|---|---|---|---|
| Not particularly brilliant, brownish tints; in very thin leaflets iridescent, carmine-red. | Brown-black, dark green. $\beta = 1.61$. | Transverse sections show almost no pleochroism. In longitudinal sections very strong, a and b differing but slightly. In *longitudinal sections* parallel to the $c'$-axis (= the shorter sides of the rectangle). $a =$ yellow *pale brown;* *perpendicular to the $c'$-axis* (parallel to the longer sides). $c = dark\ brown\ to\ black.$ Absorption $c > b > a$. | Primary constituent I. O. Partly in large crystals (in eruptive rocks) often cracked or shattered, or with broad opaque border; or in minute irregular leaflets, especially in the crystalline schists; or distributed through the ground-mass constituent II. O., as in the basalts and other rocks. | Generally with quartz and orthoclase; hornblende, more rarely augite and olivine. | Generally free from inclosures; yet often numbers of epidote needles arranged in tufts (comp. decomposition), or long thin rutile needles arranged very regularly at 60°; apatite, zircon. | Into *chloritic minerals* very commonly *with epidote and calcite.* In this decomposition the biotite loses its brown color, and becomes green; lenticular calcite separates between the leaves, and needles of epidote appear. (See Figs. 80 and 81.) In the decomposition of biotite also a separation of ferric hydroxide or magnetite about the periphery. | *In nearly all rocks.* *In many* as *essential primary* constituent. One of the first-formed of minerals. As *decomposition-product* of augite, hornblende, rarely of olivine. As *contact-mineral* in metamorphic schists. | Easily recognizable by eminent cleavage and exceedingly powerful pleochroism. Distinguished from: *hornblende* in that the transverse sections are not pleochroitic (and by the investigation i. e. p. l.)— the longitudinal sections can be distinguished by the oblique extinction to be proven on hornblende; *chlorite* in that chlorite is always green, never so well crystallized, feebler pleochroitic, and generally arranged in tufts. |

# DETERMINATION OF ROCK-FORMING MINERALS.

| Name. | Chemical composition and reactions. | Specific gravity. | Cleavage. | Ordinary combinations and form of the cross-section. | Twins. | Optical orientation. | Character and strength of double-refraction. | Direction of extinction. |
|---|---|---|---|---|---|---|---|---|
| b. Rubellan. | Like biotite (meroxene); rich in iron. | See meroxene. | See meroxene. | Large thin hexagonal tables. | | Large axial angle. | See meroxene. | |
| c. Phlogopite. | A magnesian mica, *nearly free from iron.* According to Tschermak, a mixture of $K_6(Al_2)_3 Si_6O_{24}$, $H_8Si_{10}O_{24}$, and $Mg_{12}Si_6O_{24}$ in the proportion of nearly $3:1:4$. | 2.75–2.97. | See meroxene. | See meroxene. | See meroxene; also twins after $\infty P$ with individuals lying near one another. | A P. $\parallel \infty P\infty$ a nearly $\perp oP$. $c : a = 2\tfrac{1}{2}°$. Dispersion $\rho < v$. Axial angle about $15°$. | Negative like meroxene. | Like meroxene, always parallel extinction. |
| d. Anomite. | According to Tschermak, a mixture of $H_2K_4(Al_2)_3 Si_6O_{24}$ and $Mg_{12}Si_6O_{24}$ in proportion of $1:1$ or $2:1$. | | See meroxene; also here the "gliding-planes" very commonly discernible. One of the gliding-planes parallel $\infty P\infty$. | See meroxene. | | A.P. $\perp \infty P\infty$ (mica I class). a nearly $\perp oP$. Axial angle about $12$–$16°$ and less. Dispersion $\rho > v$. | Negative. | ditto. |

# TABLES FOR DETERMINING MINERALS.

| Polariza-tion-colors. | Color and power of refracting light. | Pleo-chroism. | Structure. | Associa-tion. | Inclosures. | Decomposi-tion. | Occur-rence. | Remarks. |
|---|---|---|---|---|---|---|---|---|
| | Brown-ish red, brick-red. | | Often appears as a foreign inclosure; only primary constituent I.O. *Is only an altered (pyrogene?) biotite.* | With augite, olivine plagio-clase, nephe-line, or leucite. | Augitic needles, ferric hydrate, and microlites regularly arranged at 60° as in meroxene. | Depositing ferric hydroxide. | In basalts and lavas. | Dis-tinguished from biotite only by the color. |
| See mer-oxene. | Yellow, pale brown, red-brown, like mer-oxene. Relief marked. | Very strong, yet weaker than mer-oxene. | Mostly in thin irregular leaflets. | With calcite and ser-pentine. | Very poor; as in rubellan, regular layers of thread-like needles. | Becoming green, like meroxene. | In *granular* rarely compact *lime-stones*, dolo-mites, and in serpen-tine rocks. | Differs from meroxene only in chemical composition and color. |
| ditto. | Red-brown. | ditto. | ditto. | With olivine, augite, and actino-lite. | | Becoming green to colorless as above. At the beginning of the decomposi-tion it becomes opaque, and contains numbers of brown grains inclosed. | Rare in olivine-fels. | |

| Name. | Chemical composition and reactions. | Specific gravity. | Cleavage. | Ordinary combinations and form of the cross-section. | Twins. | Optical orientation. | Character and strength of double-refraction. | Direction of extinction. |
|---|---|---|---|---|---|---|---|---|
| e. Muscovite (and sericite). | $H_4K_2(Al_2)_3 Si_6O_{24}$. Not attacked by acids. | 2.76–3.1. | *Very perfect* $\parallel oP$; "sliding-planes" (gleitfläche) as in meroxene. | Rarely crystallized in rocks; hexagonal tables. | See meroxene. | $A.P. \perp \infty P \infty$ (mica I. class). $\mathfrak{a}$ differing but little from $c'$ nearly $\perp oP$. Dispersion $\rho > v$. Axial angle generally large, 60–70°. (See Fig. 18.) | Strongly negative. | Like magnesiamica with parallel extinction; apparently rhombic. |
| 2. Talc. | $H_2Mg_3 Si_4O_{12}$. Not attacked by acids. Al-reaction. | 2.69–2.8. | Eminent $\parallel oP$ (imperfect $\infty P$). | Never in crystals; in rocks mostly in minute irregular leaflets like mica. | | $A.P. \parallel \infty P \infty$ $\parallel$ to a *fracture-line* (schlaglinie). $\mathfrak{a}$ nearly $\perp oP$. (According to Tschermak axial angle about 17°.) | Feebly negative. | Apparently rhombic? |

# TABLES FOR DETERMINING MINERALS.

| Polarization-colors. | Color and power of refracting light. | Pleochroism. | Structure. | Association. | Inclosures. | Decomposition. | Occurrence. | Remarks. |
|---|---|---|---|---|---|---|---|---|
| Exceedingly *brilliant, iridescent* (red to yellow colors). | Colorless, light green, oil-green. | | As primary constituent I. O. in large leaves and tables, in tufted and stellate aggregates. As secondary product in aggregates of minute irregular leaflets. In crystalline schists in minute irregular leaflets. | With quartz, orthoclase, biotite, tourmaline. | Very poor; rarely rutile needles, hematite tablets, or tourmaline columns. Zircon. | | As *primary* constituent in *granites*, especially tourmaline granites, and in *crystalline schists;* especially prominent in gneiss, mica-schist, and clay schists. As primary constituent nowhere else in eruptive rocks. As *decomposition-product* in the feldspars, chiastolite, liebenerite, etc. | Easily recognizable by the highly eminent cleavage and brilliant polarization-colors; yet difficult to distinguish with the microscope from talc. *Sericite* is only a muscovite, appearing like talc, soft, greasy to the touch, non-elastic and occurring in compact aggregates of minute irregular leaflets, in certain semi-crystalline schists. |
| See muscovite. | Colorless, white, light green. | | Mostly in *irregularly disposed* interlaced or *rosette-shaped stellate aggregates* of minute leaflets. | With quartz, orthoclase, mica, or with augite and olivine. | Very poor. Biotite, actinolite. Like muscovite. | | As primary constituent in many crystalline schists. Not common. As secondary product in the decomposition of augites and hornblendes poor in iron, especially enstatite before occurring in olivine-fels and serpentines. | Difference between muscovite and talc: *Muscovite* occurs generally in large individuals remarkable for the basal cleavage, or in separate leaves. *Talc*, however, occurs generally in aggregates of compact intertwined minute leaflets arranged in stellate groups. The microchemical investigation of isolated leaflets with hydrofluo-silicic acid is the only safe one. |

# DETERMINATION OF ROCK-FORMING MINERALS.

| Name. | Chemical composition and reactions. | Specific gravity. | Cleavage. | Ordinary combinations and form of the cross-section. | Twins. | Optical orientation. | Character and strength of double-refraction. | Direction of extinction. |
|---|---|---|---|---|---|---|---|---|
| **3. Chlorite Group.** | | | | | | | | |
| *a.* Ripidolite. (Chlorite in restricted sense.) | Mixture of $p$ ($2H_2O$ . $3MgO$ . $2SiO_2$) + $q$ ($2H_2O$ . $2MgO$ . $Al_2O_3$ . $SiO_2$). $p:q = 1:2$. | 2.78– 2.95. | Very perfect $\parallel oP$. | Leaflets and six-sided tablets $\infty P$, $oP$ like hexagonal. If monoclinic, then $\infty P$, $\infty P\infty$, $oP$. | | Apparently *hexagonal* (optically-uniaxial), often clearly optically-biaxial, with very small axial angle. $a \perp oP$. | Feebly *negative.* | Cleavage-leaflets like isotrope. Longitudinal sections with parallel extinction. |
| *b.* Helminth. | Decomposed by $H_2SO_4$. | | ditto. | Long vermicular curled columns. | Six-sided leaflets with re-entrant angles. | | | |
| *c.* Pennin-ite. | See *a*. $p:q = 3:2$. Decomposed by HCl. | 2.61– 2.77. | ditto. | Crystals like rhombohedra $oP$. $R$ or $3R$ or $\infty R$ . $R$. | Penetration *three-lings*. (Biaxial parts. Visible in three positions differing by $120°$ in leaves $\parallel oP$.) | Often clearly optically-*biaxial.* | Sometimes positive, sometimes negative; very feeble. | Longitudinal sections with parallel extinction. Cleavage-leaflets sometimes isotrope, sometimes double-refracting. |
| *d.* Kaemmererite. | Contains $Cr_2O_3$. | 2.617– 2.76. | ditto. | Irregular leaflets apparently $P$ . $oP$. | | Clearly optically-*biaxial.* | | |
| *e.* Clinochlore. | $p:q = 2:3$. More difficultly decomposed by acids than the above. | 2.65– 2.78. | ditto. "Sliding planes" (gleitflächе) similar to mica. | Crystals of monoclinic habit $\infty P$ . $\infty P\infty$ . $oP$, etc. $\infty P$ quite $120°$. In large leaves. | Commonly in *twins* and three-lings. Twinning plane a face of the hemipyramid $3P$. | $A.P. \parallel \infty P\infty$, often also $\perp \infty P\infty$; $c$ quite $\perp oP$. Varying about $12$-$15°$ from the normal to $oP$. Large axial angle. Dispersion $\rho < v$. | Generally *positive.* | $c : c = 12$-$15°$. |
| *f.* Chloritoid and *g.* Sismondine. | $H_2R(Al_2)SiO_7$; $R = FeO$ and some MgO. Decomposed by concentrated $H_2SO_4$. | 3.52– 3.56. | $\parallel oP$. Not so perfect as in the others. | ditto. Tablets. | Commonly *tablets* of thin leaves developed twin-like, which are placed at $120°$ to each other. | $A.P. \parallel \infty P\infty$, r. M. differs about $12°$ from the $\perp oP$. | Negative. Feeble. | $a : c = 5$-$12°$. |

# TABLES FOR DETERMINING MINERALS.

| Polarization-colors. | Color and power of refracting light. | Pleochroism. | Structure. | Association. | Inclosures. | Decomposition. | Occurrence. | Remarks. |
|---|---|---|---|---|---|---|---|---|
| *Feebly* brilliant, bluish, blue to green. | Light to *dark green.* $\mu = 1.575.$ | Very feeble. | The chlorites do not for the most part occur as rock-constituents in large lamellary hexagonal tablets like the micas, but like talc in *aggregates of minute irregular leaflets* either singly or disposed in radial groups. | As primary constituent with quartz, orthoclase, biotite, and muscovite. | Very poor. Hematite and hydrated ferric oxide, and needles of rutile and actinolite. | | Primary. More commonly in leaflets in chloritic schists, as *decomposition-product* of mica, augite, hornblende, and garnet. | Difficult to distinguish from decomposed or green-colored mica. The chlorites as rock-constituents are extremely difficult to distinguish from each other. Clinochlore alone (also ottrelite) is well characterized through the pronounced pleochroism as well as the common twinning; more easily determined by optical examination. *Ottrelite* is marked by the greater hardness, less perfect cleavage, absence of laminations, and richness of inclosures; also distinguished by chemical quantitative analysis. |
| | | | | | | As *decomposition-product* after mica and hornblende, and interpenetrated in minerals of the crystalline schists. Rare. | | |
| See ripidolite. | Leek to bluish green. | Feeble. Green shades. | ditto. | ditto. | | | *Rare* as rock-constituent as above, in leaves. | |
| | *Peach* to *blood-red.* | | Often interpenetrated with clinochlore. | With olivine, augite, and chromite. | | By decomposition is decolorized and resembles talc. | Rarely in serpentines. | |
| More brilliant than in the other chlorites. Indigo-yellow. | *Dark oil* to *bluish green.* | Often very *strong.* In sections ⊥ oP yellow; ∥ c light green, yellowish green. ⊥ c blue-green, dark-green. | In larger leaves, yet not so marked by lamellæ as mica. | With quartz, orthoclase, and mica. With augite, hornblende, olivine, or serpentine. | ditto. | | Primary. Common in crystalline schists, as chloritic schist, and secondary in serpentine. | |
| See clinochlore. | Dark green. | See clinochlore. ∥ c yellowish green. ⊥ c greenish blue. | ditto. | With quartz, orthoclase, and mica. With augite, rutile, titanite, glaucophane. | Fluid inclosures very common. Rutile needles. | | Chloritoid in certain semi-crystalline schists. Sismondine rarely in glaucophane-eclogite. | |

# DETERMINATION OF ROCK-FORMING MINERALS.

| Name. | Chemical composition and reactions. | Specific gravity. | Cleavage. | Ordinary combinations and form of the cross-section. | Twins. | Optical orientation. | Character and strength of double-refraction. | Direction of extinction. |
|---|---|---|---|---|---|---|---|---|
| *k*. Ottrelite. | $H_6R_3(Al_2)_2 Si_4O_{24}$. $R = Fe, Mn$. Attacked by $H_2SO_4$ only with difficulty. | 4.4 (?). | $oP$ very perfect. Besides, according to $\infty P$, with an angle of 110–120° (Becke). | Thin spherical tablets; rounded cross-sections $\perp oP$ rare. Elongated rectangles if the sections are inclined to $oP$. | See sismondine; *poly synthetic twinning-striations* $\frac{1}{2} oP$. (Fig. 82.) | Optically biaxial; 1. M. *rather sharply inclined to the perfect cleavage-planes*; small axial angle. | Very feebly negative. | Commonly parallel to the longer axis of the cross-section. |

2. MONOCLINIC

*aa*. PLANE OF OPTIC AXES GENERALLY $\perp \infty P\infty$; PERFECT

| 1. *a*. Orthoclase. | $K_2Al_2 Si_6O_{16}$. Not attacked by acids. Small amount of Na, Ca, Fe, Mg. | 2.50–2.59 (2.57). | *Eminent* $\frac{1}{2}oP$ and $\infty P\infty$. Cleavage-angle 90°. | In grains, or partly columnar: $oP, \infty P\infty, \infty P.2P\infty, 2P\infty.P$, and partly of large or more rarely minute tabular crystals. $\infty P\infty, \infty P, oP 2P\infty, P\infty$. | Very common, especially after the following three laws: most commonly 1. *The Carlsbad law*. Twinning-plane $\infty P\infty$ combined or interpenetrated in the direction of the *b*-axis. 2. *Baveno* law. Twinning-plane $2P\infty$, especially in the columnar examples. 3. Rarely the *Manebach* law. | A.P. generally $\perp \infty P\infty$, equally inclined with $oP$ and forms with the vertical axis an angle of 69° 11'. $c = b$ $a : \dot{a} = 5°$. True axial angle = 69°. (See Fig. 14.) Axial dispersion $= \rho > \nu$. In sections parallel $\infty P\infty$ or $\infty P\infty$ i. cond. a distorted biaxial interference-figure visible. A.P. is rare. | Rather feebly negative. | In sections or cleavage-leaflets $\parallel \infty P\infty$ a direction of extinction varies from the edge $oP$: $\infty P\infty = a : a$ about 5° 18'. Sections parallel *b*, that is, from the zone $oP$: $\infty P\infty$, of course have a parallel extinction. |

# TABLES FOR DETERMINING MINERALS.

| Polarization-colors. | Color and power of refracting light. | Pleochroism. | Structure. | Association. | Inclosures. | Decomposition. | Occurrence. | Remarks. |
|---|---|---|---|---|---|---|---|---|
| Not brilliant, similar to ripidolite. | Greenish black; in sections light to grayish green. | Rather *powerful*; ‖ *oP* lavender-blue, bluish green, ‖ *e* greenish blue, yellowish green. | Compare with "Inclosures." In large tablets of a black color (rather hard). Cleavage ‖ *oP* never so very perfect as in the other chlorites; besides this, however, always a cleavage ‖ to the *c*-axis. | With quartz, mica (muscovite), rutile needles, garnet. | Generally exceedingly *rich in inclosures* of colorless *quartz granules*, rutile needles, and earthy particles. | | Rare, in semi-crystalline and metamorphic schists. | *Ottrelite is triclinic* (Renard). Cleavage after *oP*; also not after ∞ *P*, but in two directions cutting each other at an angle of about 130°, and in a third direction at right angles to one of these. |

## CRYSTALS.
### CLEAVAGE ‖ *oP* AND ∞*P*∞, ANGLE NEARLY 90°.

| Polarization-colors. | Color and power of refracting light. | Pleochroism. | Structure. | Association. | Inclosures. | Decomposition. | Occurrence. | Remarks. |
|---|---|---|---|---|---|---|---|---|
| Rather brilliant, not, however, so bright as in quartz. In very thin sections and in microlites the polarization-colors of orthoclase are dull, generally bluegray, as, e.g., nephe-line. | Rarely colorless, clear as water; generally white or *opaque from decomposition*, gray; tinged red from ferric oxide or hydroxide. *index low* | | Orthoclase in large crystals or grains I.O. and smaller granules, rarely filaments, II.O. in eruptive rocks; always in grains in crystalline schists. *Penetrations with plagioclase* are common, generally ‖ ∞*P*∞; graphic-granite-like, with quartz (micro-pegmatite). (See Fig. 63, *e*.) Zonal structure rare; also inclosures zonally disposed. | With quartz, biotite, muscovite, and hornblende, rarely augite, plagioclase, elæolite. | As a rule very poor. Hematite, biotite leaflets, fluid inclosures, apatite needles, zircon. | Mostly perfectly decomposed, the crystals opaque, and non-transparent; into kaolin with formation of muscovite or epidote. | One of the most common constituents of the granular and porphyritic *older* eruptive rocks. Essential primary constituent in granite, syenite, quartzose porphyry, and accessory in nearly all plagioclase rocks; moreover, in the crystalline schists, especially the *gneisses*; here often glassy, as sanidine. | The large crystals can be easily distinguished from the other colorless optically-biaxial minerals by the twinnings in sections ‖ *oP* and ∞ *P*∞, and by the oblique extinction parallel ∞ *P*∞. The threadlets of orthoclase and sanidine, so often appearing in the ground-mass of rocks, have often a marked similarity to nepheline. |

| NAME. | Chemical composition and reactions. | Specific gravity. | Cleavage. | Ordinary combinations and form of the cross-section. | Twins. | Optical orientation. | Character and strength of double-refraction. | Direction of extinction. |
|---|---|---|---|---|---|---|---|---|
| *b. Sanidine* | | | As above; crystals *furrowed*. | Sanidine in minute, long, narrow threads, as microlites, or large crystals, never in grains. Form of cross-sections parallel $oP$ and $\infty P\infty$ long and thread-like; parallel $\infty P\infty$ distorted hexagons whose sides correspond to $oP . \infty P . \infty P\infty$. In columnar types of the crystals: rectangular sections if at right angles to $oP . \infty P\infty$; octagonal if besides these also $2P\infty$ is present. (See Fig. 83.) | Twinning-plane = $oP$. (See Fig. 28.) Cross-sections of twins: *a*. In the Carlsbad twins the rectangular sections at right angles $\infty P\infty$ divided into halves parallel to the edges $oP/\infty P\infty$ and $\infty P/\infty P\infty$. *b*. In the Baveno twins the quadratic sections at right angles $\infty P\infty$ are divided into halves by the diagonals. | Parallel $\infty P\infty$: $b = b$ $a : \mathfrak{a}$ equals 5°. | | |

# TABLES FOR DETERMINING MINERALS.

| Polarization-colors. | Color and power of refracting light. | Pleochroism. | Structure. | Association. | Inclosures. | Decomposition. | Occurrence. | Remarks. |
|---|---|---|---|---|---|---|---|---|
| | Sanidine is always *colorless*, *clear as water*. $\beta\rho = 1.5237$. | | Sanidine in large crystals I. O. and minute threads II.O. in eruptive rocks. The large crystals are often crumbled or fused, and with an exceedingly beautiful zonal structure, seen particularly well. i. p. p. i. Inclosures are common, arranged in zones. | Sanidine like orthoclase; besides with augite, nepheline, and leucite, never with muscovite. | Sanidine generally *very rich in inclosures*, especially *vitreous inclosures*, generally zonally disposed, augite-microlites, apatite needles. | Almost always fresh, rarely opaque. In andesites and trachytes a decomposition into opal. | Essential primary constituent of the trachytes, rhyolites, phonolites, and the glasses of the orthoclase rocks; accessory in nearly all of the *younger* plagioclase rocks. | and certain melilites. The isotrope hexagonal transverse sections are wanting on orthoclase. Grains of orthoclase in isotrope sections are easily distinguished from quartz by the condenser, as in orthoclase cross-sections one of the optic axes is visible. Orthoclase is distinguished from plagioclase by the optical orientation and absence of the polysynthetic striation. |

168   DETERMINATION OF ROCK-FORMING MINERALS.

bb. Plane of Optic Axes | $\infty P \infty$;

| Name. | Chemical composition and reactions. | Specific gravity. | Cleavage. | Ordinary combinations and form of the cross-section. | Twins. | Optical orientation. | Character and strength of double-refraction. | Direction of extinction. |
|---|---|---|---|---|---|---|---|---|
| 1. Monoclinic Augite Group. | | (3.17-3.41) | | | | | | |
| a. *Ordinary* *and* *basaltic* *Augite.* | $RSiO_3$ $R = Mg$, Ca, Fe, and $Fe_2O_3$ and $Al_2O_3$. Mixture of Ca Mg $Si_2O_6$ + Ca Fe $Si_2O_6$ + Mg $Al_2SiO_6$. (Tschermak.) $Fe$-rich augites. Not attacked by acids. | 3.34-3.38. | Eminent $\infty P$. | Rarely in grains; in crystals: $\infty P \cdot \infty P \infty$, $\infty P \infty \cdot P$, and sometimes $P \infty \cdot oP$ and $-P$. $\infty P = 87°6'$. Sections at right angles to the *c*-axis are octagonal, with evident prismatic cleavage. The longitudinal sections distorted hexagonally with the *c*-axis parallel to the cleavage-fissures. Also rectangular parallel $\infty P \infty$; often a rhomb. (See Fig. 84.) | Very common. Twinning-plane $\infty P \infty$, also in polysynthetic twins. (See Figs. 24 and 25.) More rarely penetration-twins after: twinning-plane a face $-P \infty$; or after: twinning-plane a face $P 2$. | A.P.$\|\infty P\infty$; the r. M. $= c$ is wanting *in the obtuse angle β*, $b = b$ (See Fig. 10.) The positive axial angle, as in the rhombic augites, decreases with the iron present. Sections at right angles to the *c*-axis and parallel $\infty P \infty$ show with condenser one optic axis exactly in the centre of the field. | Positive, strong. | In sections parallel $\infty P \infty$ $c : c =$ about 39°. Varies from 39° to 54°. a : to edge $oP/\infty P\infty$ $= a : a =$ about 22°. Sections $\|b$ have parallel extinction. In sections inclined to $\infty P \infty$ $c : c$ decreases to 0° parallel $\infty P \infty$. |

## TABLES FOR DETERMINING MINERALS.

**Eminent Cleavage after $\infty P = 87°$.**

| Polarization-colors. | Color and power of refracting light. | Pleochroism. | Structure. | Association. | Inclosures. | Decomposition. | Occurrence. | Remarks. |
|---|---|---|---|---|---|---|---|---|
| *Very brilliant*, especially in the light-colored, yellow to red. | In sections *green to brown*, often violet to brown in the basalts. The same crystal often shows several colors. (Comp. "structure.") $\beta\rho = 1.69$. | *Generally very feeble*, yet augite is strongly pleochroitic as in the phonolites and then resembles hornblende. Absorption feeble $c > a > b$. $a$ about $= b$. | In large crystals I. O. and columns in microlites II. O. The first very commonly show a zonal structure, e.g. with brown layers which in turn are often again composed of numberless thin layers. As a consequence of this varying constitution of both core and layers, optical differences, as in directions of extinction and polarization-colors, are frequent. (See Fig. 45.) As with orthoclase, the successive layers in twins of augite run equally and unimpeded through both individuals. Augites often show the so-called "hour-glass" formation where sections $\perp \infty P \infty$ divide into four fields of which each two lying opposite extinguish at the same instant. (See Figs. 46 and 47.) Augite crystals are often fused, also commonly separated into large aggregates, the so-called "augite-eyes," or needles radially grouped. | Principally with plagioclase, nepheline, leucite, with or without olivine and biotite. Rarely with orthoclase, hornblende, and quartz. | Vitreous inclosures are common, as are also gas-pores and apatite needles. Rarely with Magnetite. | Augite crystals are commonly decomposed into a product of chloritic material, calcite, ferric hydrate, epidote, and quartz. Perfect pseudomorphs of one or more of these minerals after augite are common.— Into opal.— More rarely the metamorphosis into hornblende (uralitizing) wherein the form of augite remains with hornblendic cleavage. Finally the rare metamorphosis into serpentine, with formation of talc and chlorite. | As essential primary constituent in many younger prophyritic eruptive rocks: diabases, melaphyrs, augite-andesites, and all basaltic rocks; also common in andesites, trachytes, phonolites. Rare and in larger grains in the older granular eruptive rocks, and in crystalline schists. | Easily distinguished from other optically-biaxial minerals by the important oblique extinction $c : c$ and prismatic clearage with angle of 87°; especially in transverse sections; more difficult when granular; in sections inclined to the $c$-axis the cleavage-angle approaches that of hornblende. Easily distinguished from epidote by the color, direction of extinction, relief, and polarization-colors. If augite is perfectly colorless, the polarization-colors are very brilliant and resemble olivine. |

| Name. | Chemical composition and reactions. | Specific gravity. | Cleavage. | Ordinary combinations and form of the cross-section. | Twins. | Optical orientation. | Character and strength of double-refraction. | Direction of extinction. |
|---|---|---|---|---|---|---|---|---|
| b. Diallage. | See augite. | 3.23–3.34. | $\infty P$ (87°) concentrically arranged after $\infty P\infty$. | Rarely in clearly-defined crystals, mostly in large tabular or granular individuals, fibrous parallel to the $c$-axis. | $\| \infty P\infty$ polysynthetic; not rarely after $oP$. | | See augite. | |
| c. Omphacite. | See augite. Rich in $Al_2O_3$. | 3.3. | See augite, also separation $\| \infty P\infty$, yet not so perfect as in diallage. | Only in grains | Rare. | | See augite. | |
| d. Diopside. | More CaO than MgO, poor in $Al_2O_3$. Mixture of $CaMgSi_2O_6$ and $CaFeSi_2O_6$. (Tschermak.) | 3.3. | ditto. | ditto. | ditto. | ditto. | ditto. | ditto. |
| e. Sahlite. | Pale green augite, poor in Fe. | 3.2–3.3. | Separation after $oP$ together with cleavage after $\infty P$ and $\infty P\infty$. | In grains and long columns with separation at right angles to the longest axis; generally without terminal planes. Cross-sections resemble augite. | ditto. | ditto. | ditto. | ditto. |

# TABLES FOR DETERMINING MINERALS.

| Polarization-colors. | Color and power of refracting light. | Pleochroism. | Structure. | Association. | Inclosures. | Decomposition. | Occurrence. | Remarks. |
|---|---|---|---|---|---|---|---|---|
| See augite. | Greenish brown. | Very feeble. | Occurs only in large irregular grains. A great similarity in structure to bronzite especially as regards inclosures, separating into fibres, and twinnings. Often interpenetrated with ordinary augite, hornblende, or mica. Rare in crystals. | With plagioclase, ordinary augite, olivine, hornblende. Rarely with quartz. | As in bronzite. Inclosures of brown leaflets of göthite parallel $\infty P\infty$, otherwise poor in inclosures. | Formation of uralite common, in that diallage changes at the ends into dark green, strongly pleochroitic, hornblende fibres. Into viridite; into serpentine with formation of chlorite and talc. | Primary constituent. Common in gabbro, norite, rare in porphyritic, eruptive rocks. In serpentine and olivine-fels. Rare in crystalline schists. | Often resembles bronzite. Easily distinguished from it on sections or cleavage-leaves $]\infty P\infty$; i. c. p. l. appearance of one optic axis. |
| ditto. | Grass-green. | See augite. | Only known in fresh grains poor in inclosures; often interpenetrated with hornblende. Often enveloped by surrounding grains. | With quartz, hornblende, garnet, zoisite, disthene, rutile. | Rare. Fluid inclosures and needles of rutile. | | *In eclogites* and amphibolites. | See augite. They are distinguished from: *augite* by the paler color (small amount of Fe) and by the crystalline form; *diallage* by the lack of the perfect separation after $\infty P\infty$. |
| ditto. | ditto. | ditto. | | With olivine, chromite, diallage, and the rhombic augites. | Very rare. Vitreous inclosures. | | As primary constituent in *olivine-fels* (so-called chromium diopside). Rarely secondary as metamorphic product of garnet. (Pyrope.) | |
| Very brilliant. | Pale green to colorless. Relief marked as a consequence of the powerful refraction of light. | | | With quartz, hornblende, garnet, scapolite, plagioclase, titanite. | | Rarely changed to uralite. | In *crystalline* schists. | |

# DETERMINATION OF ROCK-FORMING MINERALS.

| Name. | Chemical composition and reactions. | Specific gravity. | Cleavage. | Ordinary combinations and form of the cross-section. | Twins. | Optical orientation. | Character and strength of double-refraction. | Direction of extinction. |
|---|---|---|---|---|---|---|---|---|
| f. Acmite. | $Na_2Fe_2Si_4O_{12}$. | 3.53–3.55. | Eminent $\infty P$, 87°; imperfect $\infty P\infty$. | In grains or columns $\infty P$, $\infty P\infty$, $\infty P\infty$, elongated by predominance of faces $\infty P\infty$. | $\infty P\infty$ common. | A.P. ‖ $\infty P\infty$. Large axial angle. Sections or *leaves* ‖ $\infty P\infty$ show a distorted axial *picture of a biaxial mineral*. | See augite. Positive. | $c:c$ = very small *angle* = 2–7°. |
| g. Wollastonite. | $CaSiO_3$ by HCl perfectly *decomposed with separation of amorphous* $SiO_2$. | 2.78–2.91. | Parallel $\infty P\infty$, $oP$, and $P\infty$. | $\infty P$ = 87°. Only in *prisms, irregular, elongated, fibrous*, following the *b*-ortho-axis. | ditto. | A.P. ‖ $\infty P\infty$. Apparent axial angle = about 70°. (Compare Fig. 11.) | Positive. strongly. | $c$ forms with $oP$ towards the front, 32° 12′. $a:c$ = 12°. |

*cc.* **Perfect Cleavage**

| 2. Hornblende Group. a. *Ordinary and basaltic* Hornblende. | $m\,RSiO_3$ + $n\,R_2O_3$. R=Ca, Mg, Fe. $R_2$ = $Al_2$, $Fe_2$. Only those rich in Fe partially attacked by acids. | 3.1–3.3. | Highly eminent $\infty P$, 124° 11′; imperfect $\infty P\infty$ and $\infty P\infty$. | $\infty P$, $\infty P\infty$, and $oP$. $P$ or $P\infty$ almost always in crystals, rarely in grains. Transverse sections generally *hexagonal*, also octagonal, longitudinal sections, as in augite. (Fig. 86.) | ditto. | A.P. ‖ $\infty P\infty$. The 1. M. = $a$ falls in the obtuse angle β, $b = b$ (see Fig. 9). True axial angle about 79°, the positive axial angle becoming larger with increased percentage of iron. Parallel $oP$ and $\infty P\infty$ side appearance of one optic axis on the circumference of field. Feeble dispersion ρ < υ. | Strongly *negative*, yet somewhat feebler than augite. | $c:c$ = about 15°. Varies from 2–18°. $a:c$ = 75°. $a:b$ = 29° 58′. $c:c$ = 13–15° in green hornblendes, and = 11–13° and less in brown. |
| b. Smaragdite. | See uralite. | | | | | | | |

# TABLES FOR DETERMINING MINERALS.

| Polarization-colors. | Color and power of refracting light. | Pleochroism. | Structure. | Association. | Inclosures. | Decomposition. | Occurrence. | Remarks. |
|---|---|---|---|---|---|---|---|---|
| See augite. | Dark brown, dark green. $\beta$ above 1.7. | Rather strong. $c$ dark brown; $a$ brownish green. Absorption $c > b > a$. | In large crystals in the syenites, often with fibrous terminations. In minute crystals of yellow and dark green color in the trachytes and phonolites. | With elæolite, sodalite, microcline, and biotite. | Earthy particles. | | Not rare in *elæolite-syenites, phonolites,* and *trachytes.* | |
| Very brilliant. | Colorless, yellowish white. Relief *marked* | | In aggregates of fibrous individuals in tufts or radially disposed. | With calcite, green augite, granite. | Fluid inclosures. | | As decomposition-product or contact-mineral rare in granular chalks metamorphosed from eruptive rocks. Rare in elæolite-syenites and phonolites. | Resembles tremolite, but distinguishable by the prismatic angle, solubility in acids, and gelatinizing; difficult to distinguish from zeolites as scolecite, e.g. |

$\infty P = 124°$.

| | | | | | | | | |
|---|---|---|---|---|---|---|---|---|
| Less brilliant than in augite; yellow to greenish brown. | Green to brown $\beta\rho = $ 1.62. | Generally very strong. $a = $ yellow-green or honey-yellow; $b = $ yellow-brown; $c = $ black or greenish brown. Absorption $c > b > a$. | In large *crystals or grains* I. O. More rarely in small crystals and microlites II.O. The green hornblendes are often fibrous; the brown often beautifully developed in zones. The brown hornblende of the younger eruptive rocks often shows a broad opaque margin (see Fig. 44), or pseudomorphs of augite and magnetite after hornblende occur. The green hornblendes are often interpenetrated with augite. | With orthoclase, plagioclase, quartz, biotite; more rarely with augite and olivine. With omphacite, garnet, zoisite, rutile. | Poor in inclosures. Fluid inclosures, glass, gas-pores, earthy particles, apatite needles. | Becomes finely fibrous and bleached through decomposition into epidote, calcite, ferric hydroxide, then often surrounded by a wreath of magnetite; always as augite. Metamorphoses into biotite, chlorite. | Primary essential constituent. In granular and porphyritic eruptive rocks: syenite, diorite (green hornblende), porphyrite, trachyte (brown, more rarely green, hornblende). Accessory in basalts(brown H.), rare and in olivine-fels (green H.). Common in crystalline schists(green, more rarely brown, H.). As essential constituent in amphibolite, hornblendic schists, certain gneisses, eclogite (so-called smaragdite). | Easily distinguished from: *augite* by the prismatic cleavage-angle, slight inclination of $c : c$, and powerful pleochroism; *biotite* on sections at right angles to the vertical axis. In biotite the cleavage and powerful dichroism is wanting in such sections ($\parallel oP$). |

# DETERMINATION OF ROCK-FORMING MINERALS.

| Name. | Chemical composition and reactions. | Specific gravity. | Cleavage. | Ordinary combinations and form of the cross-section. | Twins. | Optical orientation. | Character and strength of double-refraction. | Direction of extinction. |
|---|---|---|---|---|---|---|---|---|
| c. Actinolite and | $CaMg_3Si_4O_{12} + CaFe_3Si_4O_{12}$ *Al-free Fe-poor* (Tschermak). $\overline{RSiO_3}$ R = predominating Mg, less Ca, and a little Fe. | 3.026–3.160 | As above; separation at right angles to the *c*-axis. | *Long prisms*, generally without terminations $\infty P, \infty P\infty$. | Rare. | See Hornblende. | | $c : c$ generally 15°. |
| d. Tremolite. | $3MgSiO_3 + CaSiO_3$. MgO predominating. *Unattacked* by acids. | 2.93–3. | $\infty P$ like hornblende. Separation at right angles to the *c*-axis. | $\infty P, \infty P\infty$ generally in long narrow prisms. | Rare. Like hornblende. | See hornblende. | | $c : c = 15°$. |
| e. Arfvedsonite. | $Na_2(Fe)_2Si_4O_{12}$. Insoluble in acids. | 3.33–3.59 | $\infty P$ like hornblende. | In large grains. | | See hornblende. | | |
| f. Glaucophane (Gastaldite). | $Na_2(Al)_2Si_4O_{12}$. *Contains Ca, Mg, Fe*. Nearly unattacked by acids. | 3.1. | Like hornblende. Separation at right angles to the *c*-axis | Elongated prisms, generally without terminal planes. | | See hornblende. | | $c : c = 6\frac{1}{2}$ –7°. |
| g. Uralite (Smaragdite in part). | Like ordinary green hornblendes. | 3.1–3.3. | Like *hornblende;* often, however, showing in addition the augite-cleavage quite perfectly. | See "Structure;" single fibres show $\infty P$ = about 124°. Part *in the form of augite* or in *irregular large grains.* | | See hornblende. | | |

# TABLES FOR DETERMINING MINERALS.

| Polarization-colors. | Color and power of refracting light. | Pleochroism. | Structure. | Association. | Inclosures. | Decomposition. | Occurrence. | Remarks. |
|---|---|---|---|---|---|---|---|---|
| See hornblende. | *Light to dark green.* | c dark green, a yellowish green, feebler than in the hornblendes, generally only in green tints. c > b > a. | Generally occurring in *long narrow needles* or grains, often fibrous at the termination. | With quartz, mica, chlorite, rutile. | Very poor. | Often perfect pseudomorphs of biotite, chlorite, and ferric hydroxide after actinolite are observed. | Rather common in certain non-feldspathic crystalline schists, in talcose, mica-chloritic schists, in serpentines. | Distinguished from ordinary green hornblende by chemical means; actinolite always occurs in long columns, not like hornblende in short crystals. |
| Very brilliant. | *Colorless*, relief marked. | | In long columns, the termination often in sheaf-like fibres; in tufted aggregates, rarely in grains. | With calcite; with olivine, hornblende, diallage. | Very poor. | Into calcite and talc. | As contact-mineral in limestones; as primary constituent (also rarely secondary) in crystalline schists and serpentines. | Compare wollastonite. |
| See hornblende. | *Blue-green.* | Very strong. | In irregular, often fibrous grains and long columnar individuals. | With orthoclase, microcline, elæolite, sodalite. | | | Rarely in elæolite rocks. | Distinguished from hornblende by chemical composition and color. |
| See hornblende. | *Indigo-, lavender-blue.* | Very strong. a = white, b = violet-blue, c = dark blue. Absorption c > b > a. | Mostly in long fibrous needles, often interpenetrated with green hornblende. | With quartz, hornblende, garnet, zoisite, chlorite, omphacite, rutile, titanite. | Rutile needles and gas-pores are common. | | Rare in crystalline schists, eclogites, amphibolites, mica and chlorite schists. | |
| Generally aggregate polarization, as the separate hornblende threads have not the same optical orientation. | Dark to *light green.* | Partly strong, partly weak. | Finely-fibrous decomposition-product of *augite* and *diallage*, often of the form of augite and with remnants of the augite or diallage yet fresh. The fibres show the prismatic angle of hornblende. (See Fig. 85.) | With plagioclase, olivine, diallage, augite. | | | In gabbros and serpentines; in augitic porphyries. | Compare with diallage and ordinary hornblende. An ordinary green hornblende occurring in eclogite was also called *smaragdite*. |

176   DETERMINATION OF ROCK-FORMING MINERALS.

*dd.* CLEAVAGE ∥ $oP$ AND $\infty \breve{P} \infty$

| Name. | Chemical composition and reactions. | Specific gravity. | Cleavage. | Ordinary combinations and form of the cross-section | Twins. | Optical orientation. | Character and strength of double-refraction. | Direction of extinction. |
|---|---|---|---|---|---|---|---|---|
| Epidote. | $H_2Ca_4(R_2)_3$ $Si_6O_{26}$ $(R_2 = (Al_2)$ $(Fe_2)$. Slightly attacked by HCl. | 3.32–3.5. | *Highly eminent* ∥ $oP$, and *perfect* $\infty \breve{P} \infty$ forming an angle of 115° 24′. | Generally very small prisms, elongated *in the direction of ortho-diagonal axis*, the combination $\infty P$. $oP$, $\breve{P}\infty$, $\infty\breve{P}\infty$ predominating. (See Fig. 89.) The *longitudinal sections* parallel $\infty\breve{P}\infty$ are *hexagonal*. The transverse sections at right angles to $c$ and sections parallel $oP$; $\infty\breve{P}\infty$ are long and narrow, rectangular or hexagonal, with one pair of sides longer; in grains. | Rare microscopically. Twinning plane $\infty P\infty$. (See Figs. 26 and 88.) | A.P. ∥ $\infty \breve{P}\infty$ at right angles to the elongation of the crystal. $b = \bar{b}$, 1. M. = a nearly coinciding with $c$. Sections ∥ $\infty \breve{P}\infty$ show a biaxial interference-figure, as the 2. M. is at nearly right angles. (See Fig. 87.) | Strongly negative. | $a : c =$ 2° 10′ $c : a =$ 27° 47′ $= c : oP$. |

*ee.* CLEAVAGE IMPERFECT $\infty \breve{P}$ OR

| Titanite. | $CaSiTiO_5$; contains FeO. Decomposed by $H_2SO_4$; $TiO_2$ dissolved with formation of gypsum. | 3.4–3.6. | $\infty P$ 133° 52′, $\breve{P}\infty$ 113° 30′, imperfect. | Mostly crystals: $\infty P$, $oP$, ½$\breve{P}\infty$; ½$\breve{P}\infty$ or ¾$P_2$ prominent with $oP$, $\breve{P}\infty$, ½$\breve{P}\infty$. $\breve{P}\infty$, or in *acute wedge-shaped grains*. Such are characteristic *crystal cross-sections*. (See Fig. 90.) | Rather common; contact- or penetration-twins; twinning-plane = $oP$. (See Fig. 27.) | A.P. ∥ $\infty \breve{P}\infty$ 1. M. = $\bar{c}$ at nearly right angles to ½$\breve{P}\infty$; *very strong dispersion* of the axes. $\rho > v$. (See Fig. 13.) | Strongly positive. | $a : c =$ 39° 17′ $\bar{a} : \bar{b} =$ 21°. |

# TABLES FOR DETERMINING MINERALS. 177

ANGLE 115°.

| Polarization-colors. | Color and power of refracting light. | Pleochroism. | Structure. | Association. | Inclosures. | Decomposition. | Occurrence. | Remarks. |
|---|---|---|---|---|---|---|---|---|
| Very brilliant, yellow to red. | *Lemon-yellow, yellowish green* very marked. Relief very marked. $\beta = 1.72-1.75$. | Rather *powerful* in the *thicker prisms*. $\mathfrak{a}$ = very pale yellow, $\mathfrak{b}$ = brown to yellowish green, $\mathfrak{c}$ = green to lemon-yellow. Absorption $\mathfrak{b} > \mathfrak{c} > \mathfrak{a}$. | Generally in long minute prisms, lying in chloritic matter, or in pseudomorphs, more rarely in grains. | With quartz, orthoclase, plagioclase, hornblende, biotite, augite with chlorite. | Very poor. Fluid inclosures. |  | Secondary mineral. Common as decomposition product of the feldspars, hornblende, biotite, more rarely of augite, in eruptive rocks and crystalline schists bearing these minerals, also often as primary constituent in the latter. | Similar to augite, distinguished from it by the even parallel extinction in sections parallel to the longest development (= $b$-axis) and slight inclination of $\mathfrak{a} : \mathfrak{c}$. The yellow color, powerful refraction of light, and brilliant polarization-colors are characteristic for epidote. |

$p\infty$; ACUTE WEDGE-SHAPED CROSS-SECTIONS.

| Feeble, gray—i.e. like original color; much weaker than augite and hornblende. $\beta\rho = 1.905$. Relief *very* marked. | *Pale yellow, reddish brown* to colorless. | Rather strong in the darker colored varieties. $\mathfrak{a}$ = reddish brown. $\mathfrak{c}$ = greenish yellow. $\mathfrak{c} > \mathfrak{b} > \mathfrak{a}$. Weaker than in the hornblendes. | *Rough surface of section* is characteristic for titanite. Commonly associated and interpenetrated with augite and hornblende. One of the minerals first formed in the eruptive rocks. | With orthoclase, plagioclase, hornblende, augite, biotite, chlorite, quartz, and other accessory minerals. | Very poor. | Rarely pseudomorphs of calcite after titanite. | As *primary* accessory constituent in eruptive rocks. Granite (rarely), syenite, phonolite, leucitophyr, elæolite-syenite, trachyte, mica- and hornblende-andesite, diorite and in crystalline, especially hornblendic schists. Secondary as decomposition-product of ilmenite and titaniferous magnetite. | Easily recognizable by the almost constant wedge-shaped cross-sections, powerful refraction of light, and rough surface. |

| Name. | Chemical composition and reactions. | Specific gravity. | Cleavage. | Ordinary combinations and form of the cross-section. | Twins. | Optical orientation. | Character and strength of double-refraction. | Direction of extinction. |
|---|---|---|---|---|---|---|---|---|
| Gypsum. | $CaSO_4 + 2H_2O$. Difficultly soluble in acids. | 2.2–2.4. | *Highly eminent clino-diagonal*, perfect according to $-P$. | In granules or *elongated prismatic individuals*, crystals $\infty P . \infty P \infty$. $-P$. | Very rare in *microscopic* individuals. | A.P. $\| \infty P \infty$. I. M. $=$ a. One optic axis nearly $\perp \infty P \infty$. One forms 83° with $c$, the other 22°. | Strongly *negative*. | $a : c =$ 52° 30'. $c : c =$ 37° 30'. |

## II. b. 3. Minerals Crystallizing

### α. Long Columnar Crystals, Colorless or of a Blue Color.

| Disthene. (Cyanite.) | $Al_2SiO_5$ Acids have no action. | 3.48–3.68. | *Highly eminent* $\| \infty P \infty$, perfect $\infty P \infty$, and parallel $oP$. (*Gleit-fläche.*) | Grains, or *elongated prisms*, $\infty P \infty$, $\infty P \infty$ predominating. $\infty P \infty$ with an angle of 106° 15', rarely with terminal planes. Transverse sections rectangular or hexagonal if $\infty 'P$ or $\infty P'$ is added to the above combination. | Common; *more rarely* on microscopic individuals. Twinning plane either: 1. $\infty P \infty$ repeated; 2. At right angles to the $c$-axis; 3. At right angles to the $b$-axis; 4. Parallel $oP$, caused by pressure, and repeated. | A.P. forms with the edge $\infty P \infty : oP$ an angle of 30°; with $\infty P \infty : oP$ an angle 60° 15', and like the I. M. $=$ a is at right angles to $\infty P \infty$. (See Fig. 16.) Large axial angle, about 80°. Feeble dispersion of the axes, $v < p$. In sections parallel $\infty P \infty$ a biaxial interference-figure with negative middle line is visible. | Rather strongly *negative*. | In sections parallel $\infty P \infty$ $c : c =$ 30°. |

# TABLES FOR DETERMINING MINERALS.

| Polarization-colors. | Color and power of refracting light. | Pleochroism. | Structure. | Association. | Inclosures. | Decomposition. | Occurrence. | Remarks. |
|---|---|---|---|---|---|---|---|---|
| Very brilliant. *Iridescent*. | *Colorless*, secondary, often colored by iron compounds. | | In minute granules, and tangled or parallel fibrous aggregates of needles. Rarely in crystals. | Rarely with clastic constituents as quartz granules or mica leaflets. | Fluid inclosures. | | As *simple rock*, granular or compact. | |

## in the Triclinic System.

**OR GRAINS. CLEAVAGE** $\infty \bar{P} \infty$ , $\infty P \infty$ **AND** $oP$.

| Exceedingly brilliant. | *Colorless*, *azure-blue*, often spotted. $\beta\rho = 1.72$. Relief marked. | If blue rather *strongly* pleochroitic, especially parallel $\infty \bar{P} \infty$, $\mathfrak{c} =$ blue. $\mathfrak{a} =$ white. | In long prisms or irregular grains, traversed by number less fissures parallel or at right angles to the chief axis, often irregularly or completely colored blue. Rarely in aggregates of thin needles or filaments; the needles cracked and broken at right angles to the chief axis. | With quartz, mica, garnet, omphacite, hornblende, rarely with orthoclase. | Very poor; fluid inclosures. | Rare. Surrounded by a marginal zone of a brownish, finely fibrous, felt-like decomposition-product. | Rare. Primary accessory constituent in crystalline schists, granulite, eclogite, and especially in many micaceous schists. | If colorless, it is often difficult to distinguish from sillimanite, with which it commonly occurs; only possible by the determination of the position of the axes of elasticity. |

## β. Broad Tabular Crystals or Grains,

| Name. | Chemical composition and reactions. | Specific gravity. | Cleavage. | Ordinary combinations and form of the cross-section. | Twins. | Optical orientation. | Character and strength of double-refraction. | Direction of extinction. |
|---|---|---|---|---|---|---|---|---|
| Triclinic Feldspars. 1. Potassium Feldspar. Microcline. (Microperthite, so-called fibrous orthoclase.) | See *orthoclase*. | 2.54– 2.57 (2.56). | Highly eminent ‖ $oP$. Eminent parallel $\infty \check{P} \infty$, $\infty' P$, $\infty P'$. | Very similar to orthoclase, $\infty \check{P} \infty . oP . \infty' P . \infty P'$ predominating. | Rare. Countless *thin lamellæ of orthoclase are developed parallel to $\infty \check{P} \infty$ and at right angles to it, so that in sections parallel oP a latticed interpenetration of two systems of striations is visible, which is exceedingly characteristic for microcline.* Besides, lenticular lamellæ and irregular lines of polysynthetic twinned *albite* are so interpenetrated that the $oP$-planes of both species of plagioclase fall in one plane. (See Figs. 91–93.) | A. P. at right angles to $oP$; its cross-section with $\infty \check{P} \infty$ forms with the obtuse edge $oP . \infty \check{P} \infty$ 5–6° in the obtuse angle *dc*. Cleavage-leaflets parallel $\infty \check{P} \infty$ show one of the optic axes more clearly; the axial plane is somewhat inclined to the plane $\infty \check{P} \infty$. | Rather strongly negative. In leaflets parallel $\infty \check{P} \infty$; positive double-refraction. | c with the normal to $\infty \check{P} \infty =$ 15° 26'; a cleavage-leaflet parallel $oP$ *does not therefore extinguish parallel like orthoclase*, but gives an extinction to the edge $oP : \infty \check{P} \infty$ = $+15$–16°; parallel $\infty \check{P} \infty$ = $+4$–5°. |

# TABLES FOR DETERMINING MINERALS. 181

COLORLESS. CLEAVAGE PARALLEL $oP$ AND $\infty \breve{P} \infty$.

| Polarization-colors. | Color and power of refracting light. | Pleochroism. | Structure. | Association. | Inclosures. | Decomposition. | Occurrence. | Remarks. |
|---|---|---|---|---|---|---|---|---|
| Exceedingly brilliant. | *Colorless*. Relief not so marked as in orthoclase. | | In rocks only in grains; commonly interpenetrated with quartz, like graphic-granite, also with sodalite and elæolite. Compare the twinning development. An orthoclase or feldspar corresponding to microcline was called *microperthite;* this contains countless exceedingly thin lamellæ of a triclinic feldspar closely related to albite, which can be especially well observed in sections parallel $\infty \breve{P} \infty$, or $\infty \breve{P} \infty$, as spindle-shaped cross-sections. (See Fig. 93.) | *a.* With orthoclase, elæolite, sodalite, augite, and hornblende. *b.* With quartz, orthoclase, biotite, hornblende, muscovite. *c.* With these and garnet, cyanite. | Generally very poor; of minerals; hornblende, biotite, zircon, apatite. | Fibrous decomposition with opacity as in orthoclase. | As primary essential constituent with orthoclase in: *a.* Elæolite-syenite; *b.* In different granites, especially graphic-granite; and *c.* In crystalline schists (as microperthite, also called fibrous orthoclase), especially in granulite and gneisses. | Distinguished from: *orthoclase* by the oblique extinction on $oP$, and the interpenetration of twins; *the other triclinic feldspars* by the latticed structure (interpenetration of twins) parallel $oP$ and optical properties. |

182     DETERMINATION OF ROCK-FORMING MINERALS.

| Name. | Chemical composition and reactions. | Specific gravity. | Cleavage. | Ordinary combinations and form of the cross-section. | Twins. | Optical orientation. | Character and strength of double-refraction. | Direction of extinction. |
|---|---|---|---|---|---|---|---|---|
| 2. Plagioclase, Calcium-Sodium Feldspars: *a.* Albite (and oligoclase albite). | Ab. $Na_2Al_2Si_6O_{16}$ with traces of Ca and K, 1–2%. Not attacked by acids. $SiO_2 = 68\%$. $Ab_8An_1$. | 2.61– 2.63 (2.62). | Eminent parallel $oP$ and $\infty\check{P}\infty$; imperfect $\infty\bar{P}$ and $P_l$. Right edges $of$ : $\infty\check{P}\infty = 93° 36'$. | $\infty\check{P}\infty$, $oP$. $\infty'P, \infty\bar{P}$. $P_l\infty$, $P_l$ very similar to orthoclase. (See Fig. 94.) | Almost always twinned. 1. Albite law. *Twinning-plane* $\infty\check{P}\infty$ and generally *polysynthetic;* therefore in sections from the zone $of':\infty\bar{P}\infty$ the single individuals *appear as fine lamellæ with varied polarization-colors.* Only those sections *parallel* $\infty\check{P}\infty$ show *no* twinning-striations. Two such polysynthetically-twinned albite individuals are often again combined according to the Carlsbad orthoclase twinning-law. 2. Pericline law. *Twins according to the law: axis of rotation the b-axis.* *composition plane* the rhombic section, i.e., *the plane so cutting the rhomboidal prism* $\infty'P$. $\infty P'$ *that the plane angles which these planes form with* $\infty\check{P}\infty$ *are equal to each other.* The twinning-edge hereby forms with the edge $oP$. $\infty\check{P}\infty$ an angle of 13–22°. Such twins are often again united after the Manebach orthoclase law. Also $oP$ as composition plane. *By combining both laws* (1 *and* 2) *a latticed structure* i. p. p. l. is observed in sections inclined to $\infty\check{P}\infty$, *recalling that of microcline.* Compare Figs. 29 and 30. | A. P. forms with the *c*-axis an angle of 96° 16', with the normal to $\infty\bar{P}\infty$ an angle of 16° 17'. 1.M. = t. Dispersion feeble $\rho < v$; large axial angle. Cleavage-leaflets parallel $\infty\check{P}\infty$ show quite complete distorted interference-figure (appearance of the positive middle line perpendicular to $\infty\check{P}\infty$); yet, because of the large axial angle, in the position of 45° the hyperbolas do not lie in the field. c inclined to the sharp edge $oP : \infty\check{P}\infty$. (See Fig. 97.) | Rather strongly positive. | On cleavage pieces: *parallel* $oP$ *the obliqueness of extinction to the edge* $oP$ : $\infty\check{P}\infty = +3° 54'$ to $+4° 51'$ $(+4° 30')$; *parallel* $\infty\check{P}\infty$ also = $+15°33'$ to $+20°$ $(+19°)$. |

# TABLES FOR DETERMINING MINERALS.

| Polarization-colors. | Color and power of refracting light. | Pleochroism. | Structure. | Association. | Inclosures. | Decomposition. | Occurrence. | Remarks. |
|---|---|---|---|---|---|---|---|---|
| For the most part very brilliant. Not so powerful as in quartz; in very thin sections feeble, blue-green. | Colorless, clear as water. Relief feebly defined. $\beta\rho = 1.537$. | | In large grains, rarely in crystals; often inter-penetrated with orthoclase and quartz. Compare microcline. In eruptive rocks as thin fibres. | With calcite, quartz, mica, and orthoclase; chlorite, more rarely with hornblende. | Very poor; fluid inclosures. | Rarely decomposed. Fibrous, opaque decomposition. See oligoclase. | Common in *granular limestones*. In *crystalline schists*, in many semi-crystalline *gneisses*, phyllites, sericite-schists. Rare in eruptive rocks, in grains in diorite, in fibres in many andesites and porphyries. | The polysynthetic twinning after $\infty P\infty$ is peculiar to all plagioclase, and is exceedingly characteristic for them. The triclinic feldspars can be distinguished from each other accurately only by chemical analysis or by determination of the obliqueness of extinction on $oP$ and $\infty P\infty$ on cleavage-pieces from grains or larger crystals. It is therefore impossible to specify with accuracy the minute plagioclase threads occurring in the ground-mass of the eruptive rocks; one can at best determine, by measuring the obliqueness of extinction in sections, whether they belong to a plagioclase approximating albite or anorthite in composition. |

| Name. | Chemical composition and reactions. | Specific gravity. | Cleavage. | Ordinary combinations and form of cross-section. | Twins. | Optical orientation. | Character and strength of double-refraction. | Direction of extinction. |
|---|---|---|---|---|---|---|---|---|
| b. Oligoclase. | $SiO_2$ = 62–66. per cent. But little K. = $Ab_5An_1$ to $Ab_3An_1$. | 2.62–2.65. (2.63.) | Most perfect $\|oP$, also after $\infty \check{P} \infty$ like albite. $oP$. $\infty \check{P} \infty$ right = 93° 28'. | See albite. | Always polysynthetic twinning according to the *Albite law;* also according to the *Pericline law.* | Very similar to albite. In cleavage-planes parallel $\infty \check{P} \infty$ the axial points lie still farther beyond the field than in albite. c is inclined to the obtuse edge $oP : \infty \check{P} \infty$. (See Fig. 98.) | See albite. | Parallel $oP$ to the edge $oP : \infty \check{P} \infty$ = + 1° 10' ($Ab_3An_1$ = + 1° 4'); parallel $\infty \check{P} \infty$ to the edge $oP : \infty \check{P} \infty$ = 2–4°, ($Ab_3An_1$ = 4° 36'). |
| c. Andesine. | $Ab_3An_1$ to $Ab_1An_1$. | 2.65. | ditto. | ditto. | See albite. | Similar to oligoclase, yet with the axial plane more strongly inclined (above 15°) to the obtuse edge $oP : \infty \check{P} \infty$. Dispersion $\rho < v$. | ditto. | Parallel $oP$ to the edge $oP : \infty \check{P} \infty$ − 1° 57' to − 2° 19'; parallel $\infty \check{P} \infty$ − 4° 50' to − 8°. |

# TABLES FOR DETERMINING MINERALS.

| Polarization-colors. | Color and power of refracting light. | Pleochroism. | Structure. | Association. | Inclosures. | Decomposition. | Occurrence. | Remarks. |
|---|---|---|---|---|---|---|---|---|
| See albite. | Colorless, clear as water or clouded, white, grayish white. | | In large grains or crystals I. O, and as minute, elongated, and narrow threads (cross-sections of thin tablets). Zonal development (see Fig. 102) and zonally disposed inclosures. Almost always twinned polysynthetically. Twinning and concentric development occurred simultaneously as in orthoclase. | With orthoclase, hornblende, biotite, augite, olivine. | Fluid inclosures rare, and vitreous inclosures common in the younger eruptive rocks, augite- and apatite-microlites. | Generally fresh in the younger eruptive rocks, in the older fibrous and clouded. Metamorphosis into epidote called saussurite; into muscovite similar to orthoclase; observed also in nearly all plagioclase. | As primary essential or accessory constituent in eruptive rocks, granite, diorite, diabase, gabbro, trachyte, andesite, also basalts, and in crystalline schists, e g. gneiss. | See albite. |
| ditto. | ditto. | | See oligoclase. (Comp. Fig. 102.) | With sanidine, orthoclase, augite, hornblende, biotite, quartz. | ditto. | Mostly fresh. | As primary essential constituent in tonalite. (quartz-diorite), in andesites, especially dacites and augite-andesites, porphyrites, syenites, also in crystalline schists. | ditto. |

185

# DETERMINATION OF ROCK-FORMING MINERALS.

| NAME. | Chemical composition and reactions. | Specific gravity. | Cleavage. | Ordinary combinations and form of the cross-section. | Twins. | Optical orientation. | Character and strength of double-refraction. | Direction of extinction. |
|---|---|---|---|---|---|---|---|---|
| *d.* Labradorite. | $Ab_1An_1$ to $Ab_1An_3$. $SiO_2 =$ 55.5 — 49 per cent. Decomposable by HCl. | 2.68 -2.70 (2.69). | See orthoclase; often change of color on $\infty \bar{P}\infty$. | Mostly in large grains; rarely in crystals; as orthoclase. | The albite and pericline laws combined are common. The individuals twinned $\|\infty \bar{P}\infty$ again twinned after the Carlsbad law or according to $\infty \bar{P}\infty$ or $oP$. See structure. | In planes $\|\infty \bar{P}\infty$ (right) a side appearance of one optic axis and indication of the lemniscates; axial point invisible; parallel $oP$ side appearance of the other axis, the axial point also invisible. *Dispersion* $\rho > v$. (See Fig. 99, *a* and *b*.) | Like orthoclase. | On $oP =$ $- 4° 30'$ to $- 6° 54'$ ($Ab_1An_1$ $= -- 5°$ 10'); on $\infty \bar{P}\infty =$ $- 16° 40'$ to $- 21° 12'$ ($Ab_1An_1$ $= - 16°$). |
| *e.* Bytownite. | $Ab_1An_3$ to $An$. $SiO_2 =$ 49–45 per cent. More easily soluble in HCl than *d*. | 2.70 -2.73 (2.71). | | Like labradorite. | | Similar to labradorite. Cleavage-leaflets $\|oP$ and $\infty \bar{P}\infty$ show the side appearance of one optic axis, the axial point not falling within the field. Dispersion $\rho > v$. (See Fig. 100, *a* and *b*.) | Like labradorite. | *Parallel* $oP =$ $- 14.5°$ to $- 20°$, ($Ab_1An_3$ $= - 17°$ 40'); *parallel* $\infty \bar{P}\infty =$ $- 27°$ to $- 32°$, $Ab_1An_3 =$ $- 29° 38'$. |

# TABLES FOR DETERMINING MINERALS.

| Polarization-colors. | Color and power of refracting light. | Pleochroism. | Structure. | Association. | Inclosures. | Decomposition. | Occurrence. | Remarks. |
|---|---|---|---|---|---|---|---|---|
| Generally very brilliant. | Like orthoclase. | | In grains and large crystals I. O. and microlites II. O. Compare inclosures and decomposition. If labradorite is twinned according to the Albite and Pericline laws, a latticed structure similar to that of microcline appears i.p. l., yet the twinning filaments in labradorite are clearly distinguishable. | With diallage, hypersthene, olivine, also with quartz, augite, hornblende, biotite. | Hornblende, olivine, diallage, magnetite, ilmenite. Especially prominent are the countless inclosures of long acicular opaque microlites disposed parallel to the vertical axis or also to the edge $oP . \infty \check{P} \infty$; also brownish tablets (ferric oxide? brookite?) which lie with their longer direction perpendicular to the microlites, or countless minute colorless to greenish granules, so that the labradorite appears opaque. | Like orthoclase. Commonly into epidote and muscovite. | Primary essential constituent in norite, gabbro, dolerite, especially in dacite, basalts, and diorites. | Like albite. |
| | Like labradorite. | | | With hornblende, augite, biotite, diallage, hypersthene, etc. | Like labradorite, yet with no microlites and leaflets. | | Primary essential constituent in eruptive rocks, diorite, gabbro, andesites. | |

| Name. | Chemical composition and reactions. | Specific gravity. | Cleavage. | Ordinary combinations and form of the cross-section. | Twins. | Optical orientation. | Character and strength of double-refraction. | Direction of extinction. |
|---|---|---|---|---|---|---|---|---|
| f. Anorthite. | $CaAl_2Si_2O_8 \cdot An$. $SiO_2 =$ 45-43 per cent. Easily soluble in HCl without formation of amorphous $SiO_2$. | 2.73- 2.75 (2.75). | Perfect $oP$ and $\infty \check{P} \infty$. $P : M$ right = 94° 10'. | Like albite. | | 1. M. = c nearly perpendicular to $2, \check{P} \infty$. Dispersion $\rho > v$. Leaflets $\vert oP$ and $\infty \check{P} \infty$ show a side appearance of one or the other of the optic axes. Axial point on margin of the field. (Comp. Fig. 101, a and b.) | Like albite. | Parallel $oP =$ $- 36°$ to $- 42°$. $An =$ $- 37°$. Parallel $\infty \check{P} \infty$ $= - 37°$ to $- 43°$. $An =$ $- 36°$. |

## DISTINCTION BETWEEN

The plagioclases from b to e inclusive are, as is well known, isomorphous mixtures of the terminal members, albite (Ab) and anorthite (An). As there are all possible intermediary stages between these two in chemical composition (oligoclase, andesine, labradorite, bytownite being only names for such members), transitions in the physical properties, specific gravity, and especially the optical orientation, are also shown.

As has been demonstrated by M. Schuster, one can directly determine the proportional mixture of the feldspar to be determined, i.e., the plagioclase itself, by observing the directions of extinction in cleavage-leaflets parallel $oP$ and $\infty \check{P} \infty$.

## C. Aggre-

Aggregates never show a simultaneous extinction, i.e., total darkness, i. p. p. l. '(between crossed nicols during a complete revolution), as the axes of elasticity of the exceedingly minute individuals forming the aggregate are irregularly distributed. In a complete horizontal revolution of the stage, therefore, the separate individuals extinguish in succession, and the entire aggregate does not extinguish as a unit in revolving from 90° to 90°. If the aggregates are radially fibrous, an interference-cross is visible i. p. p. l.

In the following pages something will be given concerning the most difficultly determinable

| Polariza-tion-colors. | Color and power of refracting light. | Pleochroism. | Structure. | Associa-tion. | Inclosures. | Decompos-ition. | Occur-rence. | Remarks. |
|---|---|---|---|---|---|---|---|---|
| See labrador-ite. | Color-less, clear as water, like labrador-ite. | | Like labradorite. | With labra-dorite, augite, hyper-sthene, olivine. | Like oligoclase. | Generally fresh, as in other plagioclase. | Rather rare. Primary essential con-stituent in eruptive rocks. In basaltic rocks and augite-andesites, gabbro, norite. In crys-talline schists, amphibo-lites, gneiss. | |

## THE SPECIES OF PLAGIOCLASE.

The oblique extinctions given have reference to the usual setting up of a plagioclase (the $oP$-plane falling from above forward and inclined from left to right) and always to the obtuse edge $oP : \infty \check{P} \infty$, i.e., the plane $\infty \check{P} \infty$ lying to the right. The symbol $+$ prefixed indicates, on cleavage-leaflets parallel $oP$, that the direction of extinction as regards the right prismatic edge is inclined towards the obtuse $oP : \infty \check{P} \infty$; on cleavage-leaflets parallel $\infty \check{P} \infty$, that it is inclined towards the edge $oP : \infty \check{P} \infty$, the same as the section of the plane $,\check{P}, \infty$ with $\infty \check{P} \infty$. The symbol $-$ indicates in both cases the opposite direction.

## gates.

crypto-crystalline aggregates. Their determination is rendered unusually difficult by the minuteness of the separate individuals; often the chemical investigation is the only safe means of determination. All aggregates here introduced are secondary minerals, decomposition-products, and often inclose fresh remnants of the original mineral. From those minerals already studied aggregates (crypto-crys-talline also) are often formed; so, e.g., from talc, muscovite, tridymite, siderite: these have been discussed already under the appropriate headings.

| Name. | Chemical composition and reactions. | Specific gravity. | Color and power of refracting light. | Optical properties. | |
|---|---|---|---|---|---|
| 1. Serpentine. | $H_2Mg_3Si_2O_9$ + aq. Completely *decomposed* by HCl. | 2.5–2.7. | Green, more rarely yellow, brown, reddish-brown, black. $\beta = 1.574$. | Partly amorphous, partly showing aggregate polarization. The variety *antigorite* rhombic (?). (See "structure.") $a = 1$. M. $\perp oP$; i.e., perpendicular to the direction of perfect cleavage. | Polarization-colors feeble. *Antigorite* negative double-refracting, feebly pleochroitic. Dispersion clear, but feeble. $\rho > \nu$. |

| Structure. | Association. | Occurrence. | Decomposition-product. | Remarks. |
|---|---|---|---|---|
| *The mesh-structure is characteristic.* The decomposition begins on the walls of the olivine fissures; generally yellowish-green threads shoot out at right angles; thus a sort of net is formed embracing within its meshes particles of fresh olivine, which are subject to the further decomposition. The interior of the meshes generally appears filled with tufted serpentine threads. The mesh-structure is yet further advanced, in that between the single fields earthy particles are deposited. In *other* serpentines the serpentine substance is arranged in form of large often very regular leaflets lying at nearly right angles, showing the optical behavior of the so-called *antigorite;* here the mesh-structure is wanting. In decomposition magnetite is separated, also ferric oxide and hydroxide. The serpentines are often impregnated with amorphous silicic acid or chalcedony. | With olivine, rhombic or monoclinic augite, hornblende, garnet, magnetite, chromite, chlorite, magnesite. | Massive, as decomposition-product of olivine-fels; in pseudomorphs after olivine, in olivine-bearing eruptive rocks, and schists. As decomposition-product of olivine, Al-free augite, and hornblende. | For the most part of *olivine* and *augite free from alumina* and *hornblende.* | Difficult to distinguish from the bastite and chloritic decomposition-products of augite. |

| Name. | Chemical composition and reactions. | Specific gravity. | Color and power of refracting light. | Optical properties. |
|---|---|---|---|---|
| 2. Viridite. Partly chloritic, partly serpentine-like aggregates, as: *a.* Delessite; *b.* Chlorophæite; *c.* Green earth (Grünerde). | \multicolumn{4}{l}{The augites especially and the hornblendes, also garnet and biotite, often decompose into dirty to brownish-green fibrous aggregates, or, as in green earth, granular, called by the comprehensive term *viridite*. An exact specification with the microscope is impossible on account of the minuteness of the threads and grains. The viriditic aggregates show aggregate polarization, and often a feeble pleochroism; sometimes they are finely radial and concentric or tangled fibrous, and again exceedingly fine-grained or more or less laminated aggregates. The three minerals,} |
| 3. Bastite. | \multicolumn{4}{l}{*Green. Compare with these* the rhombic pyroxenes. The decomposition of rhombic pyroxene crystals or grains into bastite or a bastite-like aggregate is very like that of serpentine. Here also the decomposition begins on the fissures, especially the separation-clefts parallel *oP*, and progresses into a threading parallel} |
| 4. Chalcedony. | $SiO_2$. Small percentage of $H_2O$. | See quartz. | Colorless, transparent, often colored by ferric oxide or hydroxide. $n = 1.547$. | See quartz. |

| Structure. | Association. | Occurrence. | Decomposition-products. | Remarks. |
|---|---|---|---|---|
| $a$, $b$, $c$ occurring in such crypto-crystalline aggregates occur very commonly in pseudomorphs after augite. According to the chemical composition, $a$ is a hydrous FeMg alumina silicate, and from the high percentage of alumina resembles the chlorites; $b$ and $c$ are iron-magnesium silicates, hydrous and poor in alumina. Very widely distributed in the decomposed basic eruptive rocks and crystalline schists. | | | For the most part from monoclinic augite and hornblende, garnet, biotite, etc. | |
| to the $c$-axis. As a consequence of the regular disposition of these threads it is often possible to determine them as bastite by studying i. c. p. l. Compare optical orientation under "Bastite" (page 150). | | | From the rhombic pyroxenes. | |
| Chalcedony is for the most part a mixture of amorphous and micro- or crypto-crystalline silicic acid. The aggregates are either fine-grained or tangled fibrous; also often radial. In the last case, quartz individuals elongated according to the chief axis are combined to form a ball, and such aggregates brilliantly-polarizing show the interference-cross between crossed nicols. | Especially in quartz-orthoclase-biotite rocks, with opal and tridymite. | Secondary mineral, common in the acidic eruptive rocks, especially rhyolite, dacite, quartz-porphyries; also in other decomposed eruptive rocks, as basalt, andesite, melaphyr, porphyrite, in cavities, clefts, and irregular parts in the ground-mass. | A long series of minerals, especially the feldspars and augite, yield on decomposition chalcedony, together with other products. | The primary radial quartz sphærulites are to be distinguished from the chalcedony always appearing as decomposition-product; these are direct eliminations from the eruptive magma, and can be recognized as primary products from the nature of the limitations (Abgrenzung). |

| Name. | Chemical composition and reactions. | Specific gravity. | Color and power of refracting light. | Optical properties. |
|---|---|---|---|---|
| 5. Zeolites. | Of these, analcime has been already studied. (Compare Regular Minerals.) | | | |
| a. Natrolite. | $Na_2Al_2Si_3O_{10} + 2H_2O$. | 2.17–2.26. | Colorless, clear as water. Relief not marked. | Rhombic. |
| b. Scolecite. | $CaAl_2Si_3O_{10} + 8H_2O$. | 2.2–2.39. | ditto. | Monoclinic or triclinic. |
| c. Stilbite. | $H_4CaAl_2Si_6O_{18} + 3H_2O$. | 2.1–2.2. | ditto. | Monoclinic. |
| d. Desmine. | $CaAl_2Si_6O_{16} + 6H_2O$. | 2.1–2.2. | ditto. | ditto. |
| e. Chabasite. | $R_2CaAl_2Si_5O_{15} + 6H_2O$. $R_2 = \frac{3}{4}H + \frac{1}{4}K$. All, a to e, are easily soluble in HCl, with separation of gelatinous silica. | 2.07–2.15. | ditto. | Rhombohedral or triclinic. Rhombohedral cleavage. |
| 6. Carbonates. | Of these, calcite, dolomite, magnesite, siderite, have been studied under the "Hexagonal Minerals." These occur also in extremely fine-grained or radial aggregates. | | | |
| Aragonite. | $CaCO_3$. Easily soluble in HCl with effervescence. | 2.9–3. | Colorless, transparent. | *Rhombic*. Polarization-colors as in calcite, *often iridescent*. Cleavage parallel $\infty \bar{P}\infty$ and $\infty P$. A.P. $\| \infty \bar{P}\infty$; $\mathfrak{a} = c$. |

| Structure. | Association. | Occurrence. | Decomposition-product. | Remarks. |
|---|---|---|---|---|

Besides analcime the following often occur as decomposition-products:

| Structure. | Association. | Occurrence. | Decomposition-product. | Remarks. |
|---|---|---|---|---|
| Almost always *in aggregates of long acicular crystals, generally radially disposed with brilliant polarization-colors.* A.P. $\mid \infty \bar{P} \infty$; $c = c$. | Compare occurrence. With augite, olivine, magnetite, hornblende, biotite, feldspar, etc., i.e. their decomposition-product; with calcite and aragonite. | *Secondary minerals,* especially prominent in the *bubble-cavities* (see Fig. 103) of feldspar-, nepheline-, and leucite-basalts; the basanites, tephrites, phonolites, and also in trachytic and andesitic eruptive rocks. | The zeolites occur generally as decomposition-products of the feldspars, of nepheline, leucite, and hauyn. | The distinctions are best effected by the microchemical examination. $b$ to $d$ inclusive can be accurately distinguished only by determining the relation of the axes of elasticity to the crystallographic axes |
| Ditto. Generally in needles radially disposed. $a : c = 11\text{-}12°$. | | | | |
| Tabular crystals in radial groups. 1. M. $= c = b$. | | | | |
| As above. A. P. $\mid \infty \bar{P} \infty$. $b : c = 34°$. 1. M. with $d = $ about $5°$. | | | | |
| In rhombohedra. Polarization-colors like feldspar. Forms more granular aggregates. | | | | |

Siderite is very common in spherical, radial, and concentric aggregates. Besides these rhombohedral carbonates very commonly as decomposition-product occur:

| Structure. | Association. | Occurrence. | Decomposition-product. | Remarks. |
|---|---|---|---|---|
| Partly in large grains or in *radial fibrous tufts of long needles.* | With calcite and zeolites. See occurrence. | Common in basic eruptive rocks in cavities and geodes. | Decomposition-product of calcareous silicates. | Characterized by solubility with evolution of $CO_2$, and by crystalline form; easily distinguished from calcite by the latter property. |

# BIBLIOGRAPHY TO PART II.

The following larger text-books and treatises are not embraced in this bibliography:

E. COHEN. Sammlung von Mikrophotographien zur Veranschaulichung der mikroskopischen Structur von Mineralien und Gesteinen, aufgenommen von J. Grimm in Offenburg. Stuttgart, Schweizerbart'sche Verlagshandlung. 1883. 80 Tafeln.

FISCHER. Kritische mikroskop.-mineralogische Studien. 3 Hfte. Freiburg i. Br. 1869–1873.

F. FOUQUÉ et A. MICHEL LÉVY. Minéralogie micrographique roches éruptives françaises. Paris, 1879. a. Atlas LV Pl.

H. ROSENBUSCH. Mikroskopische Physiographie der petrographisch wichtigen Mineralien. Stuttgart, Schweizerbart'sche Verlagshandlung. 1873. Mit 10 Tafeln.

— Mikroskopische Physiographie der massigen Gesteine. Stuttgart, Schweizerbart'sche Verlagshandlung. 1877.

F. ZIRKEL. Die mikroskopische Beschaffenheit der Mineralien und Gesteine. Leipzig, W. Engelmann. 1873.

— Microscopical Petrography. Washington, 1876. w. XII Pl.

### Acmite and Aegirine.

TSCHERMAK. Tschermak's Mineral. Mitth. 1871. 33.
BECKE. Tschermak's Mineral. u. petr. Mitth. N. F. I. 1878. 554.
KOCH. N. Jahrbuch f. Min. u. Geol. 1881. I. Beil.-Bd. 156.
TÖRNEBOHM. Förh. geol. Fören. i Stockholm. 1883. VI. 383 and 542. Comp. Ref. N. Jahrb. f. Min. u. Geol. 1883. II. 370.
MÜGGE. N. Jahrb. f. Min. u. Geol. 1883. II. 189.
MANN, N. Jahrb. f. Min. u. Geol. 1884. II. 172.

### Actinolite (Smaragdite, Karinthine).

TSCHERMAK. Tschermak's Min. Mitth. 1871, 37 and 44.
v. DRASCHE. Tsch. Min. Mitth. 1871. 85.
RIESS. Tsch. Min. u. petr. Mitth. N. F. 1878. I. 185, 192.
CH. WHITMAN CROSS. Tsch. Min. u. petr. Mitth. 1881. III. 386.
BECKE. Tsch. Min. u. petr. Mitth. 1882. IV. 234, 360.
— Tsch. Min. u. petr. Mitth. 1882. V. 157.

### Albite.

LOSSEN. Zeitschr. d. deutsch. geol. Ges. 1867. XIX. 509 and 1879. XXXI. 441.
SCHUSTER. Tsch. Min. und petr. Mitth. N. F. 1881. III. 153.
BÖHM. Tsch. Min. und petr. Mitth. N. F. 1883. V. 202.

### Almandine (ordinary Garnet).

DRASCHE. Tsch. Min. Mitth. 1872. 2. 85.
WICHMANN. Pogg. Ann. f. Phys. u. Chem. 1876. CLVII. 282.
DATHE. Zeitschr. d. deutsch. geol. Ges. 1877. XXIX. 274.
RIESS. Tsch. Min. u. petr. Mitth. 1878. I. 186.
SZABO. N. Jahrb. f. Min. u. Geol. 1880. I. Beil.-Bd. 302.
SCHRAUF. Groth's Zeitschr. f. Kryst. 1882. 323.
RENARD. Bull. du Musée royal d'hist. nat. de Belgique. 1882. I.
v. LASAULX. Sitzungsber. d. niederrhein. Ges. in Bonn. 1883.

### Analcime.

TSCHERMAK. Sitzungsber. Wien. Akad. d. Wiss. 1866. LIII. 260.

### Andalusite.

JEREMEJEFF. N. Jahrb. f. Min. u. Geol. 1866. 724.
ZIRKEL. Zeitschr. d. deutsch. geol. Ges. 1867. XIX. 68. 180.
ROSENBUSCH. Die Steiger Schiefer. Strassburg, 1877.
POHLIG. Zeitschr. d. deutsch. geol. Ges. 1877. XXIX. 560, and Tsch. Min. u. petr. Mitth. 1881. III. 344.
TELLER u. JOHN. Jahrb. d. kk. geol. R.-Anst. Wien, 1882. XXXII. 589.
MÜLLER. N. Jahrb. f. Min. u. Geol. 1882. II. 205.

### Andesine.

v. RATH. Zeitschr. d. deutsch. geol. Ges. 1864. XVI. 294.
SCHUSTER. Tsch. Min. u. petr. Mitth. 1881. III. 173.
BECKE. Tsch. Min. u. petr. Mitth. 1882. V. 149, 160.

### Anomite.

TSCHERMAK. Gr. Zeitschr. f. Kryst. 1878. 31.
BECKE. Tsch. Min. u. petr. Mitth. 1882. IV. 331. V. 151.

### Anorthite.

BECKE. Tsch. Min. u. petr. Mitth. 1882. IV. 246.
SCHUSTER. Tsch. Min. u. petr. Mitth. 1881. III. 208.

### Anthophyllite.

TSCHERMAK. Tsch. Min. Mitth. 1871. 37.
CH. WHITMAN CROSS. Tsch. Min. u. petr. Mitth.´1881. III. 388.
BECKE. Tsch. Min. u. petr. Mitth. N. F. 1882. IV. 331. 450.
SJÖGREN (on Gedrit). Comp. Ref. N. Jahrb. f. Min. u. Geol. 1883. II. 366.

### Apatite.

ROSENBUSCH. Nephelinit v. Katzenbuckel. Freiburg i. Br. 1869.
ZIRKEL. Basaltgesteine. Bonn, 1870. 72.
— N. Jahrb. f. Min. u. Geol. 1870. 806, 821.
HAGGE. Ueber Gabbro. In.-Diss. Kiel, 1871. 58.
KREUTZ. Tsch. Min. u. petr. Mitth. N. F. 1884. VI. 149.

### Arfvedsonite.

KŒNIG. Gr. Zeitschr. f. Krystall. 1877; 423.

### Augite (ordinary and basaltic).

WEDDING. Zeitschr. d. deutsch. geol. Ges. 1858. 380.
BÜTSCHLY. N. Jahrb. f. Min. u. Geol. 1867. 700.
TSCHERMAK. Sitzungsber. d. Wien. Akad. d. Wiss. 1869. LIX.
— Tsch. Min. Mitth. 1871. 28.
ROSENBUSCH. Neph. v. Katzenbuckel. 1869.
ZIRKEL. Basaltgesteine. 1870. 8.
VRBA. Zeitschr. "Lotos" Prag. Jahrg. 1870.
DATHE. Zeitschr. d. deutsch. geol. Ges. 1874. XXVI. 1.
LAGORIO. Andesite d. Kaukasus. Dorpat, 1878. Ref. N. Jahrb. f. Min. u. Geol. 1880. I. 209.
V. WERVEKE. N. Jahrb. f. Min. u. Geol. 1879. 482. 822.
BECKE. Tsch. Min. u. petr. Mitth. 1882. IV. 365.
KREUTZ. Tsch. Min. u. petr. Mitth. 1884. VI. 141.

### Bastite.

TSCHERMAK. Tsch. Min. Mitth. 1871, 20.
HAGGE. Ueber Gabbro. Kiel, 1871. 27.
STRENG. N. Jahrb. f. Min. u. Geol. 1872. 261.
DRASCHE. Tsch. Min. Mitth. 1873. 5.

### Bronzite (comp. with Serpentine).

TSCHERMAK. Sitzungsber. d. Wien. Akad. d. Wiss. 1869. LIX. 1. 1.
— Tsch. Min. Mitth. 1871. 17.
STRENG. N. Jahrb. f. Min. u. Geol. 1872. 273.
SCHRAUF. Gr. Zeitschr. f. Kryst. 1882. 321.
BÜCKING. Gr. Zeitschr. f. Kryst. 1883. VII. 502.
BECKE. Tsch. Min. u. petr. Mitth. 1883. V. 527.
ROSENBUSCH. N. Jahrb. f. Min. u. Geol. 1884. I. 197.

### Bytownite.

SCHUSTER. Tsch. Min. u. petr. Mitth. 1881. III. 202.
BECKE. Tsch. Min. u. petr. Mitth. 1882. V. 168.
RENARD. Bull. d. Musée roy. d'hist. nat. belgique. 1884. III. 10.

### Calcite.

OSCHATZ. Zeitschr. d. deutsch. geol. Ges. 1855. VII. 5.
STELZNER. Ueber Gesteine v. Altai. Leipzig, 1871. Aus Cotta: D. Altai. p. 57.
INOSTRANZEFF. Tsch. Min. Mitth. 1872. I. 45.
ROSENBUSCH. N. Jahrb. f. Min. u. Geol. 1872. 64.
LEMBERG. Zeitschr. d. deutsch. geol. Ges. 1872. 226. 1876. 519.
LAGORIO. Mikrosk. An. ostbaltischer Gebirgsarten. Dorpat, 1876.
O. MEYER. Zeitschr. d. deutsch. geol. Ges. 1879. XXXI. 445.
RENARD. Bull. Acad. royal des Sciences belg. 1879. XLVII. Nr. 5. Comp.
   Ref. N. Jahrb. f. Min. u. Geol. 1880. II. 146.

### Cancrinite.

A. KOCH. N. Jahrb. f. Min. u. Geol. 1881. I. Beil.-Bd. 144.
TÖRNEBOHM. Geol. Fören. i Stockholm Förh. 1883. VI. 383. Comp. Ref. N.
   Jahrb. f. Min. u. Geol. 1883. II. 370. 542.

### Chalcedony.

REUSCH. Pogg. Ann. f. Ph. u. Chem. 1864. CXXIII. 94.
BEHRENS. Sitzungsber. d. Wien. Akad. d. Wiss. 1871. LXIV. Dec. 1.

### Chiastolite.

ZIRKEL. Zeitschr. d. deutsch. geol. Ges. 1867. 68.
POHLIG. Zeitschr. d. deutsch. geol. Ges. 1877. XXIX. 545. 563.
— Tsch. Min. u. petr. Mitth. 1881. III. 348.
CH. WHITMAN CROSS. Tsch. Min. u. petr. Mitth. 1881. III. 381.
MÜLLER. N. Jahrb. f. Min. u. Geol. 1882. II. 205.

### Chloritoid (Sismondine).

TSCHERMAK u. SIPOCZ. Gr. Zeitschr. f. Kryst. 1879. 506 and 509.
v. FOULLON. Jahrb. d. kk. geol. R.-Anst. Wien, 1883. XXXIII. 207.
BARROIS. Ann. de la Soc. géol. du Nord. Lille, 1883. XI. 18. Comp. Ref. N. Jahrb. f. Min. u. Geol. 1884. II. 68.

### Chromite.

DATHE. J. Jahrb. f. Min. u. Geol. 1876. 247.
THOULET. Bull. Soc. minér. Paris, 1879. 34.

### Cordierite.

WICHMANN. Zeitschr. d. deutsch. geol. Ges. 1874. XXVI. 675.
v. LASAULX. N. Jahrb. f. Min. u. Geol. 1872. 831.
— Gr. Zeitschr. f. Kryst. 1883. VIII. 76.
SZABO. N. Jahrb. f. Min. u. Geol. 1880. I. Beil.-Bd. 308.
HUSSAK. Sitzungsber. d. Wien. Akad. d. Wiss. 1883. April.
CALDERON y ARAÑA. Bal. d.l. Comis. d. Mapa. geolog. Madrid, 1882.

### Corundum.

ZIRKEL. N. Jahrb. f. Min. u. Geol. 1870. 822.
TELLER u. JOHN. Jahrb. d. kk. geol. R.-Anst. Wien, 1882. XXXII. 589.
WICHMANN. Verhandl. d. kk. geol. R.-Anst. Wien, 1884. 150.

### Couseranite (Dipyr).

ZIRKEL. Zeitschr. d. deutsch. geol. Ges. 1867. XIX. 202.
GOLDSCHMIDT. N. Jahr. f. Min. u. Geol. 1881. I. Beil.-Bd. 225.

### Diallage.

G. ROSE. Zeitschr. d. deutsch. geol. Ges. 1867. 280, 294.
TSCHERMAK. Tsch. Min. Mitth. 1871. 25, and Sitzungsber. d. Wien. Akad. d. Wiss. 1869. LIX. 1. 1.

V. DRASCHE. Tsch. Min. Mitth. 1871. 1.
HAGGE. N. Jahrb. f. Min. u. Geol. 1871. 946.
STRENG. N. Jahrb. f. Min. u. Geol. 1872. 377, 379.
V. RATH. Verh. d. niederrhein. Ges. f. Nat. u. Heilkde. Bonn. 8. Mz. 1875.
DATHE. Zeitschr. d. deutsch. geol. Ges. 1877. XXIX. 274.
SCHRAUF. Gr. Zeitschr. f. Kryst. 1882. 323.
V. WERVEKE. N. Jahrb. f. Min. u. Geol. 1883. II. 97.
KLOOS. N. Jahrb. f. Min. u. Geol. 1884. III. Beil.-Bd. 19.

### Diopside (Omphacite and Sahlite).

TSCHERMAK. Tsch. Min. Mitth. 1871. 21.
V. DRASCHE. Tsch. Min. Mitth. 1871. 58.
V. KALKOWSKY. Tsch. Min. Mitth. 1875. II.
DATHE. N. Jahrb. f. Min. u. Geol. 1876. 225, 337.
RIESS. Tsch. Min. u. petr. Mitth. 1878. I. 168.
BECKER. Zeitschr. d. deutsch. Geol. Ges. 1881. XXXIII. 31.
BECKE. Tsch. Min. u. petr. Mitth. 1882. IV. 297.
SCHRAUF. Gr. Zeitschr. f. Kryst. 1882. 321.

### Disthene (Cyanite).

V. KOBELL. Pogg. Ann. f. Phys. u. Chem. 1869. CXXXVI. 156.
V. LASAULX. N. Jahrb. f. Min. u. Geol. 1872. 835.
RIESS. Tsch. Min. u. petr. Mitth. 1878. I. 165, 195.
BECKE. Tsch. Min. u. petr. Mitth. 1882. IV. 225, 231.

### Dolomite.

INOSTRANZEFF. Tsch. Min. Mitth. 1872. 48.
LEMBERG. Zeitschr. d. deutsch. geol. Ges. 1876. 519.
O. MEYER. Zeitschr. d. deutsch. geol. Ges. 1879. 445.
RENARD. Bull. Acad. royal Belg. XLVII. 5. Mai 1879. Comp. Ref. N. Jahrb.
   f. Min. u. Geol. 1880. II. 146.

### Elæolite.

SCHEERER. Pogg. Ann. f. Phys. u. Chem. 1863. CXIX. 145.
ZIRKEL. N. Jahrb. f. Min. u. Geol. 1870. 810.
V. WERVEKE. N. Jahrb. f. Min. u. Geol. 1880. II. 141.
KOCH. N. Jahrb. f. Min. u. Geol. 1880. I. Beil.-Bd. 140.

### Enstatite.

TSCHERMAK. Tsch. Min. Mitth. 1871. 17.
STRENG. N. Jahrb. f. Min. u. Geol. 1872. 273.
TRIPPKE. N. Jahrb. f. Min. u. Geol. 1878. 673.
TELLER u. JOHN. Jahrb. d. kk. geol. R.-Anst. Wien, 1882. XXXII. 589.

### Epidote.

ZIRKEL. Zeitschr. d. deutsch. geol. Ges. 1869. XIX. 121.
v. LASAULX. N. Jahrb. f. Min. u. Geol. 1872. 837.
BECKE. Tsch. Min. u. petr. Mitth. 1879. II. 25, 34.
— Tsch. Min. u. petr. Mitth. 1882. IV. 264.
v. KALKOWSKY. Tsch. Min. u. petr. Mitth. 1876. II. 87.
REUSCH. N. Jahrb. f. Min. u. Geol. 1883. II. 179.
TÖRNEBOHM. Geol. Fören. i Stockholm Förh. VI 185. Comp. Ref. N. Jahrb. f. Min. u. Geol. 1883. I. 245.
BACHINGER. Tsch. Min. u. petr. Mitth. 1884. VI. 44.
KÜCH. Tsch. Min. u. petr. Mitth. 1884. VI. 119.

### Fluorite.

LASPEYRES. Zeitschr. d. deutsch. geol. Ges. 1864. XVI. 449.

### Glaucophane.

HAUSMANN. Göttinger gel. Anz. 1845. 195.
BODEWIG. Pogg. Ann. f. Phys. u. Chem. 1876. CXLVIII. 224.
LUEDECKE. Zeitschr. d. deutsch. geol. Ges. 1876 XXVIII. 248.
BECKE. Tsch. Min. u. petr. Mitth. 1879. II. 49, 71.
WILLIAMS. N. Jahrb. f. Min. u. Geol. 1882. II. 201.
STELZNER. N. Jahrb. f. Min. u. Geol. 1883. I. 208.
BARROIS. Ann. Soc. géol. du Nord. Lille, 1883. XI. 18. Comp. Ref. N. Jahrb. f. Min. u. Geol. 1884. II. 68.
v. LASAULX. Sitzungsber. d. niederrhein. Ges. F. Nat. u. Heilkunde. Bonn, 1884. 3. XII.

### Graphite.

ZIRKEL. Zeitschr. d. deutsch. geol. Ges. 1867. 68.
— Pogg. Ann. f. Phys. u. Chem. CXLIV. 1871. 319.
RENARD. Bull. du Musée royal d'hist. nat. Bruxelles, 1882. I. 47. Comp. Ref. N. Jahrb. f. Min. u. Geol. 1883. II. 68.

### Gypsum (and Anhydrite).

HAMMERSCHMIDT. Tsch. Min. u. petr. Mitth. 1883. V. 245.

### Hauyn (comp. Nosean).

ZIRKEL. Basaltgesteine. 1870. 79.
— N. Jahrb. f. Min. u. Geol. 1870. 818.
VOGELSANG. Mededeel. d. k. Akad. v. Wetenschapp. Amsterdam, 1872 (2).
SAUER. Zeitschr. f. d. gesammt. Naturwiss. Halle, 1876. XIV.
DOELTER. Tsch. Min. u. petr. Mitth. 1882. IV. 461.

### Hematite.

G. ROSE. Zeitschr. d. deutsch. geol. Ges. 1859. XI. 298, 306.
KOSMANN. Zeitschr. d. deutsch. geol. Ges. 1864. XVI. 665.
ZIRKEL. Basaltgesteine. 1870. 71.

### Hercynite.

v. KALKOWSKY. Zeitschr. d. deutsch. geol. Ges. 1881. XXXIII. 533.

### Hornblende (ordinary and basaltic).

ZIRKEL. Zeitschr. d. deutsch. geol. Ges. 1867. 99. 119.
— Zeitschr. d. deutsch. geol. Ges. 1871. 43.
— Basaltgesteine. 1870. 74.
TSCHERMAK. Sitzungsber. d. Wien. Akad. d. Wiss. 1869. LIX. 1. 1.
— Tsch. Min. Mitth. 1871. 38.
RIESS. Tsch. Min. u. petr. Mitth. 1878. 165.
SOMMERLAD. N. Jahrb. f. Min. u. Geol. 1882. II. 139.
BECKER. N. Jahrb. f. Min. u. Geol. 1883. II. 1.
STRENG. XXII. Bericht d. oberhess. Ges. f. Natur- u. Heilkunde. Giessen, 1883.
KLOOS. N. Jahrb. f. Min. u. Geol. 1884. III. Beil.-Bd. 24.

### Hypersthene.

KOSMANN. Sitzungsber. d. niederrhein Ges. f. Natur- u. Heilkunde. Bonn, 3. Febr. 1869.
— N. Jahrb. f. Min. u. Geol. 1869. 374 and 1871. 501.
HAGGE. N. Jahrb. f. Min. u. Geol. 1871. 946.
TSCHERMAK. Tsch. Min. Mitth. 1871. 17.

# BIBLIOGRAPHY TO PART II.

NIEDZWIEDZKI. Tsch. Min. Mitth. 1872. 253.
BECKE. Tsch. Min. u. petr. Mitth. 1878. I. 244.
BECKE. Tsch. Min. u. petr. Mitth. 1883. V. 527.
FOUQUÉ. Santorin. Paris, 1879.
BLAAS. Tsch. Min. u petr. Mitth. 1881. III. 479.
TELLER u. JOHN. Jahrb. d. kk. geol. R.-Anst. Wien. 1882. XXXII. 589.
ROSENBUSCH. Gesteine v. Ekersund. N. Magaz. f. Naturvidenskaberne. XXVII. 4. Heft.
HAGUE u. IDDINGS. Amer. Journ. of Science. 1883. XXVI. 222. Ref. N. Jahrb. f. Min. u. Geol. 1884. I. 225.
CH. WHITMAN CROSS. The same. XXV. 1883. 139. Ref. N. Jahrb. f. Min. u. Geol. 1884. I. 228.
KRENNER. Gr. Zeitschr. f. Kryst. 1884. IX. 255.

### Ilmenite.

LASPEYRES. N. Jahrb. f. Min. u. Geol. 1869. 513.
ZIRKEL. Basaltgesteine. Bonn, 1870. 70.
SANDBERGER. N. Jahrb. f. Min. u. Geol. 1870. 206.
STRENG. N. Jahrb. f. Min. u. Geol. 1872. 385.
GÜMBEL. D. paläolith. Eruptivgest. d. Fichtelgebirges. München, 1874. 35.
DATHE. Zeitschr. d. deutsch. geol. Ges. 1874. XXVI. 1.
COHEN. Reisen in Südafrika. Hamburg, 1875. 2. Friedrichsen'sche Jahresber. der geograph. Ges. Comp. Ref. N. Jahrb. f. Min. u. Geol. 1876. 213.
v. LASAULX Verh. d. naturw. Ver. d. preuss. Rheinlande u. Westphal. 1878. XXXV.
SAUER. N. Jahrb. f. Min. u. Geol. 1879. 575.
CH. WHITMAN CROSS. Tsch. Min. u. petr. Mitth. 1881. III. 401.
CATHREIN. Gr. Zeitschr. f. Kryst. 1882. 244.

### Labradorite.

VOGELSANG. Archiv. Néerland. 1868. III.
SCHRAUF. Sitzungsber. d. Wien. Akad. d. Wiss. Dec. 1869. LX. Bd.
STELZNER. Berg- und Hüttenmänn. Zeig. XXIX. 150.
HAGGE. N. Jahrb. f. Min. u. Geol. 1871. 946.
SCHUSTER. Tsch. Min. u. petr. Mitth. 1881. III. 183.

### Leucite.

ZIRKEL. Zeitschr. d. deutsch. geol. Ges. 1868. 97.
— Basaltgesteine. Bonn, 1870.
v. RATH. Monatsber. d. Berlin. Akad. d. Wiss. Aug. 1872.

KREUTZ. Tsch. Min. u. petr. Mitth. 1884. VI. 135.
v. CHRUSTSCHOFF. Tsch. Min. u. petr. Mitth. 1884. VI. 161.

### Liebenerite.

ZIRKEL. N. Jahrb. f. Min. u. Geol. 1868. 719.

### Magnesite.

ROSENBUSCH. N. Jahrb. f. Min. u. Geol. 1884. I. 196.

### Magnetite.

ZIRKEL. Basaltgesteine. Bonn, 1870. 67.
VELAIN. Descript. géol. d'Aden, Réunion, des îles St. Paul et Amsterdam. Paris, 1877.

### Meionite.

v. RATH. Zeitschr. d. deutsch. geol. Ges. 1866. XVIII. 608, 626. 633.
v. KALKOWSKY. Zeitschr. d. deutsch. geol. Ges. 1878. XXX. 663.

### Melanite.

FOUQUÉ. Compt. rend. 15 mars 1875.
WICHMANN. Pogg. Ann. f. Phys. u. Chem. 1876. CLVII. 282.
KNOP. Gr. Zeitschr. f. Krystall. 1877. 58.

### Melilith.

v. RATH. Zeitschr. d. deutsch. geol. Ges. 1866. XVIII. 527.
ZIRKEL. Zeitschr. d. deutsch. geol. Ges. 1868. XX. 118.
— Basaltgesteine. Bonn, 1870. 77.
HUSSAK. Sitzungsber. d. Wien. Akad. d. Wiss. April 1878.
STELZNER. N. Jahrb. f. Min. u. Geol. 1882. II. Beil.-Bd. 369.

### Meroxene (Biotite).

TSCHERMAK. Sitzungsber. der Wien. Akad. der Wiss. 1869. May. LIX.
— Gr. Zeitschr. f. Kryst. 1878. II. 18.
ZIRKEL. Basaltgesteine. Bonn, 1870. 76.
— Ber. d. kgl. sächs. Ges. d. Wiss. July 21, 1875.
v. KALKOWSKY. Die Gneissformation d. Eulengebirges. Leipzig, 1878. 28.
— N. Jahrb. f. Min. u. Geol. 1880. I. 33.

KISPATIC.   Tsch. Min. u. petr. Mitth. 1882. IV. 127.
WILLIAMS.   N. Jahrb. f. Min. u. Geol. 1882. II. 616.
BECKER.    N. Jahrb. f. Min. u. Geol. 1883. II. 1.

### Microcline (Microperthite).

DES CLOIZEAUX.   Ann. de chim. et phys. 1876. 9. 433.
DATHE.   Zeitschr. d. deutsch. geol. Ges. 1877. XXI. 274.
— Zeitschr. d. deutsch. geol. Ges. 1882. XXXIV. 12.
M. LÉVY.   Bull. d. la sociét. miner. No. 5. 1879.
BECKE.   Tsch. Min. u. petr. Mitth. 1882. IV. 196.
KOLLER.   Tsch. Min. u. petr. Mitth. 1883. V. 218.
KLOOS.   N. Jahrb. f. Min. u. Geol. 1884. II. 87.

### Muscovite (Sericite).

LOSSEN.   Zeitschr. d. deutsch. geol. Ges. 1867. XIX. 509.
WICHMANN.   Verh. des naturf. Ver. f. d. Rheinlande. XXXIV. 5. F. 4. Bd.
TSCHERMAK.   Gr. Zeitschr. f. Kryst. 1878. 40.
v. LASAULX,   N. Jahrb. f. min. u. Geol. 1872. 851.
v. GRODDECK.   Jahrb. d. kk. geol. R.-Anst. Wien, 1883. 397.

### Nepheline.

ZIRKEL.   Pogg. Ann. f. Phys. u. Chem. 1867. 298.
— N. Jahrb. f. Min. u. Geol. 1868. 697.
— Basaltgesteine. Bonn, 1870.
ROSENBUSCH.   Nephelinit v. Katzenbuckel. Freiburg, 1869. Ref. N. Jahrb. f.
    Min. u. Geol. 1869. 485.
BOŘICKY.   Archiv. d. naturw. Landesdurchforsch. Böhmens. Prag, 1874. Die
    Phonolithe. 8.

### Nosean.

v. RATH.   Zeitschr. d. deutsch. geol. Ges. 1862. XIV. 663.
ZIRKEL.   Pogg. Ann. f. Phys. u. Chem. 1867. CXXXI. 312.
ROSENBUSCH.   Nephel. v. Katzenbuckel. 1869. 35.
BOŘICKY.   Archiv. d. naturw. Landesdurchforsch. Böhmens. Prag, 1873. Die
    Basaltgesteine. 27.
— The same. 1874. Die Phonolithe. 10.

### Oligoclase.

ZIRKEL.   Zeitschr. d. deutsch. geol. Ges. 1867. XIX. 100.
M. SCHUSTER.   Tsch. Min. u. petr. Mitth. 1881. III. 164.
MÜGGE.   N. Jahrb. f. Min. u. Geol. 1881. II. 107.

### Oligoclasalbite.

SCHUSTER.  Tsch. Min. u. petr. Mitth. 1881. III. 159.

### Olivine.

TSCHERMAK.  Sitzungsber. d. Wien. Akad. d. Wiss. 1866. LIII. 260.
— Sitzungsber. d. Wien. Akad. d. Wiss. 1867. July. LVI.
ZIRKEL.  Basaltgesteine. Bonn, 1870. 55.
— Zeitschr. d. deutsch. geol. Ges. 1871. 59.
HAGGE.  Ueber Gabbro. Kiel, 1871. N. Jahrb. f. Min. u. Geol. 1871. 946.
ROSENBUSCH.  N. Jahrb. f. Min. u. Geol. 1872. 59.
DATHE.  N. Jahrb. f. Min. u. Geol. 1876. 225, 337.
PENCK.  Zeitschr. d. deutsch. geol. Ges. 1878. XXX. 97.
BRÖGGER.  N. Jahrb. f. Min. u. Geol. 1880. II. 187.
COHEN.  N. Jahrb. f. Min. u. Geol. 1880. II. 31, 52.
V. FOULLON.  Tsch. Min. u. petr. Mitth. 1880. II. 181.
BECKER.  Zeitschr. d. deutsch. geol. Ges. 1881. XXXIII. 31.
BECKE.  Tsch. Min. u. petr. Mitth. 1882. IV. 322, 355, 450.
— Tsch. Min. u. petr. Mitth. 1882. V. 163.
SCHRAUF.  Gr. Zeitschr. f. Kryst. 1882. 321.
KREUTZ.  Tsch. Min. u. petr. Mitth. 1884. VI. 142.

### Opal.

M. SCHULTZE.  Verh. d. naturf. Ver. d. preussischen Rheinlande u. Westphalens. 1861. 69.
G. ROSE.  Monatsber. d. Berlin. Akad. d. Wiss. 1869. 449.
BEHRENS.  Sitzungsber. d. Wien. Akad. d. Wiss. 1871. LXIV. I. Abth.
VELAIN.  Descript. géolog. d'Aden, Réunion . . . Paris, 1877. 32, 322.
KISPATIČ.  Tsch. Min. u. petr. Mitth. 1882. IV. 122.

### Orthoclase (Sanidine).

REUSCH.  Pogg. Ann. f. Phys. u. Chem. 1862. CXVI. 392, and 1863. CXVIII. 256.
ZIRKEL.  Pogg. Ann. f. Phys. u. Chem. 1867. CXXXI. 300.
— Sitzungsber. d. Wien. Akad. d. Wiss. 1863. XLVII. 237, 246.
— N. Jahrb. f. Min. u. Geol. 1866. 775.
— Zeitschr. d. deutsch. geol. Ges. 1867. XIX. 87.
LASPEYRES.  Zeitschr. d. deutsch. geol. Ges. 1864. XVI. 392.
S. WEISS.  Beitr. z. Kenntn. d. Feldspathbildung. Haarlem, 1866.
ROSENBUSCH.  Verh. d. Naturf. Ver. Freiburg. VI. 1, 95, 98, 103.
STRENG.  N. Jahrb. f. Min. u. Geol. 1871. 598.

### Ottrelite.

v. LASAULX. N. Jabrb. f. Min. u. Geol. 1872. 849.
TSCHERMAK u. SIPÖCZ. Gr. Zeitschr. f. Kryst. 1879. 509.
BECKE. Tsch. Min. u. petr. Mitth. 1878. I. 270.
RENARD et VALLÉE POUSSIN. Ann. de la Soc. géol. Belgique. VI. Mém. 51.
 N. Jahrb. f. Min. u. Geol. 1880. II. 149.

### Perowskite.

BOŘICKY. Sitzungsber. der math.-naturw. Classe d. k. böhm. Ges. d. Wiss.
 1876. Comp. Ref. N. Jahrb. f. Min. u. Geol. 1877. 539.
HUSSAK. Sitzungsber. d. Wien. Akad. d. Wiss. math.-nat. Classe. April 1878.
STELZNER. N. Jahrb. f. Min. u. Geol. 1882. II. Beil.-Bd. 390.

### Phlogopite.

TSCHERMAK. Gr. Zeitschr. f. Kryst. 1878. 33.

### Picotite.

ZIRKEL. Basaltgesteine. Bonn, 1870. 97.
STELZNER. N. Jahrb. f. Min. u. Geol. 1882. II. Beil.-Bd. 393.

**Pinite** (and other decomposition-products of Cordierite).

WICHMANN. Zeitschr. d. deutsch. geol. Ges. 1874. XXVI. 675.

### Plagioclase.

TSCHERMAK. Sitzungsber. d. Wien. Akad. d. Wiss. L. Dec. 1864.
WEISS. Beitr. z. Kenntn. d. Feldspathbildung. Haarlem, 1866.
ROSE. Zeitschr. d. deutsch. geol. Ges. XIX. 1867. 289.
STELZNER. N. Jahrb. f. Min. u. Geol. 1870. 784.
ZIRKEL. Zeitschr. d. deutsch. geol. Ges. 1871. XXIII. 43, 59, 94.
— Basaltgesteine. Bonn, 1870. 28.
HAGGE. Ueber Gabbro. Kiel, 1871.
STRENG. N. Jahrb. f. Min. u. Geol. 1871. 598, 715.
COHEN. N. Jahrb. f. Min. u. Geol. 1874. 460.
v. RATH. Monatsber. d. Berlin. Akad. d. Wiss. 24. Feb. 1876.
ROSENBUSCH. Verh. d. naturforsch. Ges. Freiburg i. Br. VI. 1, 77.
PENCK. Zeitschr. d. deutsch. geol. Ges. 1878. XXX. 97.
PFAFF. Sitzungsber. d. phys.-med. Societ. z. Erlangen. 1878.
SCHUSTER. Tsch. Min. u. petr. Mitth. 1881. III. 117.
— Tsch. Min. u. petr. Mitth. 1882. V. 189.

HOEPFNER.  N. Jahrb. f. Min. u. Geol. 1881. II. 164.
BECKE.  Tsch. Min. u. petr. Mitth. 1882. IV. 253.
KLOCKMANN.  Zeitschr. d. deutsch. geol. Ges. 1882. 373.
V. WERVEKE.  N. Jahrb. f. Min. u. Geol. 1883. II. 97.
KREUTZ.  Tsch. Min. u. petr. Mitth. 1884. VI. 137.

### Pleonaste.

TELLER u. JOHN.  Jahrb. d. kk. geol. R.-Anst. Wien, 1882. XXXII. 589.

### Protobastite (Diaclasite).

TSCHERMAK.  Tsch. Min. Mitth. 1871. 1. Heft. 20.
STRENG.  N. Jahrb. f. Min. u. Geol. 1872. 273. Anm. 2.

### Pyrope.

DOELTER.  Tsch. Min. Mitth. 1873. 13.
SCHRAUF.  Gr. Zeitschr. f. Kryst. 1882. 321 and 1884. II. 21.

### Quartz.

H. CLIFTON SORBY.  Quart. Journ. geol. Soc. Nov. 1858. XIV. 453.
ZIRKEL.  N. Jahrb. f. Min. u. Geol. 1868. 711.
— Pogg. Ann. f. Phys. u. Chem. 1871. CXXXXIV. 324.
ROSENBUSCH.  Reise n. Südbrasilien. Freiburg i. Br., 1870.
BEHRENS.  N. Jahrb. f. Min. u. Geol. 1871. 460.
LEHMANN.  Verh. d. niederrhein. Ges f. Nat. u. Heilkunde. Bonn, 1874. XXXI.
— Verh. d. naturhist. Ver. d. preuss. Rheinlande u. Westphalens. 1874. XXXIV.
V. CHRUSTSCHOFF.  Tsch. Min. u. petr. Mitth. 1882. IV. 473.
BOŘICKY.  Archiv d. naturw. Landesdurchf. Böhmens. 1882. IV. No. 4. 12.

### Ripidolite (Chlorite, Helminth).

O. MEYER.  Zeitschr. d. deutsch. geol. Ges. 1878. XXX. 1, 24.

### Rubellan.

HOLLRUNG.  Tsch. Min. u. petr. Mitth. 1883. V. 304.

### Rutile.

SAUER.  N. Jahrb. f. Min. u. Geol. 1879. 569.
— N. Jahrb. f. Min. u. Geol. 1880. I. 227, 279.
V. WERVEKE.  N. Jahrb. f. Min. u. Geol. 1880. II. 281.

CATHREIN.  N. Jahrb. f. Min. u. Geol. 1881. I. 169.
— Gr. Zeitschr. F. Kryst. 1883. VIII. 321.
H. GYLLING.  N. Jahrb. f. Min. u. Geol. 1882. I. 163.
PICHLER u. BLAAS.  Tsch. Min. u. petr. Mitth. 1882. IV. 513.
SANDBERGER.  N. Jahrb. f. Min. u. Geol. 1882. II. 192.
V. LASAULX.  Gr. Zeitschr. f. Kryst. 1883. VIII. 54.

### Serpentine (comp. Olivine).

WEBSKY.  Zeitschr. d. deutsch. geol. Ges. 1858. 277.
WEISS.  Pogg. Ann. f. Phys. u. Chem. 1863. CXIX. 458.
TSCHERMAK.  Sitzungsber. d. Wien. Akad. d. Wiss. LVI. July 1867.
ZIRKEL.  N. Jahrb. f. Min. u. Geol. 1870. 829.
J. ROTH.  Abhandl. d. Berlin. Akademie d. Wiss. 1869.
DRASCHE.  Tsch. Min. Mitth. 1871. 1.
WEIGAND.  Tsch. Min. Mitth. 1875. 183.
DATHE.  N. Jahrb. f. Min. u. Geol. 1876. 225, 337.
LEMBERG.  Zeitschr. d. deutsch. geol. Ges. 1877. XXX. 457.
BECKE.  Tsch. Min. u. petr. Mitth. 1878. I. 459, 470.
— Tsch. Minn. u. petr. Mitth. 1882. IV. 322.
HARE.  Serpentin von Reichenstein. In.-Diss. Breslau, 1879.
HUSSAK.  Tsch. Min. u. petr. Mitth. 1882. V. 61.
SCHRAUF.  Gr. Zeitschr. f. Kryst. 1882. 321.
SCHULZE.  Zeitschr. d. deutsch. geol. Ges. 1883. XXXV. 433.

### Sillimanite.

V. KALKOWSKY.  Die Gneissform. d. Eulengebirges. Leipzig, 1878.
SCHUMACHER.  Zeitschr. d. deutsch. geol. Ges. 1878. 427.
BECKE.  Tsch. Min. u. petr. Mitth. 1882. IV. 189.

### Scapolite.

MICHEL LÉVY.  Bull. Soc. minér. France. 1878. No. 3 and 5.
BECKE.  Tscherm. Min. u. petr. Mitth. 1882. IV. 369.
TÖRNEBOHM.  Geol. Fören. i Stockholm Förhandl. VI. 185. Comp. Ref. N. Jahrb. f. Min. u. Geol. 1883. I. 245.
CATHREIN.  G. Zeitschr. f. Kryst. 1884. IX. 378.

### Sodalite.

V. RATH.  Zeitschr. d. deutsch. geol. Ges. 1866. 620.
— Verh. d. niederrhein. Ges. f. Nat. u. Heilkunde. 1876. 82.
VRBA.  Sitzungsber. d. Wien. Akad. d. Wiss. LXIX. Feb. 1874.

v. KALKOWSKY. Zeitschr. d. deutsch. geol. Ges. 1878. 663.
v. WERVEKE. N. Jahrb. f. Min. u. Geol. 1880. II. 141.
KOCH. N. Jahrb. f. Min. u. Geol. 1881. I. Beil.-Bd. 149.

### Staurolite.

PETERS u. MALY. Sitzungsber. d. Wien. Akad. d. Wiss. LVII. 1868. 15.
v. LASAULX. Tsch. Min. u. petr. Mitth. 1872. III. 173, and N. Jahrb. f. Min. u. Geol. 1872. 838.
O. MEYER. Zeitschr. d. deutsch. geol. Ges. 1878. XXX. 1.

### Talc.

v. LASAULX. N. Jahrb. f. Min. u. Geol. 1872. 823.
TSCHERMAK. Tsch. Min. Mitth. 1876. I. 65.

### Titanite.

ZIRKEL. Zeitschr. d. deutsch. geol. Ges. 1859. XI. 522, 526.
— Pogg. Ann. f. Phys. u. Chem. 1867. CXXXI. 325.
v. RATH. Zeitschr. d. deutsch. geol. Ges. 1862. XIV. 665.
— Zeitschr. d. deutsch. Geol. Ges. 1864. XVI. 256.
GROTH. N. Jahrb. F. Min. u. Geol. 1866. 46.
v. LASAULX. N. Jahrb. f. Min. u. Geol. 1872. 362.
v. WERVEKE. N. Jahrb. f. Min. u. Geol. 1880. II. 159.
MANN. N. Jahrb. f. Min. u. Geol. 1882. II. 200.
DILLER. N. Jahrb. f. Min. u. Geol. 1883. I. 187.

### Titaniferous Magnetite.

v. WERVEKE. N. Jahrb. f. Min. u. Geol. 1880. II. 141.
CATHREIN. Gr. Zeitschr. f. Kryst. 1883. VIII. 321.

### Tremolite (Grammatite).

TSCHERMAK. Tsch. Min. Mitth. 1871. 37. and 1876. 65.
BECKE. Tsch. Min. u. petr. Mitth. 1882. IV. 338.

### Tridymite.

ZIRKEL. Pogg. Ann. f. Phys. u. Chem. 1870. CXL. 492.
v. LASAULX. N. Jahrb. f. Min. u. Geol. 1869. 66.
— Gr. Zeitschr. f. Kryst. 1878. II. 254.
STRENG. Tsch. Min. Mitth. 1871. 47.
— N. Jahrb. f. Min. u. Geol. 1872. 266.

ROSENBUSCH. Verhandl. d. naturf. Ges. Freiburg i. Br. 1873. VI. 1. Hft. 96.
SCHUSTER. Tsch. Min. u. petr. Mitth. 1878. 71.

### Tourmaline.

ZIRKEL. N. Jahrb. f. Min. u. Geol. 1875. 628.
TÖRNEBOHM. Geol. Fören. i. Stockholm Förhandl. 1876. III. 218.
MEYER. Zeitschr. d. deutsch. geol. Ges. 1878. XXX. 1, 24.
WICHMANN. N. Jahrb. f. Min. u. Geol. 1880. II. 294.
DATHE. Zeitschr. d. deutsch. geol. Ges. 1882. XXXIV. 12.
PICHLER u. BLAAS. Tsch. Min. u. petr. Mitth. 1882. IV. 512.

### Uralite.

G. ROSE. Reise nach dem Ural. II. 371.
BECKE. Tsch. Min. u. petr. Mitth. 1882. V. 157.

### Viridite (Delessite, Chlorophæite).

VOGELSANG. Zeitschr. d. deutsch. geol. Ges. 1872. XXIV. 529.
KOSMANN. Verh. d. naturw. Ver. d. preuss. Rheinlande u. Westph. XXV. 239. and 289.
TSCHERMAK. Die Porphyrgesteine Oesterreichs. Wien, 1869. 42, 66, 134.
— Tsch. Min. Mitth. 1872. 112.

### Wollastonite.

FOUQUÉ. Compt. rend. 15 Mar. 1875.
LAGORIO. Andesite d. Kaukasus. Dorpat, 1878. Ref. N. Jahrb. f. Min. u. Geol. 1880. I. 209.
CH. WHITMAN CROSS. Tsch. Min. u. petr. Mitth. 1881. III. 373.
TÖRNEBOHM. Geol. Fören. i. Stockholm Fürh. 1883. VI. No. 12. 542. Comp. Ref. N. Jahrb. f. Min. u. Geol. 1884. I. 230.

### Zeolite (Analcime).

ROSENBUSCH. Nephelinit v. Katzenbuckel. Freiburg i. Br., 1869.
KLOOS. N. Jahrb. f. Min. u. Geol. 1884. III. Beil.-Bd. 37.

### Zircon.

SANDBERGER. Würzburger nat. Zeitschr. 1866./67. VI. 128 and 1883.
— Zeitschr. d. deutsch. geol. Ges. 1883. XXXV. 193.
— N. Jahrb. f. Min. u. Geol. 1881. I. 258.

ZIRKEL. N. Jahrb. f. Min. u. Geol. 1875. 628.
— N. Jahrb. f. Min. u. Geol. 1880. I. 89.
TÖRNEBOHM. Geol. Föhren. i Stockholm Förhandling. 1876. III. No. 34. and N. Jahrb. f. Min. u. Geol. 1877. 97.
MICHEL LÉVY. Bull. Soc. minéral. France. 1877. No. 5. 77.
ROSENBUSCH. Sulla presenza dello zircone nelle roccie. Atti d. R. Accadern. d. Science. Torino 1881. Vol. XVI.
BECKE. Tsch. Min. u. petr. Mitth. 1882. IV. 204.
FLETCHER. Gr. Zeitschr. f. Kryst. 1882. 80.
NESSIG. Zeitschr. d. deutsch. geol. Ges. 1883. XXXV. 118.
v. CHRUSTSCHOFF. Tsch. Min. u. petr. Mitth. 1884. VI. 172.

### Zoisite.

RIESS. Tsch. Min. u. petr. Mitth. 1878. I. 188.
BECKE. Tsch. Min. u. petr. Mitth. 1878. I. 249. and 1882. IV. 312.

# EXPLANATIONS OF CUTS ACCOMPANYING PART II.

| FIG. | | PAGE |
|---|---|---|
| 51 | ILMENITE. Grain, partly decomposed into leucoxene, with undecomposed earthy filaments interlaminated.................................. | 111 |
| 52 | OPAL. As filling of a cavity, in concentric layers, inclosing small groups of tridymite tablets. (After Fouqué.)........................ | 112 |
| 53 | HAUYN. Cross-section with opacitic border and vitreous inclosures; penetrated by a network of black lines crossing each other at right angles........................................................ | 115 |
| 54 | *a.* MELANITE cross section, zonally developed...................... | 117 |
| | *b.* ALMANDINE GRAIN, with inclosures of quartz-grains; traversed by irregular cleavage fissures.................................. | 117 |
| 55 | PYROPE GRAIN ($P$) with border of so-called *kelyphite* ($K$). From the serpentine ($S$) from Kremse, Bohemian forest. On the serpentine portion ($S$) showing the "mesh-structure" is a thin layer of fresh olivine grains, followed by the fibrous metamorphosed zone ($K'$) of *pyrope;* this has been called *kelyphite* by Schrauf, and is a "*pyrogene*" product, although regarded by others as an "*hydatogene*" product, and has been regarded as allied to an augitic mineral........ | 117 |
| 56 | PEROWSKITE GRAINS in the so-called "hacked" figures. (After Stelzner.)........................................................ | 120 |
| 57 | LEUCITE cross-section in polarized light, showing the polysynthetic striation. (After Zirkel.)...................................... | 122 |
| 58 | Cross sections of small LEUCITE crystals and grains (constituents II. order), with vitreous inclosures regularly distributed........... | 123 |
| 59 | RUTILE CRYSTAL. Knee-, heart-shaped, and polysynthetic twins. (After Reusch.)............................................... | 122 |
| 60 | ZIRCON CRYSTALS. (After Fouqué.)............................... | 124 |
| 61 | SCAPOLITE cross-section, at right angles to the chief axis, with rectangular cleavage.............................................. | 124 |

| FIG | | PAGE |
|---|---|---|
| 62 | MELILITE. *a.* Cross-sections parallel to the chief axis. The upper shows a separation into fine fibres and cleavage-fissures parallel *oP*; the under, the so-called "pflock-structure," pear-shaped and spindle-shaped canals originating from the face *oP*, which appear as a small circle in sections (parallel) *oP* (Fig. 62, *b*). Fig. 62, *c*, shows a larger cross-section of an irregular grain, wherein small leucite grains are developed. (*a* and *b* after Stelzner.)............. | 127 |
| 63 | QUARTZ. *a—d* are cross-sections of the conchoidal crystal skeleton, which occur interpenetrated with orthoclase "micropegmatitic." *a.* Section parallel to the chief axis. *b.* Section parallel to the base. *c.* Section at right angles to the prismatic edges. *d.* Section inclined to the same. (After Fouqué.) *e.* Cross-section of an orthoclase wherein quartz is developed micropegmatitic................ | 129 |
| 64 | TRIDYMITE. Crystal groups of thin hexagonal tablets overlapping each other like roof-tiles. (After Fouqué.)........ ............... | 131 |
| 65 | CALCITE GRAIN, with rhombohedral cleavage and twinning striations. After — $\frac{1}{2}R$...................................................... | 132 |
| 66 | NEPHELINE. *a.* Transverse section. *b.* Longitudinal section, with augitic inclosures zonally distributed........................... | 134 |
| 67 | APATITE. *a.* Transverse section. *b.* Longitudinal section, with cleavage-fissures and acicular inclosures parallel to the base....... | 137 |
| 68 | TOURMALINE. *a.* Longitudinal section. *b.* Transverse section zonally developed................................................... | 138 |
| 69 | TOURMALINE CRYSTAL. (After Reusch.)......... ............... | 138 |
| 70 | OLIVINE cross-section in different degrees of decomposition. *a.* With undecomposed centre. *b.* "Serpentinized" only on the edges and cleavage-fissures................................................ | 141 |
| 71 | OLIVINE cross-section. *a.* Cross section parallel *oP*. *b.* Cross-section parallel $\infty \breve{P} \infty$. (After Fouqué.)........................... | 140 |
| 72 | SILLIMANITE. *a.* Transverse section. *b.* Long, broken needle, with transverse fissures............................................. | 142 |
| 73 | STAUROLITE. Twin with inclosures of quartz granules; the + sign annexed indicates the position of the directions of vibration in the individual which is hatched ..................................... | 142 |
| 74 | ENSTATITE and BRONZITE transverse sections. *a.* Optical orientation according to Tschermak's position. *b.* According to G. v. Rath's position.................................................. | 144 |
| 75 | ENSTATITE longitudinal section, with the cleavage fissures parallel to the vertical axis partially decomposed into bastite................ | 145 |

# EXPLANATIONS OF CUTS ACCOMPANYING PART II. 217

| FIG. | | PAGE |
|---|---|---|
| 76 | ANDALUSITE cross-sections. *a.* Transverse section with rectangular cleavage-cracks, and opaque granules distributed centrally and in a cross-shape. (Similar to chiastolite.)........................... | 153 |
| 77 | CORDIERITE GRAIN, with a fibrous decomposition on the cleavage-cracks, with inclosures of sillimanite needles..................... | 155 |
| 78 | Transverse section of a twinned cordierite crystal. The apparently hexagonal crystal, composed of three individuals, divides into six fields in polarized light, two of which lying opposite extinguish together; the position of the directions of vibration is designated by a mark................................................................ | 154 |
| 79 | ZOISITE cross-sections. *a.* Transverse section. *b.* Longitudinal section, showing cleavage-fissures and fluid inclosures arranged in a series........................................................... | 155 |
| 80 | BIOTITE leaflet, parallel $oP$; the outer portions are decomposed into chlorite and contain earthy granules and epidote needles; the irregularly defined kernel is fresh......................................... | 156 |
| 81 | BIOTITE longitudinal section, showing cleavage-cracks parallel $oP$ and inclosures of calcite lenses...................................... | 156 |
| 82 | OTTRELITE. Section at right angles to $oP$, twinned polysynthetically after $oP$. The annexed $+$ indicates the position of the directions of vibration...................................................... | 164 |
| 83 | SANIDINE cross-sections. $a =$ parallel $oP$ or $\infty P \infty$. $b =$ Carlsbad twin. $c =$ Baveno twin. $d =$ parallel $\infty P \infty$ with a combination of $oP$, $\infty P \infty$, $2P \infty$, $e =$ parallel $\infty P \infty$. (After Rosenbusch.)... | 166 |
| 84 | AUGITE cross-section. *a.* At right angles to the vertical axis. *b.* Parallel to the orthopinacoid. *c.* Parallel to the clinopinacoid. (After Fouqué.).................................................. | 168 |
| 85 | URALITE cross-section. The seconary hornblende is partially developed over the augite, with a twin lamella after $\infty P \infty$. (After Becke.)........................................................ | 175 |
| 86 | HORNBLENDE cross-section. *a.* Transverse section. *b.* Parallel $\infty P \infty$. *c.* Parallel $\infty P \infty$. (After Fouqué.)..................... | 172 |
| 87 | EPIDOTE. Optical orientation. (After Klein and v. Lasaulx.) Opt. A. $=$ optic axes (for red and green), I. a first negative middle line, II. $c =$ second middle line, $b = b$ optic normals. *a.* Clinodiagonal and one direction of cleavage. *c.* Vertical axis.................. | 176 |
| 88 | EPIDOTE twin after $\infty P \infty$. (After Reusch.)...................... | 176 |
| 89 | EPIDOTE CRYSTAL. (After Reusch.).... ....................... | 176 |

## 218  DETERMINATION OF ROCK-FORMING MINERALS.

| FIG. | | PAGE |
|---|---|---|
| 90 | TITANITE. Cross-section of crystals and grains; simple individuals and twins after $oP$............................................. | 176 |
| 91 | MICROCLINE. Section parallel $oP$ shows the latticed twinning striations and lenticular albite developed within, with polysynthetic striations also..................... ............................ | 180 |
| 92 | MICROCLINE from Lampersdorf, Silesia. (After A. Beutell.) Section parallel $oP$. The microcline is in part homogeneous, in part shows the latticed structure; the larger albite bands run parallel to the edge $oP : \check{P} \infty$ and show fine twinnings striation parallel $oP : \infty \check{P} \infty$.. | 180 |
| 93 | MICROPERTHITE. $a =$ section parallel to the separation-plane corresponding $\infty \check{P} \infty$, shows a peculiar network composed of filaments refracting light powerfully, crossing each other at right angles. $b =$ section parallel $oP$, $c$ parallel $\infty \check{P} \infty$, both with entered polysynthetically twinned albite lamellæ. (After Becke.)............. | 180 |
| 94 | Plagioclase crystal showing the position of the obtuse edge $P/M$, and the bearing of the directions of extinction toward them. (After Schuster.)...................................................... | 182 |
| 95 | PLAGIOCLASE. Cross-section parallel $M(\infty \check{P} \infty)$. Right longitudinal plane ($\infty \check{P} \infty$) of a crystal correctly oriented. (Compare Fig. 94.) The obtuse edge $P : M$ lies above............................ | 182 |
| 96 | PLAGIOCLASE. Cross-section parallel $P(oP)$. Upper terminal plane ($oP$) of an oriented crystal; the obtuse edge $P : M$ lies to the right. | 182 |
| 97–101$b$. | Interference-figures of PLAGIOCLASE on cleavage-leaflets parallel $M$ and $P$. They have reference to the upper $oP$- and right $\infty \check{P} \infty$-planes of an oriented crystal (Fig. 94), and are all in the same position as Figs. 95 and 96. | |
| | Fig. 97  Albite, parallel $M(\infty \check{P} \infty)$........................ ....... | 182 |
| | 98  Oligoclase, parallel $M(\infty \check{P} \infty)$ .... .................. | 184 |
| | 99$a$  Labrador, parallel $M(\infty \check{P} \infty)$........................ | 186 |
| | 99$b$  Labrador, parallel $P(oP)$........................... | 186 |
| | 100$a$  Bytownite, parallel $M(\infty \check{P} \infty)$....................... | 186 |
| | 100$b$  Bytownite, parallel $P(oP)$........................... | 186 |
| | 101$a$  Anorthite, parallel $M(\infty \check{P} \infty)$....................... | 188 |
| | 101$b$  Anorthite, parallel $P(oP)$..........................:.. | 188 |
| | (Figs. 95–101 after Schuster.) | |
| 102 | ANDESINE. Cross-section parallel $oP$. Zonally developed. (After Becke.)............................................................ | 185 |
| 103 | AGGREGATES of acicular zeolite crystals and concentric-conchoidal carbonates as cavity-deposits.................................... | 195 |

# CUTS ACCOMPANYING PART II.

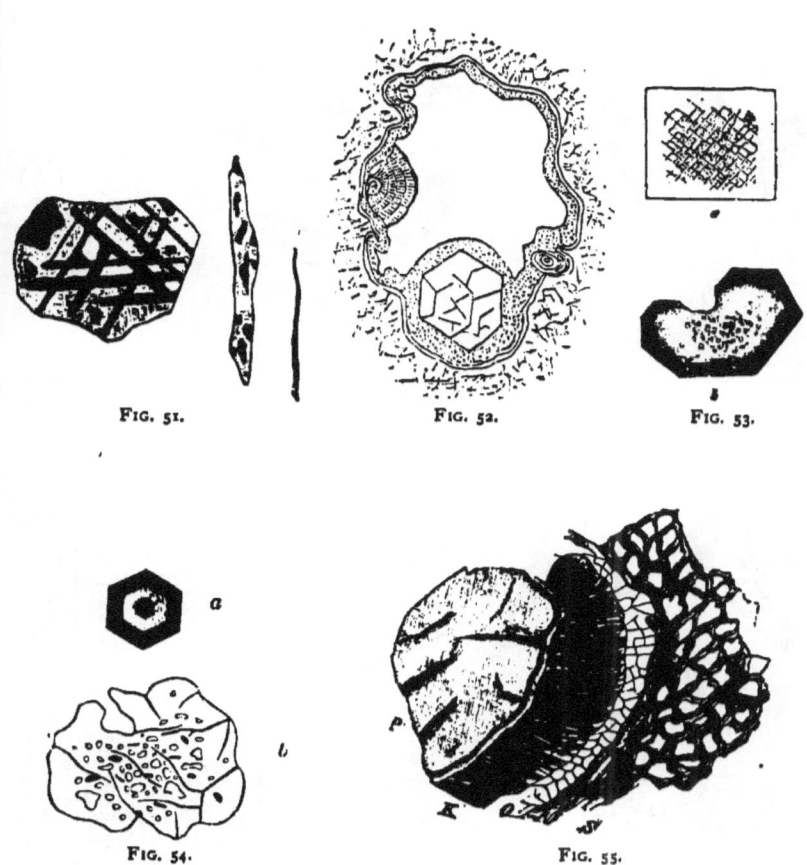

Fig. 51.　　Fig. 52.　　Fig. 53.

Fig. 54.　　Fig. 55.

220 *DETERMINATION OF ROCK-FORMING MINERALS.*

CUTS ACCOMPANYING PART II.—*Continued.*

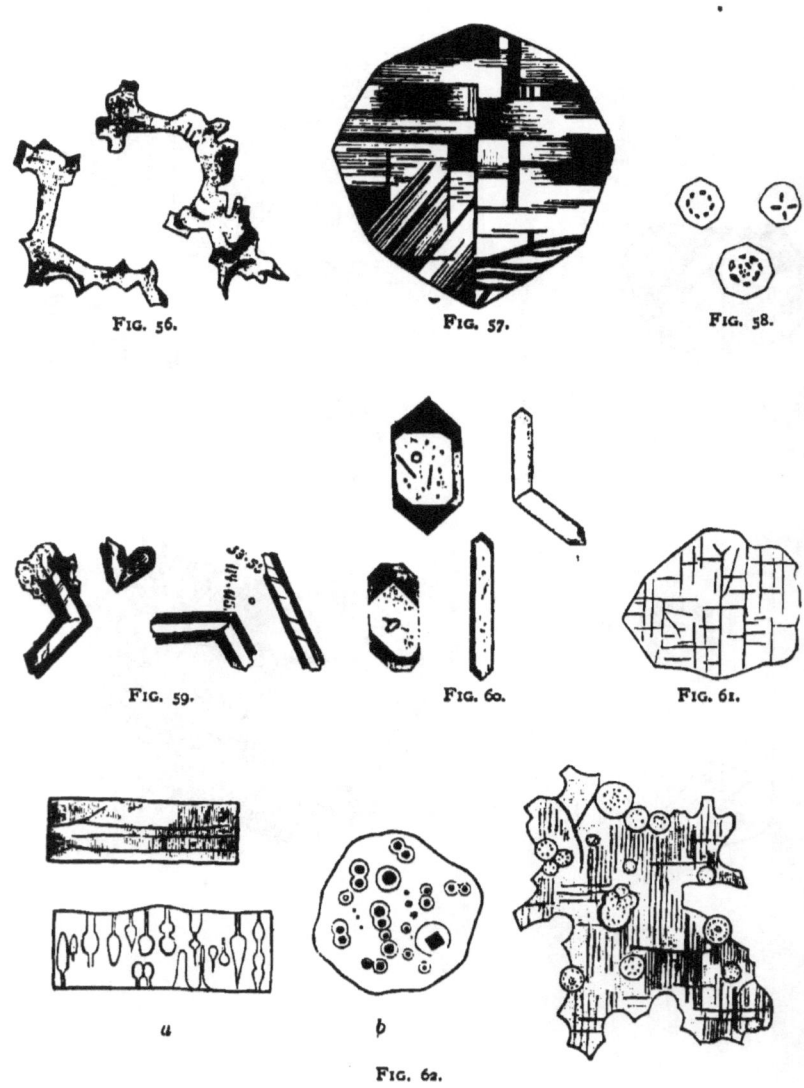

FIG. 56.   FIG. 57.   FIG. 58.

FIG. 59.   FIG. 60.   FIG. 61.

*a*   *b*

FIG. 62.

## CUTS ACCOMPANYING PART II.—*Continued.*

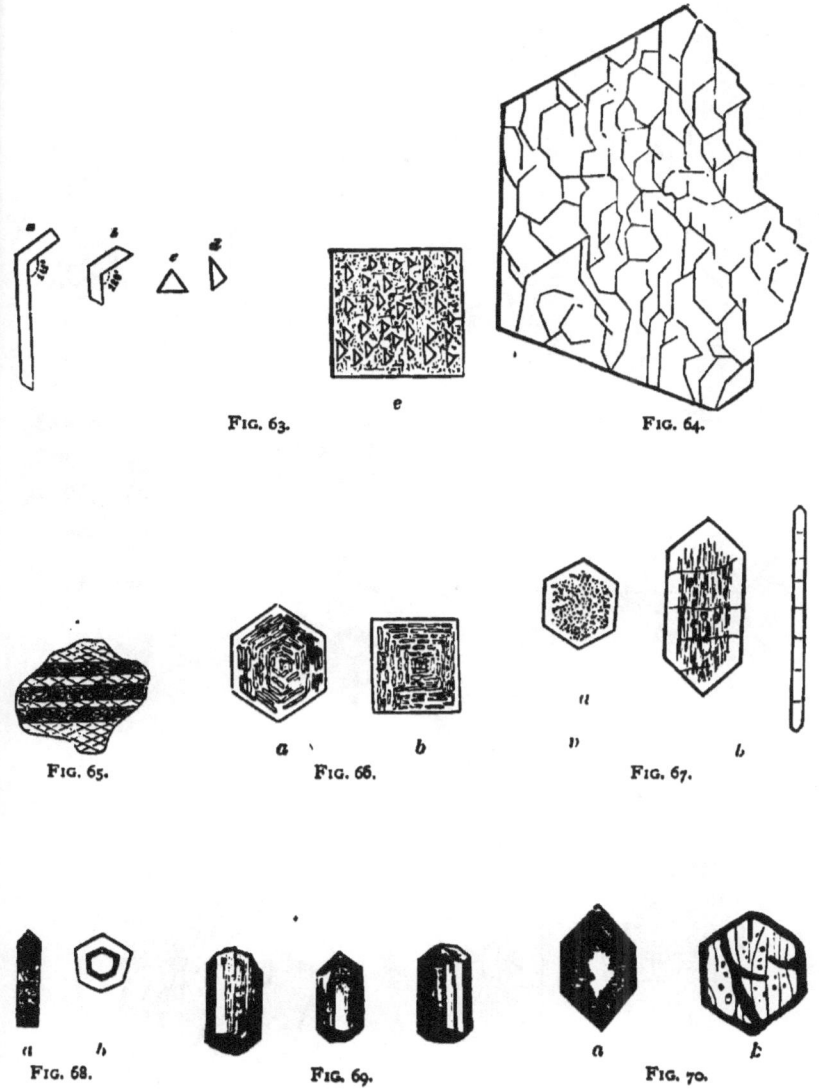

## DETERMINATION OF ROCK-FORMING MINERALS.

### CUTS ACCOMPANYING PART II.—*Continued.*

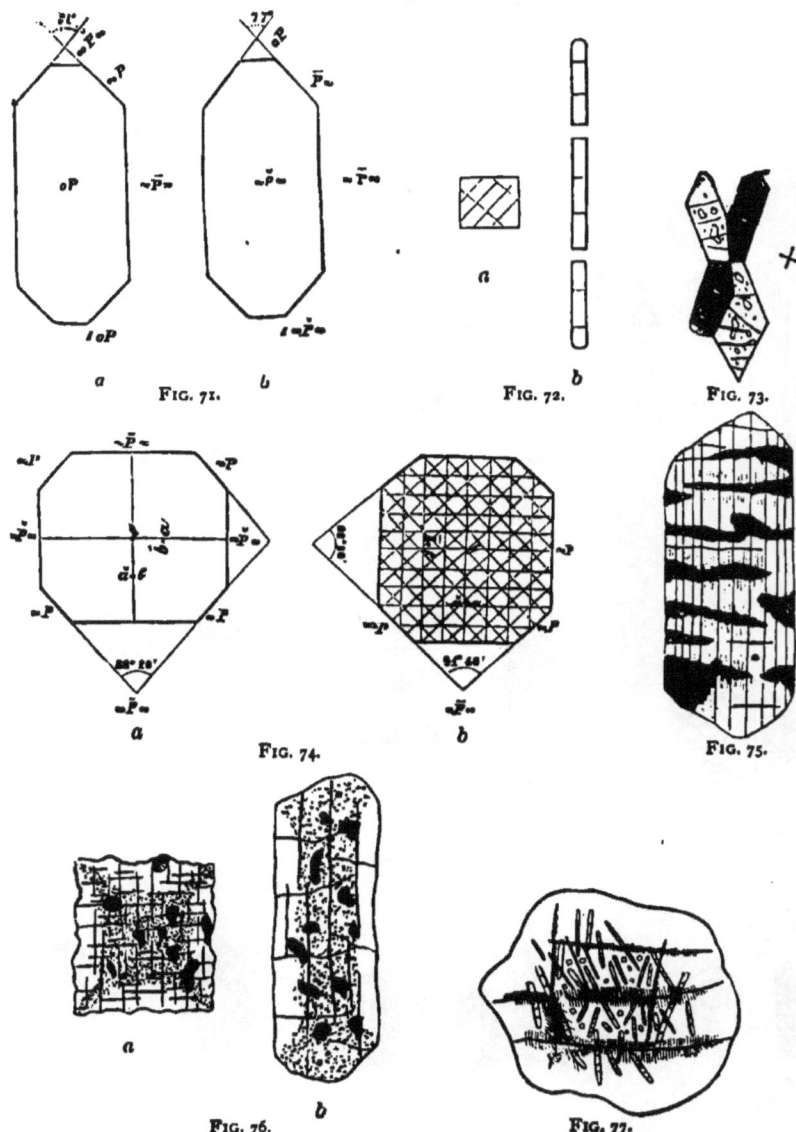

Fig. 71.  Fig. 72.  Fig. 73.

Fig. 74.  Fig. 75.

Fig. 76.  Fig. 77.

# CUTS ACCOMPANYING PART II. — *Continued.*

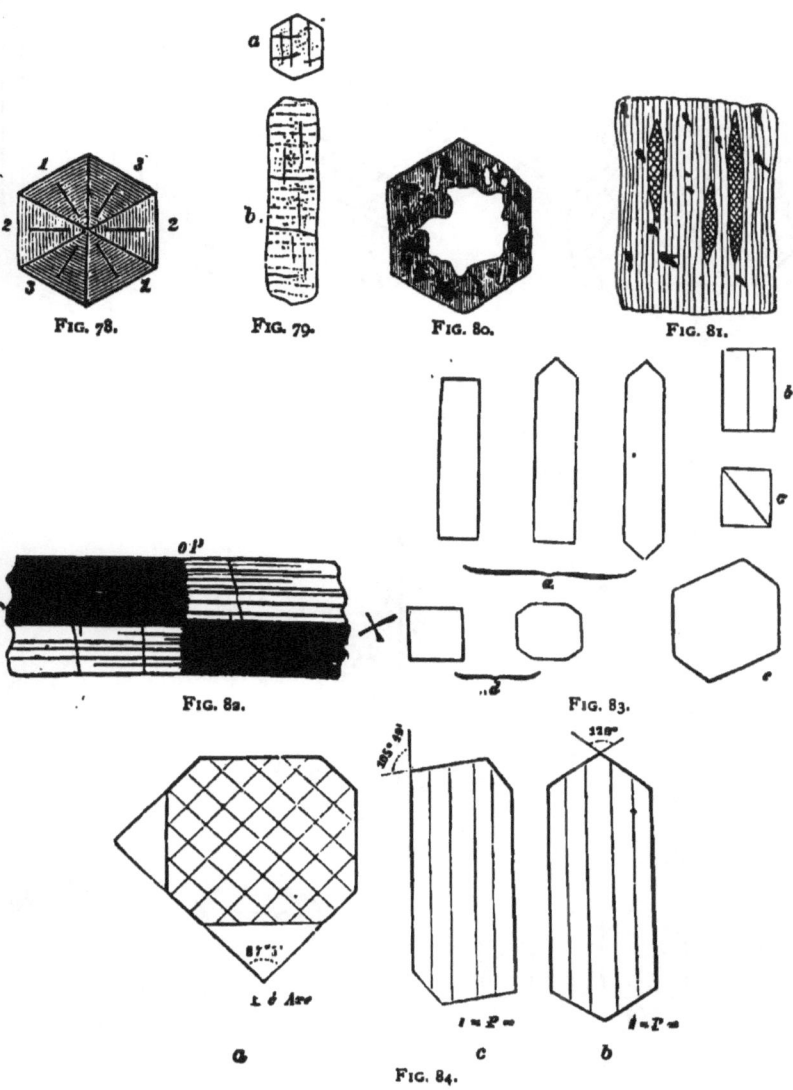

FIG. 78.   FIG. 79.   FIG. 80.   FIG. 81.

FIG. 82.   FIG. 83.

FIG. 84.

224   *DETERMINATION OF ROCK-FORMING MINERALS.*

## CUTS ACCOMPANYING PART II.—*Continued.*

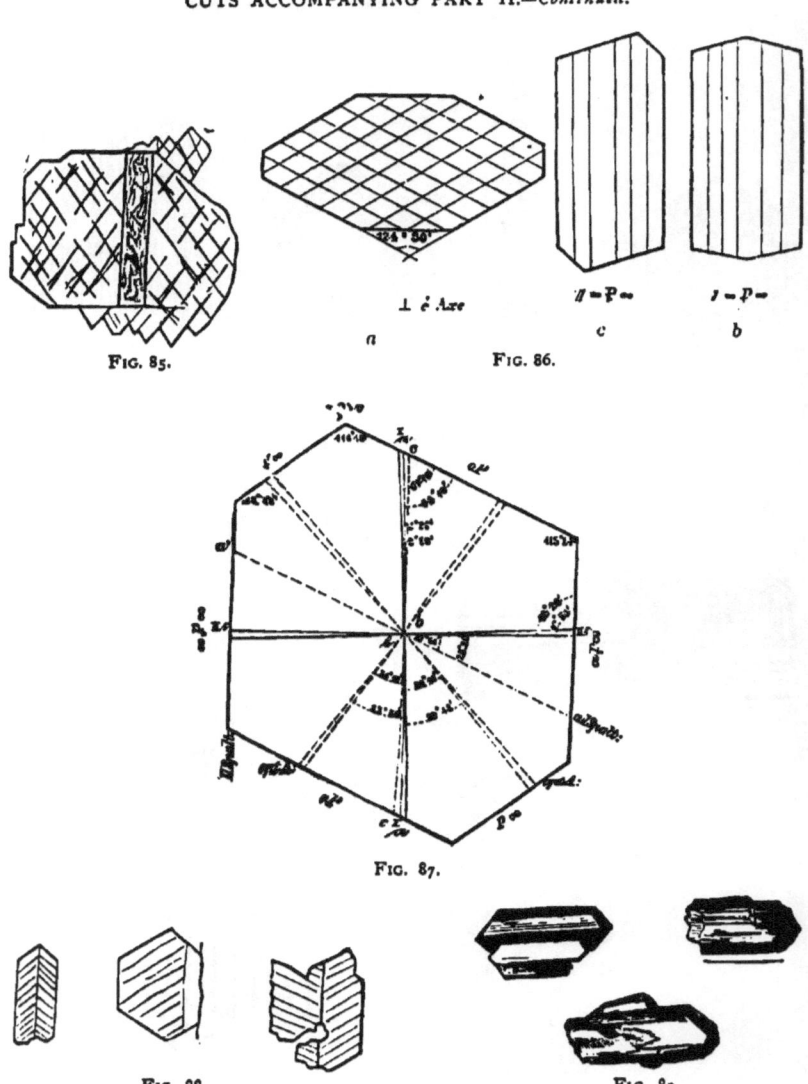

## CUTS ACCOMPANYING PART II.—*Continued.*

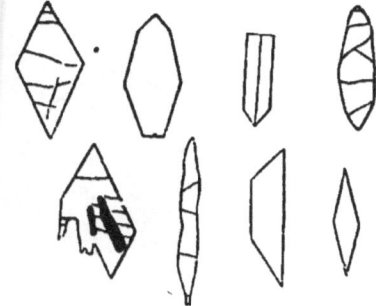

FIG. 90.

FIG. 91.

FIG. 92.

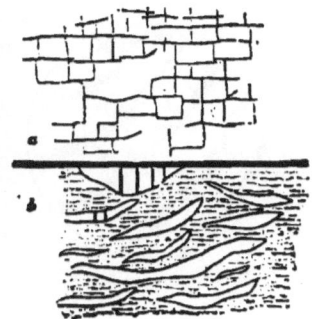

FIG. 93.

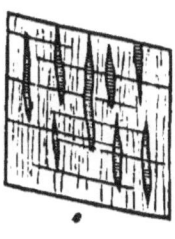

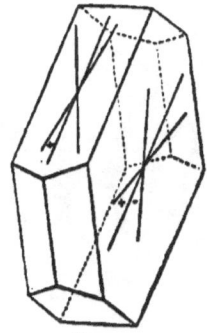

FIG. 94.

226  *DETERMINATION OF ROCK-FORMING MINERALS.*

CUTS ACCOMPANYING PART II.—*Continued.*

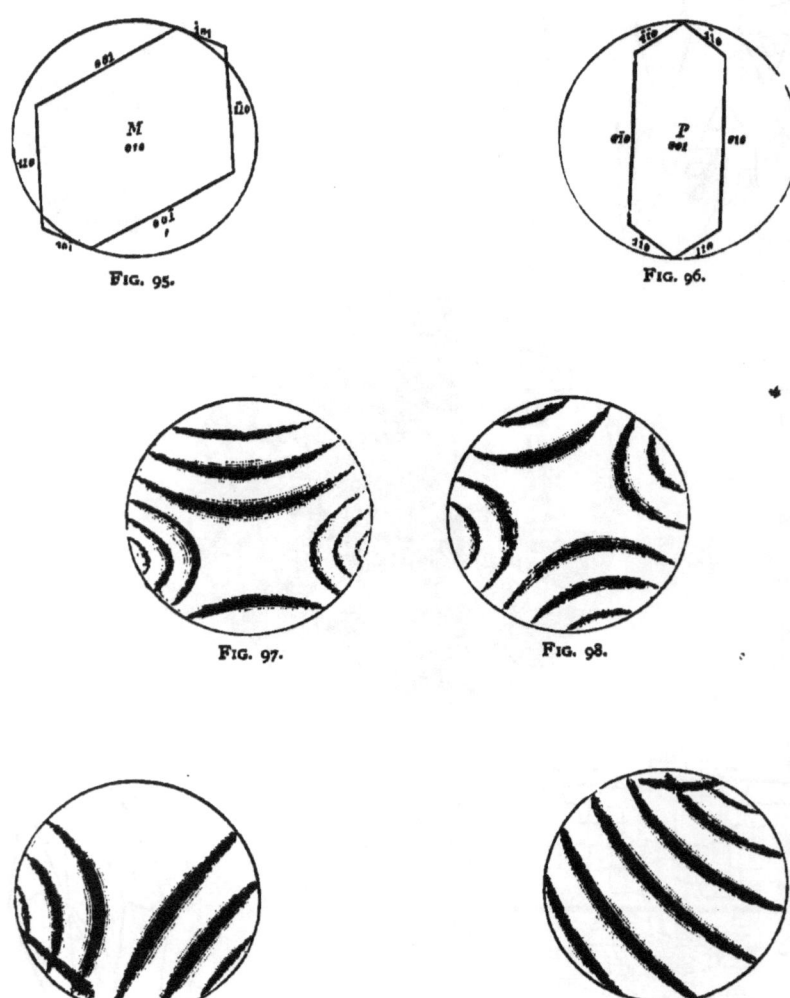

Fig. 95.

Fig. 96.

Fig. 97.

Fig. 98.

Fig. 99 *a*.

Fig. 99 *b*.

## CUTS ACCOMPANYING PART II.—*Concluded.*

Fig. 100 *a*.

Fig. 100 *b*.

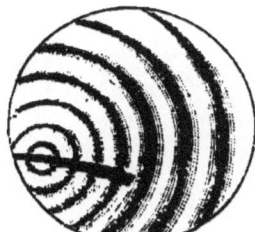

Fig. 101 *a*.

Fig. 101 *b*.

Fig. 102.

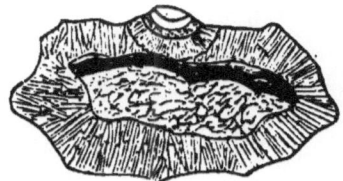

Fig. 103.

# INDEX.

## A

| | PAGE |
|---|---|
| Aegerine | 197 |
| Aggregate | 188 |
| Acmite | 172, 197 |
| Actinolite | 174, 197 |
| Albite | 182, 198 |
| Almandine | 116, 198 |
| Ammonium-magnesium Phosphate | 62 |
| Amorphous Minerals | 112 |
| ———, Behavior of, in polarized light | 17, 30, 106 |
| Analcime | 118, 198 |
| Analyzer | 8 |
| Anatase | 124 |
| Andalusite | 152, 198 |
| Andesine | 184, 198 |
| Anisotrope | 106 |
| Anomite | 158, 199 |
| Anorthite | 188, 199 |
| Anthophyllite | 22, 146, 199 |
| Apatite | 53, 136, 199 |
| Arragonite | 194 |
| Arfvedsonite | 174, 199 |
| Augite, Ordinary and basaltic | 168, 199 |
| — optical orientation of | 24, 28 |
| — shell-formed structure of | 91, 92 |
| — cleavage of | 84 |
| — interpenetrations of | 93 |
| — twins | 41 |
| Axes of elasticity, Determination of the position of | 26 |
| Axial plane, Determination of the position of the optic | 33 |
| Axial colors, Determination of the | 45 |

## B

| | |
|---|---|
| *Bachinger* | 203 |
| *Barrois* | 201 |
| Barium-mercury solution | 75 |
| Bastite | 22, 150, 192, 200 |

| | PAGE |
|---|---|
| *Becke* | 92, 164, 197–211, 213, 214 |
| *Becker* | 202, 204, 207, 208 |
| *Behrens* | 51, 59, 200, 208, 210 |
| Belonite | 87 |
| *Bertrand* | 7 |
| Biotite | 36, 89, 156 |
| Bitumen | 110 |
| *Blaas* | 205, 211, 213 |
| *Bodewig* | 203 |
| *Böhm* | 198 |
| *Bořicky* | 51, 55, 207–210 |
| *Bourgeois* | 51 |
| *Brögger* | 208 |
| Bronzite | 22, 146, 200 |
| *Bücking* | 200 |
| *Bütschly* | 199 |
| Bytownite | 186, 200 |

## C

| | |
|---|---|
| Cadmium-boro-tungstate solution | 73 |
| Cæsium alum | 63 |
| Calcite | 38, 132, 200 |
| Calcite plate | 12 |
| *Calderon* | 7 |
| — Double-plate | 12 |
| *Calderon y Araña* | 201 |
| Carinthine | 172 |
| Cancrinite | 136, 200 |
| *Cathrein* | 76, 210–212 |
| Centring adjustment on microscope | 13 |
| Chabazite | 194 |
| Chalcedony | 192, 200 |
| Chemical investigation, Methods of | 50 |
| Chiastolite | 152, 201 |
| Chlorite | 162 |
| Chloritoid | 162, 201 |
| Chlorophæite | 192, 213 |
| Chromite | 110, 118, 201 |
| *Chrustschoff* | 99, 205, 210, 213 |
| Clinochlore | 162 |

# 230  INDEX.

| | PAGE |
|---|---|
| Cohen | 1, 66, 81, 85, 197, 205, 208, 209 |
| Condenser | 10 |
| Cordierite | 40, 47, 154, 201 |
| Corrosion of the rock-forming minerals | 88 |
| Corundum | 138 |
| Couseranite | 126, 201 |
| Cross | 198, 201, 204, 205, 213 |
| Crystal formation, Disturbances in the | 87 |
| Crystallites | 86 |
| Crystallization, Determination of the systems of | 106 |
| Crystalloids | 86 |
| Cyanite | 178, 202 |

## D

| | |
|---|---|
| Dathe | 198–202, 207, 208, 211–213 |
| Decomposition of the rock-constituents | 101 |
| Delessite | 192, 213 |
| Des Cloizeaux | 207 |
| Determination of the system of crystallization of the rock-forming minerals | 106 |
| Diaclasite | 150, 210 |
| Diallage | 170, 201 |
| Dichroite | 154 |
| Diller | 212 |
| Diopside | 170, 202 |
| Dipyr | 126, 201 |
| Dispersion of the optic axes | 36 |
| Disthene | 29, 178, 202 |
| Doelter | 79, 204, 210 |
| Dolomite | 132, 202 |
| Double-refracting minerals in parallel polarized light | 17 |
| Double-refraction, Determination of the character of | 31, 34 |
| v. Drasche | 198–200, 202, 211 |

## E

| | |
|---|---|
| Eisen-kies | 108 |
| Elæolite | 134, 203 |
| Enstatite | 21, 144, 203 |
| Epidote | 24, 42, 176, 203 |
| Extinction, Oblique | 25 |
| ——, Parallel | 19 |

## F

| | |
|---|---|
| Feldspar, Shell-formed structure of | 91 |
| ——, Decomposition of | 102 |
| Fisher | 197 |
| Fletcher | 213 |
| Fluid inclosures | 94, 95 |

| | PAGE |
|---|---|
| Fluor-spar (Fluorite) | 120, 203 |
| Form of occurrence of the rock-components | 81 |
| v. Foullon | 208 |
| Fouqué | 1, 66, 76, 79, 81, 197, 205, 206, 213 |
| Fourth-undulation mica | 13 |

## G

| | |
|---|---|
| Gas-pores | 94 |
| Gastaldite | 194 |
| Gisevius | 67 |
| Glasmasse | 112 |
| Glaucophane | 174, 203 |
| Globulite | 86 |
| Goldschmidt | 66, 201 |
| Garnet | 116 |
| Graphite | 110, 204 |
| v. Groddeck | 207 |
| Groth | 16, 45, 212 |
| Green earth | 192 |
| Gümbel | 205 |
| Gylling | 211 |
| Gypsum | 178, 204 |

## H

| | |
|---|---|
| Hagge | 199, 202, 204, 205, 208, 209 |
| Hague | 205 |
| Hammerschmidt | 204 |
| Harada's apparatus | 70 |
| Hare | 211 |
| Hausmann | 203 |
| Hauyn | 54, 114, 204 |
| Heating apparatus | 15 |
| Helminth | 162, 210 |
| Hematite | 110, 138, 204 |
| Hercynite | 118, 204 |
| Hexagonal minerals | 106, 128 |
| ——, Behavior of, in polarized light | 18, 30 |
| Höpfner | 210 |
| Hollrung | 210 |
| Hornblende, Cleavage of | 84 |
| ——, Ordinary and basaltic | 172 |
| ——, Opacitic border of | 89 |
| ——, Optical orientation of | 24, 28 |
| Humboldilith | 126 |
| Hussak | 201, 206, 209, 211 |
| Hydrofluosilicic acid | 55 |
| Hypersthene | 148, 204 |
| ——, Inclosures in | 100 |
| ——, Optical orientation of | 22 |
| ——, Pleochroism of | 48 |

# INDEX.

## I

| | PAGE |
|---|---|
| *Iddings* | 205 |
| Ilmenite | 110 |
| Index of refraction, Determination of | 14, 44 |
| Inclosures of the rock-forming minerals | 93 |
| —— of gases | 94 |
| —— of fluids | 95 |
| —— of vitreous particles | 97 |
| —— of foreign minerals | 99 |
| *Inostranzeff* | 200, 202 |
| Interference-figures | 32 |
| Interpenetration of the rock-constituents | 93 |
| *Investigation*, Optical methods of | 16 |
| ——, Chemical methods of | 50 |
| Isotrope | 106 |

## J

| | |
|---|---|
| *Jeremejeff* | 198 |
| *v. John* | 198, 203, 205, 210 |

## K

| | |
|---|---|
| *v. Kalkowsky* | 202–204, 206, 211, 212 |
| Kaemmerite | 162 |
| *Kispatič* | 208 |
| C. *Klein* | 7 |
| D. *Klein* | 66, 73 |
| *Klein's* solution | 73 |
| *Klockmann* | 210 |
| *Kloos* | 202, 204, 207, 213 |
| *Knop* | 54, 206 |
| *v. Kobell* | 202 |
| *Koch* | 197, 200, 203, 212 |
| *Koenig* | 199 |
| *Koller* | 207 |
| *Kosmann* | 204, 213 |
| *Krenner* | 205 |
| *Kreutz* | 199, 205, 208, 210 |
| *Küch* | 203 |

## L

| | |
|---|---|
| Labradorite | 186, 205 |
| *Lagorio* | 199, 200, 213 |
| *v. Lasaulx* | 7, 198, 201–204, 207, 209, 211–213 |
| *Laspeyres* | 7, 45, 49, 203, 205, 208 |
| *Lehmann* | 210 |
| *Lemberg* | 200, 201, 211 |
| Leucite | 120, 122, 205 |
| Liebenerite | 136, 206 |
| *Liebisch* | 7 |
| Longulite | 86 |
| *Lossen* | 198, 207 |
| *Luedecke* | 203 |

## M

| | PAGE |
|---|---|
| Magnesite | 132, 206 |
| Magnetite | 108, 206 |
| Magnet-kies | 110 |
| *Maly* | 212 |
| *Mann* | 197, 212 |
| Margarite | 86 |
| Measurement of angles | 83 |
| Mechanical separation of the rock-forming minerals | 66 |
| —— —— by means of solutions of high specific gravity | 67 |
| —— —— by the solution of the iodides of barium and mercury | 75 |
| —— —— by the solution of the iodides of potassium and mercury | 67 |
| —— —— by the solution of cadmium boro-tungstate | 73 |
| —— —— by means of the electro-magnet | 79 |
| —— —— by means of acids | 76 |
| ——, Apparatus for | 70 |
| Meionite | 124, 206 |
| Melanite | 116, 206 |
| Mellilith | 126, 206 |
| Meroxene | 156, 206 |
| *Meyer* | 200, 202, 210–213 |
| *Michel Lévy* | 1, 28, 44, 51, 66, 76, 81, 197, 207, 211, 214 |
| Microchemical Methods | 51 |
| —— —— of Bořicky | 55 |
| —— —— of Behrens | 59 |
| Microchemical reactions with Aluminium | 62 |
| —— —— Barium | 63 |
| —— —— Boron | 65 |
| —— —— Calcium | 57, 60 |
| —— —— Chlorine | 64 |
| —— —— Fluorine | 64 |
| —— —— Iron | 57, 63 |
| —— —— Lithium | 57, 63 |
| —— —— Magnesium | 57, 62 |
| —— —— Manganese | 58, 63 |
| —— —— Phosphorus | 64 |
| —— —— Potassium | 56, 60 |
| —— —— Silicon | 65 |
| —— —— Sodium | 56, 61 |
| —— —— Strontium | 58, 63 |
| —— —— Sulphur | 64 |
| —— —— Water | 66 |
| Microcline | 180, 207 |
| Microlites | 85, 86, 207 |
| Micrometer | 14 |

# INDEX.

Micropegmatite.......................... 93
Microperthite............................ 180
Microscope............................... 7
Monoclinic minerals..................... 107
———, Behavior of, in pol. light..25, 36, 40
Morphological properties of the rock-
forming minerals..................... 81
*Mügge*........................... 197, 207
*Müller*............................. 198, 201
Muscovite..................... 36, 160, 207

## N

Natrolite ............................... 194
Nepheline....................... 53, 134, 207
*Nessig* ................................ 214
*Niedzwiedzky*.......................... 205
Nigrine................................. 122
Non-pellucid minerals................... 108
Nosean ............................ 114, 207

## O

Ocular micrometer....................... 14
*Oebbeke*............................. 66, 76
Oligoclase.......................... 184, 207
—— Albite.......................... 182, 208
Olivine.................... 45, 89, 140, 208
———, Decomposition of................. 101
Omphacite.......................... 170, 202
Opacitic border......................... 89
Opal ............................... 112, 208
Optically-uniaxial minerals..... 18, 30, 46, 106
Optically-biaxial minerals...... 20, 32, 47, 107
Orthoclase................... 25, 42, 164, 208
*Oschatz* .............................. 200
Ottrelite.......................... 164, 209

## P

*Pench*............................ 208, 209
Penninite ............................. 162
Perowskite ........................ 120, 209
*Peters*................................ 212
*Pfaff*................................. 209
Phlogopite......................... 158, 209
*Pichler* ......................... 211, 213
Picotite.......................... 118, 209
Pinite............................ 154, 209
Plagioclase ............................. 209
———, Shell-formed structure of......... 91
———, Twins of...................... 43, 44
Pleochroism ............................ 45
Pleonaste ...................... 110, 118, 210
*Pohlig*........................... 198, 201
Polarization-microscope............... 7, 8

Polarizer............................... 7
Potassium fluo-borate.................. 61
—— Mercury solution.................. 67
—— Platinum chloride.................. 61
Preparation of microscopical sections... 3
Prism, Nicol's......................... 7
Protobastite ...................... 150, 210
Pseudo-crystals........................ 89
Pyrite................................ 108
Pyrope.......................... 116, 210
Pyrrhotine............................. 110

## Q

Quartz...................... 88, 128, 210
—— wedge........................... 13
—— plate, Biot-Klein's............... 11

## R

*v. Rath*............. 198, 202, 205–207, 209, 211
Regular minerals.................. 106, 114
———, Behavior of, in pol. light..... 17, 30
*Renard* ......... 163, 198, 200, 202, 204, 209
*Reusch* ....................... 200, 203, 208
Rhombic minerals.................. 107, 140
———, Behavior of, in pol. light..... 21, 35
*Riess*.................... 198, 202, 204, 214
Ripidolite........................ 162, 210
*Rohrbach* ........................ 67, 75
*Rose*............... 201, 204, 208, 209, 213
*Rosenbusch*. 1, 7, 16, 45, 51, 76, 81, 92, 197–200,
205, 207–210, 213
*Roth*.............................. 101, 211
Rubellan......................... 158, 210
Rutile......................... 38, 122, 210

## S

Sagenite .............................. 122
Salite............................ 170, 202
*Sandberger*................... 205, 211, 213
Sanidine......................... 166, 208
*Sauer*........................ 204, 205, 210
Scapolite........................ 124, 211
Scolecite............................. 194
*Scheerer* ............................ 203
*Schönn*............................... 51
Schörl............................... 138
*Schrauf* ..... 198, 200, 202, 205, 208, 210, 211
*Schultze*........................ 13, 208
*Schulze*............................. 211
*Schumacher*.......................... 211
*Schuster*......... 198, 200, 205, 207, 209, 213
Sericite.............................. 160
Serpentine...................... 190, 211

# INDEX.

| | PAGE |
|---|---|
| Shell-formed structure of crystals | 90 |
| Siderite | 132 |
| Silico-fluorides | 56, 57, 58 |
| Sillimanite | 142, 211 |
| Single-refracting minerals. | 17 |
| *Sipòcz* | 201, 209 |
| Sismondine | 162, 201 |
| *Sjögren* | 199 |
| Smaragdite | 172, 174 |
| Sodalite | 114, 211 |
| *Sommerlad* | 204 |
| *Sorby* | 44, 210 |
| Specific gravity, Determination of | 68 |
| Spinel | 118 |
| Stage, Heating | 15 |
| —— of the polarization-microscope | 7 |
| —— scale | 14 |
| Staurolite | 39, 142, 212 |
| Stauroscopic apparatus | 7, 13 |
| *Stelzner* | 200, 203, 205, 206, 209 |
| Stilbite | 194 |
| *Streng* | 51, 200, 202, 203, 205, 208, 210, 212 |
| Structure of the rock-forming minerals | 87 |
| *Szabo* | 51, 198, 201 |

## T

| | |
|---|---|
| Talc | 160, 212 |
| *Teller* | 198, 203, 205, 210 |
| Tetragonal minerals | 106, 122 |
| —— ——, Behavior of, in pol. light | 18, 30 |
| *Thoulet* | 6, 44, 66, 81, 201 |
| Titanite | 25, 42, 176, 212 |
| Titaneisen | 102, 110, 205 |
| Titan,magneteisen | 108, 212 |

| | PAGE |
|---|---|
| *Törnebohm* | 197, 200, 203, 211, 213, 214 |
| Tourmaline | 46, 138, 213 |
| Tremolite | 174, 212 |
| Trichite | 87 |
| Triclinic minerals | 107, 178 |
| ——  ——, Behavior of, in pol. light | 28, 37 |
| Tridymite | 130, 212 |
| *Trippke* | 203 |
| *Tschermak* | 45, 197-204, 206-213 |
| Twins, Behavior of, in pol. light | 37 |

## U

| | |
|---|---|
| Uralite | 174, 213 |

## V

| | |
|---|---|
| *Valée-Poussin* | 209 |
| *Velain* | 206, 208 |
| Viridite | 192, 213 |
| Vitreous inclosures | 97 |
| *Vogelsang* | 15, 85, 204, 205, 213 |
| *Vrba* | 199, 211 |

## W

| | |
|---|---|
| *Websky* | 211 |
| *Wedding* | 199 |
| *Weigand* | 211 |
| *Weiss* | 208-211 |
| *v. Werveke* | 66, 199, 202, 203, 210-212 |
| *Wickman* | 6, 198, 201, 206, 209, 213 |
| *Williams* | 203, 207 |
| Wollastonite | 25, 172, 213 |

## Z

| | |
|---|---|
| Zeolites | 194, 213 |
| Zircon | 124, 213 |
| *Zirkel* | 1, 51, 76, 197-214 |
| Zoisite | 154, 214 |

www.ingramcontent.com/pod-product-compliance
Lightning Source LLC
Chambersburg PA
CBHW031745230426
43669CB00007B/486